JOHN McKINNEY'S NEW
DAY HIKER'S GUIDE TO
SOUTHERN CALIFORNIA

For more of John McKinney's hiking tips and trails, take a hike to www.thetrailmaster.com

John McKinney's NEW

Day Hiker's Guide
to
Southern California

OLYMPUS PRESS
SANTA BARBARA

John McKinney's New Day Hiker's Guide to Southern California

Portions of this book have appeared in the author's hiking column in the Los Angeles Times, as well as in *Sunset, Westways, Los Angeles* and *Islands* magazines.

Cover Photo: Santa Ynez Mountains, by Cara Moore
The Trailmaster Series Editor: Cheri Rae
Maps designed by Hélène Webb
Book design and typography by Jim Cook

ACKNOWLEDGMENTS
For sharing their expertise on the subjects of trails, natural history and eco-politics, I'd like to thank Ruth Kilday, master trail builder Ron Webster, and Glen Owens and the Big Santa Anita Historical Society. And another thanks to the many rangers and administrators of the Cleveland, Los Padres, San Bernardino and Angeles national forests, as well as the dedicated employees of the state and national park systems. I'd also like to single out the efforts of the Ventura, Los Angeles, Orange, and Riverside county parks departments. Southern California's natural world and its trail system have benefited immeasurably from the efforts of the state's Santa Monica Mountains Conservancy, as well as the endeavors of many more local and regional conservation groups, such as the Laguna Canyon Foundation. I salute you all!

PHOTO CREDITS
Angeles National Forest, pp. 104, 123; Avalon Chamber of Commerce, p. 277; Big Santa Anita Historical Society, p. 111; First American Title Insurance, pp. 135, 137; Bob Howells, pp. 82, 306; Joshua Tree National Park, p. 313; Los Padres National Forest, p. 29; Roy Murphy, pp. 90, 129, 235; Linda Hardie-Scott, p. 75; David M. Werk, pp. 217; all other photos by John McKinney.

CONTENTS

For inspirational stories and a complete discussion of how-to-hike, get a copy of John McKinney's *Happy Trails, Hiking The Trailmaster Way*, and visit his web site, **www.thetrailmaster.com**

A Foreword from the Field

No guidebook has had such enthusiastic field-testers! By field-testers, I mean the many readers of my former Los Angeles Times hiking column (1986-2003) who took my words to the woods, deserts and coast, then wrote to me about their experiences on the trail.

By enthusiastic I mean the high you've felt high atop a mountain, that great aerobic workout you enjoyed, the fascination in the eyes of your children when you introduced them to nature's marvels.

I like to think I'm a rather enthusiastic field-tester myself. My job, as The Trailmaster, is to take a hike and write about it. I wander the world's trails looking for lonely beaches, desert dunes, dramatic summits, hills ablaze with wildflowers. (Yes, it's a dirty job, but somebody's got to do it.)

My enthusiasm increases every time I hear parents tell me how, with the help of one of my website tips, newspaper and magazine articles, appearances on Southland radio and TV shows, or books, they introduced their children to the wonders of nature. And my enthusiasm is boosted when I learn how fellow conservationists have managed to preserve another special place to walk and to give to future generations.

Although I've taken readers on journeys afoot around America, from the Olympic rain forest to the Florida Everglades, and around the world from the mountains of Greece to the beaches of Tahiti, the hikes around Southern California invariably prompt the most reader response. Let's face facts: it's easier, faster, and a whole lot cheaper to enjoy the alpine air of Mt. Baldy than to head off to Switzerland.

When you hike Southern California, you see the world—the Mediterranean in the Santa Monica Mountains, Santa Ynez Mountains and the Channel Islands; Little Switzerland atop Mt. San Jacinto and among the tall peaks of the San Gorgonio Wilderness; the Sahara Desert in the tall dunes of the Mojave Desert.

Included in this guide are many of my favorite Southern California mountain, coast and desert hikes. Experienced hikers will recognize some familiar terrain—Mts. Baldy, San Gorgonio and San Jacinto—but will find some new trails to travel. Newcomers to the Southland, and less experienced hikers, will find helpful introductions to the land—the major mountain ranges, the forests, deserts, and the coastline. Visitors from across the nation and around the world may discover that hiking is the best way to fully experience Southern California.

Between the covers of this book are the Southland's best hikes. I wanted to increase the odds of you having a great day in the great outdoors, so I left out many walkable but not-so-wonderful trails. As you might imagine, a "professional" hiker like myself encounters a lot of turkey trails; that is to say, paths that start nowhere and go nowhere, trails battered by nature or neglected by park officials to the point where I decided that they are too unsafe for you to use.

So with all this enthusiastic field-testing—mine, yours and that of park authorities—are you holding perfection in your hands?

Nope. Trails change over time. Like every hiker, I hate seeing a good trail go bad, but regrettably it happens. The ravages of fire and flood, rampant real estate development and bureaucratic neglect can ruin a favorite path. While out hiking, if you happen across a neglected, hazardous or overgrown trail, please report it to the relevant ranger or administrator. Only if you make your concerns known will conditions improve. It's up to all of us to preserve our trails—and the precious wild land they help us explore.

I hope that in some small way this book, in addition to suggesting some enjoyable hikes, contributes to a better understanding of the unique and fragile ecology of Southern California.

Understanding Day Hiking in Southern California

The land we call Southern California is an island, ecologically isolated from the rest of the continent by a combination of geographic and climatic factors. Helen Hunt Jackson once said of Southern California: "It's an island on the land." Carey McWilliams popularized the phrase in his definitive history of the region, *Southern California: An Island on the Land*. The land's island nature is apparent when you enter it from the north or east. When you round Point Conception and the north-south orientation of California becomes east-west, it is obvious that you have entered a unique geographical province. If you come to Southern California from the east through Cajon Pass or San Gorgonio Pass, the change is immediately evident. Light is softer, the climate more temperate.

The land includes seven counties: Santa Barbara, Ventura, Los Angeles, Orange, Riverside, San Bernardino and San Diego. Usually, only those parts of San Bernardino, Riverside and San Diego counties "west of the mountains" are in Southern California, but a case can be made for including all of them and adding Imperial County as well. Some boosters insist Southern California's northern boundary is San Luis Obispo or even the Monterey County line, but geographically and ecologically it's at Point Conception. Southern California is the land south of the Transverse Range, which knifes across California toward the Pacific just north of Santa Barbara.

Southern California is protected from the Mojave Desert by the San Bernardino and San Gabriel Mountain Ranges on the east and walled off from the San Joaquin Valley by other Transverse Ranges. The lowlands are covered with alluvial fans formed by earth washed down from the mountains.

Compass directions can be confusing to both newcomers and old-timers. "Up the coast" in other parts of the world is usually taken to mean north, but it's not north in Southern California.

To travel north from L.A., you head directly into the Mojave Desert, crossing east-west trending mountains in the process. If you traveled a straight line, as the crow flies, from San Bernardino to Santa Barbara, you would travel 137 miles west and only 27 miles north.

Carey McWilliams has suggested that "The analyst of California is like a navigator who is trying to chart a course in a storm: the instruments will not work; the landmarks are lost; and the maps make little sense." California may be geographically cockeyed and Southern California even more so, but we day hikers ought to get our bearings before heading for the hills. We need to find a few landmarks and consult a map. Orienting yourself to Southern California isn't that difficult. Consult the map on the following pages, and try the accompanying geography exercise.

Santa Ynez Mts.

Santa
Barbara

Santa Monica Mts.

Los
Angeles

Channel Islands
National Park

Catalina
Island

Southern California Geography made Easy

Use the locator map above or get yourself an Auto Club map of California or similar sized map. Spread it on the floor. (This is hands-on learning, so if you have small hands, you might want to borrow a friend with larger ones.)

Put your right thumb on Santa Barbara, your right pinkie on San Diego and spread your fingers in as wide a fan as you can manage. One of the first things you may notice is that your palm covers the L.A. Basin. Keep your palm firmly pressed down on L.A. to keep the metropolis from spreading into the wilderness. Look at your thumb. Above it is Pt. Conception, the northernmost point of Southern California. Above Santa Barbara are the Santa Ynez Mountains and beyond are those parts of Los Padres National Forest we call the Santa Barbara Backcountry.

Along your index finger are the San Gabriel Mountains and the Angeles National Forest. (Careful! Don't get your finger pinched in the San Andreas

Mojave Desert

SOUTHERN
CALIFORNIA

San Gabriel Mts.

San Bernardino
Mts.

San Bernardino

Joshua Tree
National
Park

San Jacinto
Mts.

Santa Ana
Mts.

Santa Rosa
Mts.

Palomar
Mts.

Anza-Borrego
Desert State
Park

San
Diego

Cuyamaca
Mts.

MEXICO

Hélène Webb

Fault.) Your middle finger is in the San Bernardino Mountains. Near the eastern terminus of this range is Mt. San Gorgonio, the highest peak in Southern California.

Between your middle and ring fingers, paralleling the coast in Orange Country are the Santa Ana Mountains, protected by the Cleveland National Forest. At the tip of your ring finger at the north end of Anza-Borrego Desert State Park lie the Santa Rosa Mountains. Take note of the Colorado Desert and farther to the north, the vast Mojave Desert.

Due east from your pinkie is the southern part of the Cleveland National Forest, as well as the Palomar and Cuyamaca mountain ranges.

Now that you're oriented, raise that right hand of yours and pledge to preserve, protect, and enjoy these places.

How to Use this Book

First decide where you want to hike. A palm oasis? An alpine meadow? A deserted beach? Consult our Southland map. Read the capsule descriptions of the hikes in the table of contents.

Unsure of what to expect in the Santa Monica, San Bernardino or Santa Ana Mountains? Read the appropriate chapter introductions.

There are more than 150 trails in this guide. Add the suggested options and you can design hundreds more. Beneath the name of the trail is the trailhead and one or more destinations. Every day hike in this book has a soul and a goal. You provide the soul; this guide will provide the goals.

Mileage, expressed in round-trip figures, follows each destination. The hikes in this guide range from 2 to 20 miles, with the majority in the 5 to 10 mile range. Gain or loss in elevation follows the mileage. In matching a hike to your ability, you'll want to consider both mileage and elevation as well as condition of the trail, terrain, and season. Hot, exposed chaparral or miles of boulder-hopping can make a short hike seem long.

You may wish to use the following guideline: A hike suitable for beginners and children would be less than five miles with an elevation gain of less than 700 to 800 feet. A moderate hike is considered a hike in the 5 to 10 mile range, with less than a 2,000-foot elevation gain. You should be reasonably fit for these. Preteens sometimes find the going difficult. Hikes over 10 miles, and those with more than a 2,000-foot gain are for experienced hikers in top form.

Season is the next item to consider. Although Southern California is one of the few places in the country that offers four-season hiking, some climactic restrictions must be heeded. You can hike some of the trails in this guide all of the time, all of the trails some of the time, but not all of the trails all of the time. Season recommendations are based on hiker comfort and partly on legal restrictions. A few trails in this guide may be impassable in winter and spring due to high water.

An **introduction** to each hike describes what you'll see along the trail: plants, animals, panoramic views. You'll also learn about the geologic and human history of the region.

Directions to trailhead take you from the nearest major highway to trailhead parking. For trails having two desirable trailheads, directions to each are given. A few trails can be hiked one way, with the possibility of a car shuttle. Suggested car shuttle points are noted.

You may notice a slight L.A. bias to the directions (no doubt prompted by my years as Los Angeles Times hiking columnist) when you proceed "up" to Santa Barbara or "down" to San Diego. For the sake of clarity and orientation, I've chosen downtown L.A. as a reference point. It seems to me L.A. is as good a place to leave from as any.

After the directions to the trailhead, read **The hike** description. Important junctions and major sights are pointed out, but I've left you to discover the multitude of little things that make a hike an adventure. Options allow you to climb higher or farther or take a different route back to the trailhead.

It's not important that you follow the trail exactly as I've described it. Whether you hike the length of a trail and every one of its options, or snooze under the first sycamore you find, is your decision and no one else's. There's enough regimentation in your life without me telling you where you must hike. This guide is for you to plan your day in the backcountry. Don't stick your nose in this guide; stick it in some wildflowers.

On the Trail

Choose the pace that's best for you. Rest once an hour for a few minutes. To keep your momentum and to avoid stiffness, several shorter rest periods are better than one long one. Set a steady pace, one you can keep up all day. Wear a watch, not because you have an appointment with a waterfall and you have to be punctual, but because a watch gives you some idea of pace and helps you get back to the trailhead before dark.

Hiking uphill takes energy. Hiking two miles an hour up a 10 percent grade requires as much energy as hiking four miles an hour on level trail. Climbing can be especially difficult in high altitude. Altitude sickness affects some hikers at about 8,000 feet. Only a few hikes in this guide are above this elevation. Altitude can cause discomfort—shortness of breath, headache and nausea—above 5,000 feet.

Hiking alone or with company is strictly a matter of personal preference. Having two or three in your party is a definite advantage if something goes wrong; someone can go for help. Hiking with a group is a good idea for first-time hikers. Most inexperienced hikers are uncomfortable going solo. Sometimes, after a few hikes, a craving for solitude develops—by which time you should be able to take care of yourself on the trail. There's a lot to be said for solitary hiking, as the writings of Thoreau, Whitman and Muir would seem to indicate.

Alas, backcountry travelers are not always immune from urban attitudes, stresses and crimes. While most of our Southland parks and preserves are far safer than our urban environment, hikers—particularly women hikers—must be aware that unsavory characters are not unknown on the trail. Your "street smarts" coupled with your trail sense are two keys to avoiding trouble.

Know that park and national forest authorities are committed to protecting the public. Many of the "rangers" you see on patrol are California peace officers—meaning they have the authority to write citations, make arrests, etc., just like their city cop counterparts. Call on them if you feel at all uncomfortable about anyone/anything; they're dedicated to not only protecting the land, but public safety as well.

Day Hiking Through the Seasons

Many have sung praises of Southern California's Mediterranean climate. Relentless sunshine, winter and summer, is how the climate is usually stereotyped. But the semi-tropical stereotype holds true only in coastal regions and only at certain times of the year. There is nothing Mediterranean about the climate of the Mojave Desert or the San Jacinto high country. In Southern California's backcountry, seasons arrive with clarity and distinction. Day hikers can find trails that are "in season" in every month of the year.

Winter brings snow to mountains in the Angeles, San Bernardino and Los Padres National Forests. Rain visits the coastal lowlands. Deciduous trees and shrubs lose their leaves. Some animals hibernate or become torpid.

But winter doesn't mean an end to all of nature's activities in Southern California, particularly in the lowland valleys and deserts. January is a fine time to take a beach hike, to visit shores laid bare by minus tides, or to see what treasure winter storms have cast ashore. In February, the desert begins to bloom. February and March, last of the winter months, are often looked upon by many Southern Californians as the first months of spring. Day hikers are guaranteed solitude in these months. High country trails are covered with snow and those on the lower slopes are muddy going.

Spring comes early to Southern California. Even the chaparral, so dull gray in other seasons, looks inviting. Ceanothus covers the lower slopes of the Santa Barbara Backcountry, the Santa Monica Mountains and San Gabriel Mountains with its dainty white and blue blossoms. In March, the giant coreopsis on Anacapa Island grows wild. As spring temperatures increase, flowers in the hotter Colorado Desert diminish, but those in the higher Mojave Desert arrive with a flourish. In June, the flower show moves to the high country of the Transverse Ranges. Lemon lilies appear streamside and lupine everywhere. Flocks of birds go about the business of building nests, laying eggs, raising young.

In summer, snowmelt-swollen creeks water emerald-green meadows. Scarlet-stemmed snow plant emerges in the pine forests. By August, even the highest peaks have lost their mantle of snow and day hikers can stand atop their summits and sign the hiker's register. A beach hike in the middle of summer is a pleasure. With the sun on your back, the surf at your feet and miles of beach in front of you, summer seems endless.

Autumn has its critics and its fans. Some say there's little use for a day that begins with frost, becomes hot enough to sunburn your nose by noon, and has you shivering by sunset. Wiser heads, those attached to day hikers no doubt, believe autumn is the best of all seasons. The high country is crisp, but still inviting, and desert washes have cooled. Autumn colors oaks, dogwoods, willows and sycamores in the Cuyamaca and Palomar Mountains with reds and golds. There's enough color change to satisfy even the most homesick New Englander.

Maps

The Automobile Club of Southern California has seven county maps useful to the hiker, including Santa Barbara, Ventura, Los Angeles, Orange County, San Diego, Riverside and San Bernardino. Particularly useful is "Los Angeles County and Vicinity."

Because many of the hikes in this guide begin at campgrounds, the Auto Club's "Southern California Camping" map is a good one to have. The richly detailed Thomas Brothers maps will also help you get around Southern California. Use care when you select a map off the rack. Many maps sold to tourists are okay for civic sightseeing, but don't show the backcountry.

About 40 percent of the hikes in this guide take place in one of the four Southern California national forests: Los Padres, Angeles, San Bernardino and Cleveland. Forest Service maps are available at ranger stations for a small fee. They're general maps, showing roads, rivers, and trails. The Forest Service keeps its maps fairly up-to-date, so they're useful for checking out-of-date topo maps.

Each route and trail in the national forest system has a route number. A route number might look like this: 2S21. Signs, inscribed with the route number, are placed at some trailheads and at the intersection of trails to supplement other directional signs. The route numbers on your map usually correspond to the route numbers on the trail, but be careful because the Forest Service periodically changes the numbers.

Trails on Forest Service maps are drawn in red and black. Red trails are usually maintained and are in good shape. Black trails are infrequently maintained and their condition ranges from okay to faint.

Some hikers prefer topographic maps. Topos show terrain in great detail and are the best way to prevent getting lost. If, for example, you know absolutely there's a road one mile to the west that runs north and south, it can be quite a comfort. Topos show trails, elevations, waterways, brush cover and improvements. Along with a compass, they're indispensable for cross-country travel.

Hiker Safety

Alas, backcountry travelers are not always immune from urban attitudes, stresses and crimes. Most people you meet in the great outdoors are as friendly and as well-intentioned as you are, but it's not unheard of to meet a creep on the trail.

While most of our parks and preserves are far safer than our urban environment, hikers—particularly women hikers—must stay alert. Your "street smarts" coupled with your trail sense are two keys to avoiding trouble.

Know that national park, national forest, state park and regional park authorities are committed to protecting the public. Many of the "rangers" you see on patrol are peace officers—meaning they have the authority to write citations, make arrests, etc., just like their city cop counterparts.

Call on land agency law enforcement personnel if you feel at all uncomfortable about anyone/anything; they're dedicated to not only protecting the land, but public safety as well.

Safety Tips for Hikers

- Tell a trusted friend or relative where you're going. If the itinerary is at all complicated, write it down, have your friend write it down. At the very least, include a phone number for the park/place you're visiting, the trail you're taking and expected return time.
- While telling someone your plans is better than telling no one, telling someone familiar with hiking is better than dear, sweet, but trail clueless Auntie Em.
- If you're traveling a remote trail or taking an unusual route, or simply want to cover all the safety bases, leave your itinerary and an emergency contact number with the supervising ranger station.
- Sign in and out at the trailhead register. If you get in trouble, emergency workers will know where to start looking for you.
- Use caution when sharing plans with strangers. By all means small-talk about hiking or anything else, but perfect strangers don't need to know where you're spending the night or your exact plans.
- Beware of anyone who acts hostile, drunk or drugged. Don't respond to taunts or provocation of any kind.
- Hiking with one or more companions reduces the potential for harassment.
- Dress conservatively (the hiker's layered look is definitely in that category) to discourage unwelcome attention.
- Hike trails away from roads and motor vehicles. Hikers are most likely to encounter harassment in backcountry accessible to four-wheel drive vehicles; unfortunately, a small minority of the four-wheelin' crowd sometimes hassles hikers.
- Have an emergency plan. Know where the nearest ranger station and hospital emergency room is located in relation to the trail you're hiking.

Elementary Trail Courtesy

- Leave your electronic music machines at home.
- No smoking on trails.
- Resist the urge to collect flowers, rocks or animals. It disrupts nature's balance and lessens the wilderness experience for future hikers.
- Litter detracts from even the most beautiful backcountry setting. If you packed it in, you can pack it out.
- You have a moral obligation to help a hiker in need. Give whatever first aid or comfort you can, and then hurry for help.
- Don't cut switchbacks.

1. SANTA YNEZ MOUNTAINS

A FEW MILLION YEARS AGO, the Santa Ynez Mountains rose slowly from the sea. The mountains are not secretive about their origin and display their oceanic heritage in a number of ways. Tilted blocks of sedimentary rock, which aggregated tens of thousands of feet in thickness, provide the first clue to the mountains' former undersea life. Fossils of sea animals give further testimony that the mountains were once many leagues under the sea. Even the vegetation betrays the mountains' origin. The mineral-poor sandstone slopes formed in the ocean deep can support little more than dense brush, so it's the chaparral community—buckthorn, mountain lilac and scrub oak—that predominates.

The Santa Ynez Mountains are part of a series of east/west trending ranges known as the Transverse Ranges, which encircle Southern California from San Diego to Point Conception. The backbone of the Transverse Range is the San Bernardino and San Gabriel Mountains, while the Santa Ynez Mountains form the uppermost or most westerly part of the Transverse Spine. The Santa Ynez extend almost fifty miles from Matilija Canyon on the east to Gaviota Canyon on the west. Compared to other ranges in the Transverse system, the Santa Ynez are quite small, ranging from 2,000 to 4,000 feet.

From the viewpoints, hikers can decipher Santa Barbara's sometimes confusing orientation; that is to say, the east-west direction of the coastline and the mountain ranges. Even many long time Southern Californians are amused by looking south to the ocean. By all means, consider taking along a Santa Barbara county map to help get oriented.

At first glance, the range seems smothered with a formless gray mass of tortured vegetation. On closer inspection, the Santa Ynez reveals more charm. Sycamores and bays line the canyons and a host of seasonal creeks wash the hillsides. In spring, the chaparral blooms and adds frosty whites and blues to the gray-green plants. The backcountry looks particularly inviting after the first winter rains. On upper peaks, rain sometimes turns to snow.

Mountain trails mainly follow the canyons above Santa Barbara and Montecito. The network of trails generally follows streams to the top of the range. They start in lush canyon bottoms, zigzag up the hot, dry canyon walls, and follow rock ledges to the crest. Many of the trails intersect Camino Cielo (the sky road), which follows the mountain crest. From the top, enjoy sweeping views of the Pacific, Channel Island and coastal plain.

MISSION CANYON

Tunnel Trail
From Tunnel Road to Seven Falls is 2 miles round trip with 400-foot elevation gain; to Inspiration Point is 4 miles round trip with 800-foot gain

"A pleasant party spent yesterday up Mission Canyon visiting noted Seven Falls and afterward eating a tempting picnic dinner in a romantic spot on the creek's bank. To reach these falls requires some active climbing, able-bodied sliding and skillful swinging. . . ." (*Santa Barbara Daily Press,* 1887)

Seven Falls has been a popular destination of Santa Barbarans since before the turn of the 20th century. The seven distinct little falls found in the bed of Mission Creek still welcome hikers.

Tunnel Trail was used by workers to gain access to a difficult city waterworks project launched by the city of Santa Barbara. Workers burrowed a tunnel through the Santa Ynez Mountains to connect the watershed on the backside of the mountains to the growing little city. Braving floods, cave-ins and dangerous hydrogen gas, a crew labored eight years and finished the project in 1912.

This easy family hike in the foothills follows Tunnel Trail, joins Jesusita Trail for an exploration of the Seven Falls along Mission Creek and ascends Inspiration Point for sweeping coastal views.

Mission Creek provided the water supply for Mission Santa Barbara. Near the mission, which you'll pass as you proceed to Tunnel trailhead, are some stone remains of the padres' waterworks system. Mission Creek also flows through the Santa Barbara Botanic Garden, which is well worth visiting because of its fine displays of native California flora. A ramble through the Santa Barbara foothills combined with a visit to the mission and botanic garden would add up to a very pleasant day's outing.

Directions to trailhead: From Highway 101 in Santa Barbara, exit on Mission Street. Turn east to Laguna Street, then left and drive past the historic Santa Barbara Mission. From the mission, drive up Mission Canyon Road, turning right for a block on Foothill Road, then immediately turning left back onto Mission Canyon Road. At a distinct V-intersection, veer left onto Tunnel Road and drive to its end. Park along the road.

The hike: From the end of Tunnel Road, hike past a locked gate onto a paved road, which eventually turns to dirt as you leave the power lines behind and get increasingly grander views of Santa Barbara. The road makes a sharp left and crosses a bridge over the West Fork of Mission Creek.

Beyond the bridge, you'll hike a short distance under some handsome oaks to a junction. (Tunnel Trail angles northeast, uphill, leading three miles to "the sky road," East Camino Cielo.) You join Jesusita Trail and descend to Mission Creek.

At the canyon bottom, you can hike up creek into a steep gorge that was cut from solid sandstone. Geologically inclined hikers will recognize fossilized layers of oyster beds from the Oligocene Epoch, deposited some 35 million years ago. In more recent times, say for the last few thousands of winters, rainwater has rushed from the shoulder of La Cumbre Peak and cut away at the sandstone layers, forming several deep pools. If you decide to hike up Mission Creek, be careful; reaching the waterfalls—particularly the higher ones—requires quite a bit of boulder hopping and rock climbing. Even when there's not much water in the creek, it can be tricky going.

From the creek crossing, Jesusita Trail switchbacks steeply up the chaparral-cloaked canyon wall to a power line road atop a knoll. Although Inspiration Point is not all that inspiring, the view from the cluster of sandstone rocks at the 1,750-foot viewpoint is worth the climb. You can see the coastline quite some distance north and south, as well as Catalina and the Channel Islands, Santa Barbara and the Goleta Valley.

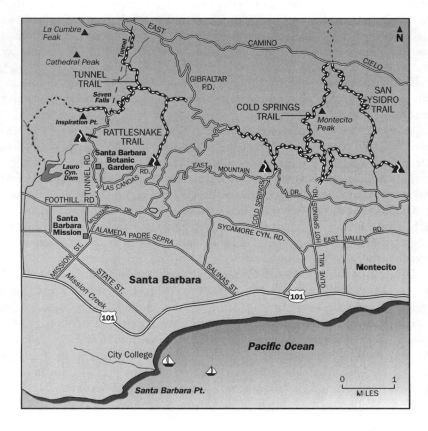

Rattlesnake Canyon

Rattlesnake Canyon Trail
From Skofield Park to Tin Can Meadow is 4.5 miles round trip
with 1,000-foot elevation gain; to Gibraltar Road is 6 miles round trip
with 1,500-foot gain

Rattlesnake Canyon Trail is serpentine, but otherwise far more inviting than its name suggests.

The joys of the canyon were first promoted by none other than the Santa Barbara Chamber of Commerce. Many a turn-of-the-century visitor to Santa Barbara resorts enjoyed hiking and riding in the local mountains. Eager to keep the customers satisfied, in 1902 the chamber purchased easements from canyon homesteaders to develop a recreation trail.

"Chamber of Commerce Trail," as the Chamber called it, was an immediate success with both tourists and locals. However, to the chamber's consternation, both the trail and the canyon itself continued to be called Rattlesnake. Chamber of Commerce Canyon sounded a bit self-serving, so the Chamber tried to compromise with an earlier name, Las Canoas Canyon, and adopted a 1902 resolution to that effect. "The name of Rattlesnake Canyon is unpleasantly suggestive of a reptile," it argued, "which is found no more plentifully there than elsewhere along the mountain range and may deter some nervous persons from visiting that most delightful locality."

In the 1960s, the city of Santa Barbara purchased the canyon as parkland. A handsome wooden sign at the foot of the canyon proudly proclaims: Rattlesnake Canyon Wilderness.

This trail explores Santa Barbara's little wilderness canyon. Red-berried toyon, manzanita with its white urn-shaped flowers, and purple hummingbird sage cloak the slopes and offer a variety of smells and textures. In the early spring ceanothus blooms, adding frosty whites and blues to the gray-green thickets. Shooting stars, larkspur, and lupine also spread their color over the slopes and meadows.

Directions to trailhead: From Highway 101 in Santa Barbara, go uptown (toward the mountains) on State Street to Los Olivos Street. Turn right and proceed a half mile, passing by the Santa Barbara Mission and joining Mission Canyon Road. Follow this road past its intersection with Foothill Road and make a right on Las Canoas Road. Follow Las Canoas to Skofield Park. Leave your car on the shoulder of the road or in the large parking area near the picnic grounds. The trail begins on Las Canoas Road near the handsome stone bridge that crosses Rattlesnake Creek.

The hike: From the sandstone bridge across from Skofield Park, hike up

Mr. & Mrs. Lyman Pope at Tin Can Shack

a brief stretch of trail and join a narrow dirt road that parallels the east side of the creek. For lovely picnicking, take any of the steep side trails down to the creek. In the early 19th century the mission padres built a dam in the bottom of the canyon, which channeled water into a stone aqueduct and diverted it into the mission's waterworks system. Portions of the aqueduct still exist and can be seen by the careful observer.

The trail zigs and zags across the creek, finally continuing along the west bank to open, grassy Tin Can Meadow. The triangular-shaped meadow gets its name from a homesteader's cabin constructed of chaparral framing and kerosene can shingles and sidings. For the first quarter of this century, Tin Can Shack was an important canyon landmark and several guidebooks of that era mention it. It was a popular destination for picnickers who marveled at the inspired architecture and posed for pictures in front of it. In 1925, a brushfire destroyed the shack and it soon disintegrated into a pile of tin.

If you're feeling energetic, hike on toward the apex of the triangular meadow where you'll find a junction. The trail bearing left takes you 0.75 mile and climbs 500 feet to its intersection with the Tunnel Trail—and incidentally to many points of interest in the Santa Barbara backcountry. To the right, Rattlesnake Canyon Trail climbs about 0.75 mile and 500 feet to its intersection with Gibraltar Road. There you will be greeted by an unobstructed view of the South Coast. Watch for strangely patterned triangular aircraft overhead. A favorite hang glider's launching peak is almost within reach.

Cold Spring Canyon

Cold Springs Trail

From Mountain Drive to Montecito Overlook is 3 miles round trip with 900-foot elevation gain; to Montecito Peak is 7.5 miles round trip with 2,500-foot gain; to Camino Cielo is 9 miles round trip with 2,700-foot gain.

After the Santa Ynez Forest Reserve was established in 1899, rangers recognized the desirability of a trail crossing the Reserve. In 1905, the Forest Service built a trail up the East Fork of Cold Springs Canyon.

And a lovely trail it is. It begins by the alder-shaded, year-round creek, then rises out of the canyon for fine coastal views.

Directions to trailhead: From Highway 101 in Montecito, a few miles south of Santa Barbara, exit on Hot Springs Road and proceed toward the foothills for 2.5 miles to Mountain Drive. Turn left. A mile's travel on Mountain Drive brings you to the Cold Springs trailhead, which begins at a point where a creek flows over a cement drainage apron.

The hike: The trail immediately crosses the creek to the east side of the canyon. It rises briefly through oak woodland, then returns to the creek. On your left, a quarter mile from the trailhead, is the easily overlooked, unsigned West Fork Trail. This century-old trail ascends 1.5 miles to Gibraltar Road.

Continuing past the West Fork trail junction, the East Fork Trail rises up the canyon wall and rejoins the creek a half mile later. Look for a fine swimming hole below you to the right. The trail then switchbacks moderately out of the canyon to Montecito Overlook. Enjoy the view of the Santa Barbara coastline and the Channel Islands.

Past the overlook, you'll cross a fire road leading down to Hot Springs Canyon, begin an uphill climb and soon encounter the Hot Springs connector trail. (The one-mile-long connector trail leads down into Hot Springs Canyon. Along the trail thrives bamboo, huge agave, banana and palm trees—remnants of landscaped gardens that surrounded Hot Springs Resort during its glory days. The trail visits the ruins of the old Hot Springs Hotel and descends to Mountain Drive. A mile's walk along one of Santa Barbara's more bucolic byways brings you back to the Cold Springs trailhead.

From the junction with the Hot Springs connector trail, Cold Springs Trail switchbacks up canyon and offers fine coastal views. A one-mile climb brings you to two eucalyptus trees (about the only shade en route!) and another 0.75 mile of travel takes you to the unsigned junction with a side trail leading to Montecito Peak (3,214 feet).

Cold Springs Trail continues a last mile to Camino Cielo. From the Sky Road, many trails lead into the far reaches of the Santa Barbara backcountry. Enjoy the grand views and return the same way.

2. Los Padres National Forest

WILDERNESS-BOUND TRAVELERS have a difficult task in deciding what to call the rugged mountain terrain arranged in a wide semi-circle around Santa Barbara. The padres left behind many names, but none of them fit. Elsewhere in Southern California, wilderness areas were named for the dominant mountain range in the vicinity. But there isn't a dominant mountain range behind Santa Barbara. Instead, there are a number of smaller ones with names like Pine and Topatopa, Sierra Madre and Santa Ynez.

So when we go, where do we say we're going?

Hikers sometimes say they're "going up to the Los Padres," an imprecise term at best, because the Los Padres National Forest includes lands as far north as Big Sur. Geologists aren't much help either. They call the land the "Transverse Ranges Geomorphic Province."

Until popular use gives mapmakers new inspiration, the best names we have are the Santa Barbara Backcountry or the Ojai Backcountry. (Even the Mt. Pinos-Frazier Park Backcountry will do.) Whatever this land of great gorges, sandstone cliffs and wide blue sky is called, it's guaranteed to please.

Most of the backcountry is in Los Padres National Forest. Together, Santa Barbara and Ventura Counties have more than a million acres of national forest land. The backcountry is under the jurisdiction of three forest districts. The Ojai District includes Sespe and Piru Creeks as well as the Sespe Condor Sanctuary. The Santa Barbara District includes the Santa Ynez and San Rafael Mountain ranges. Mt. Pinos District protects high conifer forest and includes the backcountry's highest peak, Mt. Pinos (8,831 feet).

Archeological work in the backcountry has been extensive and has contributed much to our understanding of native Chumash culture. Several thousand years before the arrival of the Spanish, an estimated 10,000 to 18,000 Chumash lived in the coastal mountains from Malibu Canyon north to San Luis Obispo. Early Spanish explorers admired Chumash craftsmen, their fine houses and wood plank canoes. But the padres and soldiers of Spain who followed the explorers forced the Chumash to give up their ancient ways. Mission life broke the spirit of the Chumash and destroyed their culture.

Gold and grass brought Americans to the backcountry. From the time of the early padres, rumors of the lost Los Padres Mine lured prospectors. Enough gold was discovered in the hills and streams to keep prospectors prospecting until well into the twentieth century, but no one ever found a big bonanza or the lost mine. Other mining endeavors were more profitable. Near the turn of the century, U.S. Borax Company mined borax from Lockwood Valley.

Lush grass on the San Joaquin side of the backcountry provided grazing for thousands of cattle. Cattle have grazed these hills since the era of the Spanish land grants, and the hiker will often surprise a few cows.

Wildfire was a major problem in the late nineteenth and early twentieth centuries. Within a twenty-year period, much of the backcountry burned, prompting the federal government to realize that the land needed protection. For fire prevention and watershed management purposes, large backcountry sections were set aside in the Pine Mountain and Zaca Lake Forest Reserve and the Santa Ynez Forest Reserve by decree of President Theodore Roosevelt. Two years later, the area became known as the Santa Barbara National Forest. In later years, acreage was added and subtracted, with the backcountry finally coming under the jurisdiction of the Los Padres National Forest in 1938.

More than 1,600 miles of trail range through the various districts of Los Padres National Forest. Nearly half of this trail system winds through the area we call the Santa Barbara Backcountry. Many of these trails have been used for centuries. Follow a trail to its end and you might be surprised at what you find. Remains of Indian camps may be found in the farthest reaches of the forest, and in remote meadows are remnants of early homesteads. Backcountry trails take you over some rough terrain—slopes are unstable and steep. Geologists classify more than half the land as "extremely sensitive" or "highly sensitive" to slippage. But what is agony for the homeowner is a delight for the hiker. As you day hike through this folded and fractured land, you might conclude that the backcountry was made for hiking, not settling.

There's more than gold in them thar hills.

MT. PINOS

Mt. Pinos Trail
From Mt. Abel to Sheep Camp is 5 miles round trip with 500-foot elevation gain; to Mt. Pinos is 10 miles round trip with 900-foot gain.
Season: April-November

The five-mile Mt. Pinos Trail offers the peak-bagger four opportunities to climb an 8,000-foot peak. Between Mts. Abel and Pinos, there are easy cross-country climbs to Grouse and Sawmill mountains. The trail passes through dense pine and fir hollows, visits historic Sheep Camp, and ascends Mt. Pinos, a blustery peak that offers views of the San Joaquin Valley, the Mojave Desert and the sprawling Los Padres National Forest high country.

You can travel from Mt. Pinos to Mt. Abel or vice versa; the Mt. Abel trailhead is much less visited.

Directions to trailhead: Exit Interstate 5 at the Frazier Park turnoff and drive west on Frazier Mountain Park Road, then Cuddy Valley Road. Five miles past the hamlet of Lake of the Woods is a junction. To reach Mt. Pinos trailhead, bear left and continue 9 miles to the Chula Vista Picnic Area. One more mile on a dirt road (closed in winter) takes you to the Condor Observation Site near the top of Mt. Pinos and the beginning (or end) of the Mt. Pinos Trail.

To reach the Mt. Abel trailhead, bear right at the above-mentioned junction and proceed 8 miles on Mil Potrero Road to Cerro Noroeste Road. Turn left and go 7 miles to the signed trailhead, 0.5 mile below the summit of Mt. Abel. Park in a safe manner along the road.

The hike: Leaving the trailhead behind, you descend a draw into a forested hollow, 0.5 mile from the start. Bear left at the signed junction here. The trail ascends Grouse Mountain, named for the resident blue grouse. Soon the trail levels and reaches a saddle on the east slope of Grouse Mountain. To ascend to the summit, scramble a short distance up the slope to your right.

The trail continues following the saddle to a junction with North Fork Trail. To reach Sheep Camp, bear right on North Fork Trail and descend a pine-covered slope past a trickling little spring. Sheep Camp, 0.5 mile from the junction, is one of the highest trail camps in Los Padres National Forest. For the day hiker, it's a pleasant picnic spot.

Return to the main trail, which soon passes close to the summit of Sawmill Mountain. It's an easy cross-country climb to bag the peak.

Continuing on the main trail, you will descend the pine-covered slopes of Sawmill Mountain, then ascend an open slope via switchbacks up balding Mt. Pinos. Stand among the gnarled pine atop the 8,831-foot summit and enjoy the view from the highest peak in Los Padres National Forest.

CHUMASH WILDERNESS

Mesa Spring Trail
From Mt. Cerro Noroeste to Quatal Canyon Road is 10 miles one-way
with 2,400-foot elevation loss; Season: April-November

A small portion of the Chumash's ancestral land is now a wilderness area—about 36,000 acres of pine forest and juniper woodland, grasslands and badlands. A highlight is Quatal Canyon, a kind of Bryce Canyon-in-miniature, complete with dramatic pinnacles and weird eroded rock formations. It is rich in vertebrate fossils, particularly from the Miocene Epoch (12 to 16 million years ago).

San Emigdio Mesa, a large flat alluvial fan forested with pinyon pine and dwarf oak, is by far the most extensive of its kind in Southern California, and recalls some of the mesas of the Great Basin.

This trail begins in a high pine forest, but passes through other ecosystems—pinyon-juniper woodland, chaparral and grassland—as it descends from Mt. Abel to Toad Spring Camp. It's a great introduction to the lay of the land, a fine overview of the Chumash Wilderness.

Directions to trailhead: This trip requires a car shuttle—either two cars or a nonhiking friend. Hikers will want to depart from the Mt. Abel trailhead and arrive at the Toad Spring Campground trailhead.

From Interstate 5 in Frazier Park, exit on Frazier Mountain Park Road and head west. The road, which becomes Cuddy Valley Road, continues to a Y-junction. The left fork leads to Mt. Pinos, but you stay right and join Mil Potrero Road. Drive 8.5 miles to Cerro Noroeste Road and turn left. Proceed 7 miles to the signed trailhead 0.5 mile below the summit of Mt. Cerro Noreoeste (Mt. Abel). Parking is not plentiful right at the trailhead, so park in a safe manner along the road.

From the Cerro Noroeste Road/Mil Potrero Road junction, continue right(west) on the latter road which, to make matters confusing, takes on the name Cerro Noroeste Road. Travel a mile to the signed turnoff for Toad Spring Campground, turning left on (Forest Road 9N09), continuing 0.3 mile to the camp, then another 0.4 mile to the unsigned trailhead on the left (south) side of the road.

The hike: Leaving signed Mt. Abel trailhead, the path descends very steeply for 0.5 mile down a draw into a forested hollow. Here there's a signed junction, with (incorrect) mileages for the trail leading left (southeast) to Mt. Pinos. You bear right on unsigned Mesa Spring Trail and descend past huge and widely spaced ponderosa pine. Scattered among the pines are silver fir, some of which are large enough and pretty enough to be the White House Christmas tree.

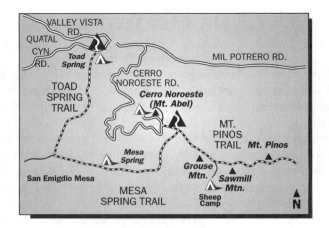

After a mile, you'll pass through a gate. (The Forest Service allows some cattle grazing on this land.) The path continues descending through a mixed transition forest of pine and oak. The area has unusual botany. Inhabitants of dry lands—coffee berry and manzanita and scrub oak—mingle with subalpine species—pine, fir and snowplant.

The path drops a couple more miles through pinyon pine country to Mesa Spring Camp, at about 6,000 feet in elevation. It's a simple trail camp with picnic tables and water. A hundred yards from camp is a huge watering trough used by bovine forest users.

Mesa Spring, Mesa Spring Camp and Mesa Spring Trail are named for San Emigdio Mesa, the pinyon-pine covered territory that you skirt as the path leaves camp. Stay right at an unsigned trail junction just below camp and continue walking for a couple miles on a flatland between the mesa on your left and the tall shoulder of Mt. Cerro Noroeste on your right.

At a (poorly) signed trail junction, you'll join Forest Service Trail 22W01, Toad Spring Trail, which leads northward 3.75 miles to Quatal Canyon Road.

The trail climbs and dips over pinyon pine- and juniper-dotted slopes. You'll get grand views west and south over the proposed Chumash Wilderness and of the Cuyama Badlands to the northwest. Best view of all is the view right below of Quatal Canyon. The pinnacle rock formations resemble those in Southwest Utah.

Toad Spring Trail, seriously eroded by motorcycles, but passable, skirts the rim of Quatal Canyon. The last mile of the trail marches steeply up and down some minor hills before reaching its terminus (or trailhead, depending on how you look at it) at Quatal Canyon Road.

PINE MOUNTAIN

Reyes Peak Trail

From Reyes Peak Roadhead to Potrero John Overlook is 3.5 miles round trip with 300-foot elevation gain; to Haddock Peak is 7.5 miles round trip with 600-foot gain; to Haddock Trail Camp is 11 miles round trip with 800-foot gain

The invigorating scent of pine, great views, and a dramatic ridgetop trail are some of the highlights of a hike atop Pine Mountain. The mountain, which straddles the Mt. Pinos and Ojai Ranger Districts in Los Padres National Forest, is made up of several 7,000-foot-plus peaks, each offering a different backcountry panorama.

For most of its length, Reyes Peak Trail stays atop, or contours just below the ridgetop connecting Reyes to its sister peaks. The well-constructed footpath is shaded the whole way by white fir, Jeffrey, ponderosa and sugar pine. Inspiring views are offered from uninspiringly named Peaks 7091, 7114 and 7416, as well as from the saddles between the summits.

Directions to trailhead: From Highway 101 in Ventura, exit on Highway 33 and head north 47 miles (32 miles past Ojai) to the signed turnoff for Pine Mountain Recreation Area. Follow the narrow paved road past some campgrounds. After 6 miles the paved surface ends and you'll continue east one more mile on a dirt road (suitable for most passenger cars) to road's end, where there's a modest amount of parking.

The hike: Follow the dirt road (closed to vehicles beyond the trailhead) about 150 yards. As the road curves southeast, join the unsigned eastbound trail that begins on the east side of the road. The trail descends slightly and soon passes below the pine- and boulder-covered summit of Reyes Peak (7,510 feet), high point of the Pine Mountain massif. Pine and fir shade the trail, which alternately follows the ridgeline and contours just below it.

You'll look down to the northwest at the farms and ranches of Cuyama Valley, and beyond to the stark Cuyama Badlands. Enjoy pine-framed views of Mt. Pinos (8,831 feet), highest peak in Los Padres National Forest. From the ridgetop, peer southwest into the Sespe River gorge.

After about 1.75 miles of travel, you'll be treated to a view of the canyon cut by Potrero John Creek. The eroded cliffs at the head of the canyon recall Utah's Bryce Canyon National Park.

Reyes Peak Trail continues east through pine and fir forest. After two more miles of travel, you'll drop into and switchback out of a hollow, and arrive at signed Haddock Peak. The peak offers good views to the south and west of the Ojai backcountry.

From the peak, the trail descends in earnest. Almost two miles of travel brings you to Haddock Trail Camp located on the banks of Piedra Blanca Creek.

Reyes Creek, Beartrap Creek

Beartrap Trail
From Reyes Creek Camp to Upper Reyes Trail Camp is 6 miles round trip with 800-foot elevation gain; to Beartrap #1 Trail Camp is 10 miles round trip with 1,100-foot gain

Reyes and Beartrap creeks are two of the many pretty watercourses that spill from the northern slopes of Pine Mountain in Los Padres National Forest. The creeks run full speed in spring and even in dry years usually have water.

Upper Reyes is a cool canyon trail camp named for a local pioneer family. Farther up the trail is Beartrap Camp, where the Reyes and others settlers established hunting camps. The fierce grizzly was lord and sovereign over these mountains until hunters eliminated the animals from the area with guns and traps.

Near the trailhead is Camp Scheideck Lodge, established in the 1890s as a hunting lodge. Now the establishment is a funky country bar, where hikers may gather post hike to quench their thirst with a beer or soft drink.

Directions to trailhead: From Interstate 5, just north of Gorman, take the Frazier Park exit and follow Frazier Mountain Road west for 7 miles to Lockwood Valley Road. Turn left and proceed 24 miles to the signed turnoff for Reyes Creek Campground. A second sign advertising Camp Scheideck Lodge is also at this junction. Turn left and follow the paved road as it crosses the Cuyama River. Caution: Crossing can be difficult during times of high water. Park in the day-use area.

The hike: From the trailhead, the path rises out of Reyes Creek Canyon. The trail leads through an interesting mixture of three life zones: chaparral, oak woodland and pine.

The trail switchbacks up to a saddle. Behind you, to the northwest, is a fine view of the tortured terrain of the Cuyama Badlands. In front of you, to the southeast, is the much more inviting forested canyon cut by Reyes Creek. From the saddle, a half-mile descent brings you to Upper Reyes Trail Camp. It's a pleasant stream-side camp, a good place to cool your heels or to take a lunch stop.

Energetic hikers will assault the switchbacks above Upper Reyes Trail Camp and climb to the ridge separating Reyes Creek from Beartrap Creek. The trail then descends to an oak- and pine-shaded camp on Beartrap Creek.

Fishbowls

Cedar Creek Trail
From Thorn Meadows to Cedar Camp is 4 miles round trip with 300-foot elevation gain; to Fishbowls is 9 miles round trip with 1,000-foot gain

The Fishbowls of Piru Creek are a deep series of potholes dredged out of the sedimentary rock creekbed by the erosive power of rushing water. You'll enjoy basking on nearby flat rocks and dreaming your life away. When you awake from your dreams, a plunge into the cold water of the Fishbowls will quickly clear your head.

This hike is one of the nicest in the Mt. Pinos area of Los Padres National Forest. The trail climbs through cedar and pine forest to the headwaters of Piru Creek. The creek springs from the slopes of Pine Mountain and bubbles through a maze of mountains. Piru Creek pools were the site of gold mining at the turn of the century. Even today, you can sometimes spot weekend prospectors looking for a flash in the pan.

Directions to trailhead: From Interstate 5 just north of Gorman, take the Frazier Park exit and follow Frazier Mountain Road west for 7 miles to Lockwood Valley Road, a dirt road suitable for most passenger cars. Proceed 7.5 miles, then turn right on signed Thorn Meadows Road (7N03B)and drive 0.5 mile to the beginning of Cedar Creek Trail on the right. Parking is along the road near the trailhead.

Cooling off in the Fishbowls

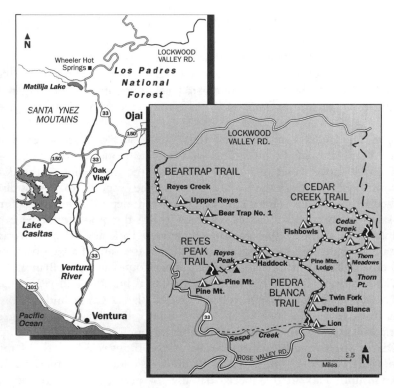

The hike: From the trailhead, head up a dirt road that is closed to vehicles. The road soon narrows to a trail, which stays near Piru Creek. It's pleasant hiking through oak woodland and scattered pines. Wallflowers, scarlet buglers and Johnny jump-ups brighten the path. Watch for the chia with its small blue flowers. A staple food of local native Americans, a single teaspoon of chia seed was reported to have been able to sustain a traveler on a 24-hour walk.

After 2 miles of pleasant hiking, you arrive at peaceful Cedar Creek Camp on a south fork of Cedar Creek in a tiny basin ringed by cedar and big cone spruce. The camp is a wonderful place for a picnic and for soaking up some shade before the climb ahead.

The trail continues up forested slopes, along the backbone of a ridge and in a long mile reaches a signed junction. To the left, a trail leads to Pine Mountain Lodge Camp. Bear right, or north, to the Fishbowls on Fishbowls Trail (22W05). The trail swoops up and down two more ridges and offers great views of the sharp forested ridges of the Mt. Pinos high country. The trail then descends steeply to Fishbowls Trail Camp, 1.5 miles from the trail junction.

The camp occupies a quiet, shady canyon cut by the headwaters of Piru Creek. From the camp, the Fishbowls area 0.25 mile upstream.

PIEDRA BLANCA

Piedra Blanca National Recreation Trail

From Lion Campground to Piedra Blanca is 3 miles round trip with 200-foot elevation gain; to Twin Forks Camp is 6 miles round trip; 600-foot gain; to Pine Mountain Lodge Camp is 11 miles round trip with 3,000-foot gain

Sparkling Piedra Blanca (White Rock) is the sort of place where Castañeda's Don Juan might lurk. The sandstone formation extends for miles between the upper reaches of Sespe River and the mountains to the north. Most of the sandstone in the Sespe area, called the Sespe Formation, is distinguished by its red color. It's a land-laid formation, deposited in layers of mud and sand on land. Unlike the red rock that guards the mouth of Sespe Creek, Piedra Blanca's thick sequences of sedimentary rock are of marine origin. These marine deposits are particularly notable in the Santa Barbara backcountry. Perhaps the most spectacular formations are found at Piedra Blanca.

Piedra Blanca Trail ascends chaparral-cloaked hillsides and visits mighty Piedra Blanca. The path then follows Piedra Blanca Creek and climbs for some distance to Pine Mountain Lodge Camp, the site of a hunting and fishing lodge that once stood on the slopes of Pine Mountain.

Directions to trailhead: From Ojai, take Highway 33 north 14 miles. Turn right on signed Rose Valley Road and continue 6 miles to Lion Campground. Park in the special day-use lot near the campground. The sometimes-signed trail begins across the creek.

The hike: Cross Sespe Creek and join Piedra Blanca Trail. The trail cuts through chaparral and wastes no time heading for Piedra Blanca. These jumbo rocks are in your sight most of the way. Like clouds, the longer you gaze at the formations, the more they assume the shape of your imagination: dragons with missing teeth, the Washington Monument. . . .

From the rocks, the trail descends sharply to an unnamed tributary of Piedra Blanca Creek, finds the creek itself and follows it up the canyon. The trail dips in and out of the narrow oak woodland that lines the creek. You pass an attractive streamside trail camp named for the dominant sandstone, Piedra Blanca, and soon come to Twin Forks Trail Camp, named for its location near the North and Middle Forks of Piedra Blanca Creek. Either Piedra Blanca or Twin Forks are nice picnic spots.

From Twin Forks, the trail twists along with the north fork of Piedra Blanca Creek. It ascends steeply for about 2 miles, then leaves the creek and climbs chaparral- and pine-covered slopes toward the top of Pine Mountain. Pine Mountain Lodge Trail Camp, located at an elevation of 6,000 feet, is cool and green, a good place to take off your shoes and sit awhile.

Sespe Creek

Sespe Creek Trail
From Lion Campground to Sespe Wilderness Boundary is 2.5 miles round trip; to Bear Canyon crossing is 9 miles round trip.

In 1992, it became official: the Sespe Wilderness. But this land near Ojai has always been a wilderness. It remained a wilderness after Don Carlos Antonio Carrillo and his Rancho Sespe cattle operation and the gold miners of the 19th century; it even retained its wilderness character when oil companies drilled wells in the 20th century.

The Sespe area had long been recognized as something special. In 1947, a 53,000-acre Sespe Sanctuary was set aside, primarily to aid the then rapidly declining condor population. After many years—in 1992, to be precise—conservationists, particularly the Keep the Sespe Wild Committee, succeeded in convincing Congress to proclaim the 219,700-acre Sespe Wilderness, as well as to designate 31.5 miles of Sespe Creek as "Wild and Scenic."

Sespe Creek, the last, large, free-flowing river in Southern California, rises on the Santa Barbara-Ventura County border and flows 55 miles from its headwaters to empty into the Santa Clara River near Fillmore. Its wildness is apparent when seen from the air; airline passengers often get a glimpse of the bold Sespe Gorge and the fractured country surrounding it when their planes fly over it on the way to and from LAX.

In some winters, the Sespe is notorious for its floods, which dislodge boulders the size of freight cars. More often it's a mellow watercourse that beckons anglers, swimmers and hikers.

Before the wilderness designation, and before late 1970s floods wiped it out, a four-wheel-drive road extended from Lion Campground to Sespe Hot Springs and then to the border of the condor refuge. The remains of Old Sespe Road (6N31) are now part of the Sespe's creekside footpath.

Backpackers bound for Sespe Hot Springs, 15 miles down-river, and to Sespe Gorge beyond trail's end, are the primary travelers on the trail. While the hot springs is too far for a day hike, the Sespe serves up some other delightful attractions—deep pools in the bends of the river, sandy beaches for sunning, sparkling, rounded, multi-colored river rock. Instead of striving for a goal on this hike, simply wander as far down-creek as you desire.

Directions to trailhead: From Ojai, follow Highway 33 north for 14 miles. Turn right onto dirt Rose Valley Road and drive 6 miles to Lion Campground. Park in the day use-hikers' parking area at road's end.

The hike: Cross Sespe Creek and follow the trail briefly north to a junction with Piedra Blanca Trail (see description on page 40). Sespe Creek Trail forks right and travels along the north bank of the creek. In the first mile

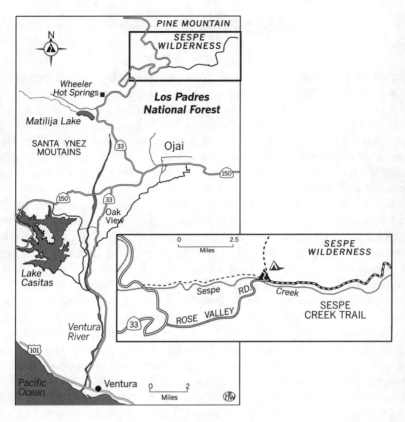

you'll cross Piedra Blanca Creek and Trout Creek before a sign welcomes you to the Sespe Wilderness.

En route, numerous right-branching side trails lead down to the river. The main trail does not cross the creek until Bear Canyon, 4.5 miles from the trailhead. This crossing is a good turnaround point, but feel free to keep hiking on the fairly level Sespe Creek Trail as far as you think you can travel and return in a day.

MATILIJA CREEK

Matilija Trail
Matilija Cyn. Rd. to Matilija Camp is 2 miles round trip with 200-foot elevation gain; to Middle Matilija Camp is 7 miles round trip with 900-foot gain; to Forest Road 6N01 is 15 miles round trip with 3,000-foot gain.
Season: Oct-June

The meaning of Matilija is unknown, but it may have been the Chumash word to describe the showy Matilija poppy, prized by the Indians for its medicinal qualities. The poppy's botanical name, *Romneya coulteri* honors two Irish scientists and longtime friends, astronomer Romney Robinson and botanist Thomas Coulter.

Coulter first collected this outstanding flower in 1831. During the early years of this century, Ojai entrepreneurs dug up Matilija poppies by the thousands and sold them in Los Angeles.

The Matilija poppy is found along many Ojai backcountry trails and often alongside the road into and out of Ojai—Highway 33. It blooms from May to July, stands three to seven feet tall and is bushy at its base. The delicate flowers have six white crinkled petals and a golden center. Matilija poppies have a strong, sweet fragrance and hikers who near a stand may smell the flower before sighting it.

The Matilija Trail has the dubious distinction of being the flash point for some of the largest fires in Southern California history. In June of 1917 the Matilija-Wheeler Springs Fire burned for five days and nights and blackened more than 30,000 acres. The 1932 Matilija Fire burned nearly a quarter million acres. One of the fire lines was Highway 33, then under construction.

The 1985 Wheeler Fire scorched much of the Ojai backcountry, including the steep terrain watered by the many forks of Matilija Creek. On the high chaparral-covered ridges, a holocaust took place. The canyon bottoms fared better in the firestorm and have made a remarkable recovery.

Matilija Trail, at its lower end, offers an ideal family outing alongside the Upper North Fork of Matilija Creek. More experienced hikers will enjoy pushing on to the canyon's upper reaches for fine ocean and mountain views. Many nice pools, cascades and flat sunny rocks offer pleasant picnic spots. Some 30,000 acres of Ojai backcountry were set aside as the Matilija Wilderness.

Directions to trailhead: Continue on Highway 33 about four miles past Ojai, and past the leftward turnoff to Matilija Hot Springs. A short mile past the hot springs, turn left on Matilija Canyon Road (Forest Service Road 5N13) and proceed 5 miles to a locked gate across the road. A parking area is located just before the gate.

The hike: Pass the locked gate and hike along the dirt road through Matilija Canyon Ranch and a private wildlife reserve. Please stay on the road and respect private property. After crossing two branches of Matilija Creek, the road turns left, but you will follow the unmarked spur that turns right and follows the creek. Within 50 yards, cross the creek twice more and begin hiking along the creek bank. A mile of nearly level walking brings you to Matilija Camp.

Matilija Camp is a nice picnic spot. Those geologically inclined will note how stream erosion in this area exposed areas of severe folding and faulting; past actions of the Santa Ynez Fault are very much in evidence.

Beyond the camp, the trail fords several small tributary creeks that feed the Upper North Fork of the Matilija, and crosses a wide meadow. The trail switchbacks above the creek for a while, then resumes again on the canyon bottom. Some level travel and few more crossings brings you to oak-shaded Middle Matilija Camp. You can lunch here and call it a day or push on upstream.

Beyond the camp, the trail crosses and re-crosses the creek half a dozen more times. The canyon floor is forested with big cone spruce, bay laurel and maple. You'll rise out of the canyon, then descend into the narrowing canyon and arrive at abandoned, but still serviceable, Upper Matilija Camp.

From this camp, the trail continues up-creek another mile, then rises steeply north out of the canyon. Switchbacks offer the hiker fine views of Old Man Mountain, the Santa Ynez range and the Pacific Ocean. The upper canyon slopes were severely burned in 1985. However, the maples at Maple Camp, the chokecherry, manzanita and scrub oak are recovering. A final steep climb brings you to the terminus of the trail at Forest Service Road 6N01 near Ortega Hill.

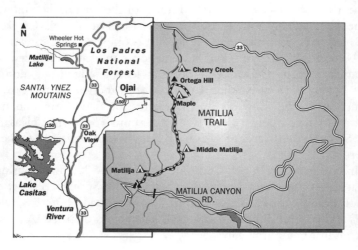

Ojai Valley

Foothill Trail
From Stewart Canyon to Gridley Road (return via Shelf Road)
is 5.5 miles round trip with 600-foot elevation gain

Ojai, nestled in a little valley backed by the Topatopa and Sulphur Mountains, has meant tranquility to several generations of settlers and citrus growers, artists, musicians and mystics. Ojai Valley was the setting for Shangri-La in the 1937 movie *Lost Horizon*.

The ten-mile-long, three-mile wide valley, surrounded by coastal mountain ranges has always had a sequestered feeling. Chumash Indians called this region Ojai, which means "nest." The meditative setting has spawned an artists colony, music festival and a number of health resorts. The environment has attracted the metaphysically minded too; the hiker can look down on the Krotona Institute of Theosophy on one side of town and the Krishnamurti Foundation on the other.

Foothill Trail offers the best view of the town and valley. From the path, hikers get great views of the harmonious Spanish architecture of Ojai, sweet-smelling citrus groves and the misty, mystical Ojai Valley.

Directions to trailhead: From the intersection of Highways 150 and 33, head east on the latter route one mile to North Signal Street in downtown Ojai. The post office and The Oaks resort are on this corner. Turn north on North Signal and drive 0.75 mile to a junction with an unsigned road on your left. A large water tower and a chain link fence are at this junction. Park along Signal.

The hike: Take a look up North Signal, which ends in another hundred yards at its meeting with Shelf Road, the dirt fire road that will be your return route. Now turn west on the paved road below the water tank. The road soon turns to gravel and you'll march past a Ventura County flood control works, the Stewart Canyon Debris Basin. Two hundred yards from the trailhead, just as your road turns north toward some residences, you'll spot a white pipe fence and a Forest Service trail sign. Join the trail, which soon dips into brushy Stewart Canyon.

The trail zigzags under oaks and a tangled understory of native and non-native shrubs. You'll cross two dirt roads then wind through a eucalyptus grove, which marks the site of the elegant Foothill Hotel, a casualty of fire in the early 1900s.

Foothill Trail turns north and ascends along the west wall of Stewart Canyon. The trail nears some private homes, crosses a paved road, then joins a dirt one and passes a water tank on your left. Shortly thereafter is a signed trail on your left for Foothill Trail 22W09 and Pratt Trail 23W09.

Continue another 100 yards on the dirt road to another signed junction with the Foothill Trail; this path you'll take east.

Foothill Trail ascends up fire-scarred slopes and over meadowland seasonally dotted with wildflowers. Keep an eye out for abundant poison oak. Just as you're beginning to wonder if this trail will ever deliver its promised views, it tops a rise and offers a first glimpse of Ojai Valley.

The trail soon descends to an unsigned junction. A connector trail leads north to Forest Road 5N11; this road heads east to Gridley Road but offers no valley views. Stay with Foothill Trail, which descends to a little seasonal creek then climbs eastward out onto open slopes for great views of Ojai. From some vantage points you can see almost the whole Ojai Valley.

About a half-mile from Gridley Road, you'll spot dirt Shelf Road 200 yards or so below Foothill Trail. Experienced bushwhackers can blaze a trail down to the road, but think twice; it's probably more trouble than the little time/distance saved. Foothill Trail, near its end, descends more steeply, its route stabilized by railroad ties. The trail emerges at a crumbling asphalt road, which you'll follow 50 yards to Gridley Road. Turn right on Gridley Road. Walk a hundred yards, cross a one-lane bridge, then descend another hundred yards to Shelf Road on your right.

Shelf Road, closed to vehicle traffic by a white pipe gate, heads east and ascends moderately into the hills. Skirting orange trees and avocado groves, Shelf Road serves up views that are just a little less dramatic than those offered by higher Foothill Trail.

Just after the road bends south, you'll reach a gate and Signal Road, which you'll follow the short distance back to the trailhead.

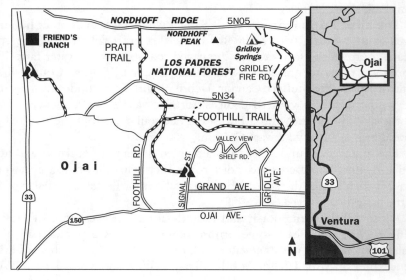

Sulphur Mountain

Sulphur Mountain Road Recreation Trail
10 miles one way with 2,300-foot elevation loss

Once upon a time, Sulphur Mountain Road was one of the Southland's great Sunday drives. Motorists loved this curvy, dirt byway back of Ojai for the superb vistas it offered of the Ojai Valley, Topatopa Mountains, coast and Channel Islands.

These days, vehicles are banned from Sulphur Mountain but the sterling views remain to anyone willing to walk a crooked mile.

Make that 10 crooked miles. A substantial length of the road has been renamed Sulphur Mountain Road Recreation Trail, and traffic restricted to equestrians, cyclists, hikers and the occasional vehicle belonging to one of the local ranchers.

The Ojai backcountry is generally assumed to be the public lands of Los Padres National Forest, which borders Ojai to the east, west and north. But south of Ojai is more backcountry—Sulphur Mountain—almost all of which is private property. The mountain, occupying a 12-mile wide by 12-mile long block of land, is surrounded by highways: Highway 33 to the west, Highway 150 on the north and east, Highways 126 and 101 on the south. These highways approach, but do not cross, Sulphur Mountain. Sulphur Mountain Road Recreation Trail (maintained by Ventura County) is the only public crossing of this terra incognita.

The ridgeline traverse of Sulphur Mountain is a one-way hike, requiring either two vehicles or the cooperation of someone to drop you at the top of Sulphur Mountain and collect you at the bottom.

It's not difficult convincing friends or family members to provide shuttle service because, while you're on the trail (3 to 4 hours), they can enjoy nearby Ojai.

Directions to trailhead: Return to Highway 33 and follow it north to the outskirts of Ojai. Bear right onto Highway 150 and motor into downtown Ojai. Proceed another 6.5 miles on Highway 150 to signed Sulphur Mountain Road. Turn right and travel 4.75 miles to the steep and winding road to a locked gate at the trailhead.

To the pickup point at trail's end: From Highway 101 in Ventura, exit on Highway 33 and drive 7.5 miles to signed Sulphur Mountain Road. Turn right and proceed 0.4 mile to the vehicle gate.

The hike: Join the road (paved at first) and hike west. Enjoy glimpses of the Ojai countryside at its most eclectic: a gazebo, a yurt, rusted farm implements, a huge red-tile-roofed hacienda.

About 1.5 miles from the trailhead, the asphalt ends and you continue

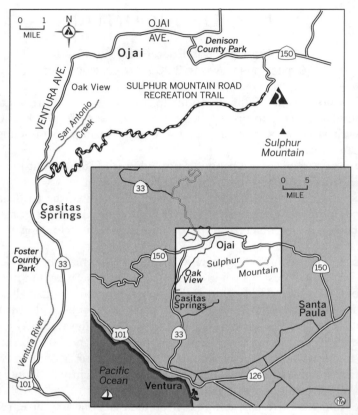

the descent on well-graded dirt road. Nearly three miles out, enjoy clear-day views of the Channel Islands and great blue Pacific.

At about mile 4, the trail delivers the first of several stunning, oak-framed panoramic vistas of the Ojai Valley. Particularly prominent in this aerial view is the Ojai Valley Inn & Country Club. Hikers growing a bit leg-weary as they approach the midpoint of this hike might start fantasizing about a massage and spa treatment at the resort.

In some years, Sulphur Mountain boasts fine spring wildflower displays—carpets of lupine and California poppies joining the profligate yellow mustard alongside the road.

The road continues dropping down the ridge and enters classic Southern California cattle country, where cows graze utterly undisturbed by passing hikers.

The last two miles of trail are steep—an elevation loss of more than 1,200 feet. All too soon, you might think, you hear the sound of traffic from Highway 33 and descend to trail's end.

Santa Paula Canyon

Santa Paula Canyon Trail

From Santa Paula Canyon to Big Cone Camp is 6 miles round trip with 800-foot elevation gain; to Cross Camp is 8 miles round trip with 900-foot gain

Waterfalls, wading pools and swimming holes are some of the attractions of tranquil Santa Paula Canyon. A trail winds along the river bed through the canyon and visits some perfect-for-a-picnic trail camps.

The lovely trail begins at St. Thomas Aquinas College, and near a malodorous oil field once owned by infamous oilman and Southern California booster Edward Lawrence Doheny. Doheny's black gold discoveries of 1892 made him an extremely wealthy man and began the first oil industry boom in Los Angeles. (Doheny's 30-room mansion is located behind iron gates just off Highway 150.)

During the Harding administration, Doheny received drilling rights on federal land in Elk Hills without undergoing the inconvenience of competitive bidding. A 1923 Senate investigation of the "Teapot Dome Scandal" uncovered Doheny's $100,000 loan to Secretary of the Interior Fall and led to Fall's conviction for accepting a bribe; Doheny, however, was acquitted of offering one.

Directions to trailhead: From the junction of Highways 33 and 150 in Ojai, head east from town on the latter road about 9.5 miles to the bridge spanning Santa Paula Creek. The trailhead is located at the entrance to St. Thomas Aquinas College/Ferndale Ranch on the north side of the road, but you continue on Highway 150 across the Santa Paula Creek bridge to a wide turnout on the south side of the highway. A sign informs you that Santa Paula Canyon Trail begins across the highway 500 feet away.

The hike: From the often-guarded Ferndale Ranch/college entrance, you'll ignore a road leading to the oil fields and follow the asphalt drive onto the college grounds. The road curves around wide green lawns and handsome classrooms. At a few junctions, signs keep you "Hikers" away from the route taken by "Oil Field Traffic." A bit more than a half-mile from the trailhead, you pass an orchard and some cows, pass through a pipe gate, and finally reach Santa Paula Creek and the true beginning of Santa Paula Canyon Trail.

The trail travels a short distance with Santa Paula Creek, crosses it, then joins a retiring dirt road—your route to Big Cone Camp. After crossing the creek again, the trail begins a moderate to stiff climb up a slope bearing the less-than-lyrical name of Hill 1989. The trail then descends to Big Cone Camp, perched on a terrace above Santa Paula Creek.

Just below the camp, the trail, now a narrow footpath, descends to the

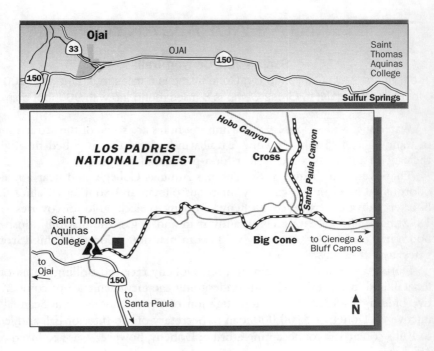

creek. As you descend, you'll look up-canyon and spot a waterfall and a swimming hole.

The trail crosses Santa Paula Creek and switchbacks up to an unsigned junction. A right at this junction leads above the east fork of Santa Paula Canyon 3.5 miles on poor, unmaintained trail to Cienega Camp. Hardy hikers will enjoy bushwhacking along to this camp set in a meadowland shaded by oak and big-cone spruce.

A left at the above-mentioned junction leads north up Santa Paula Canyon past some inviting pools. The path, sometimes called Last Chance Trail, climbs a mile to Cross, another big-cone spruce-shaded camp. Here Santa Paula Creek offers some nice falls and great swimming holes. Caution: The creek current can be quite strong on occasion.

3. Simi Hills

THE MAP IS NOT THE TERRITORY, wise explorers counsel. That old adage seems to apply to the Simi Hills, which appear as little more than narrow band between suburbs on the map, but on the ground present some challenging territory to hike.

The Simi Hills escape most hikers' attention because they are both literally and figuratively overshadowed by two other regional ranges located on this side of the Southland. The nearby Santa Susana Mountains are considerably rounder and taller than the Simi Hills. And the nearby Santa Monica Mountains have a high public profile due to associations with Malibu, movie stars and movie sets, as well as the range's national parkland status.

These comparisons aside, the Simi Hills have a distinct identity when viewed up-close. Somehow the sky-scraping sedimentary rock formations seem all the more awesome towering over flatland neighborhoods. The reddish-orange sandstone outcroppings of the Simi Hills, dating from the Tertiary and Mesozoic periods 60 to 80 million years ago, form a dramatic backdrop and its easy to see why these rugged hills were a popular setting for Western movies.

Two hundred years ago a cross atop a Simi Hills peak was a landmark to the friars and other travelers who trudged the dusty trail from mission to mission. A cross still stands atop this peak, now named Mt. McCoy, and it remains a ready reference point for Simi Valley residents.

When the Ronald Reagan Presidential Library and Museum was built in the Simi Hills, it brought national attention to the range.

It's bad news and good news and good news for hikers who heed the call of the wild in the Simi Hills. The bad news is suburbia is advancing rapidly from the floor of the Simi Valley into the once lonely hills. Just when you think—they can't possibly build a subdivision here—they do.

The good news is some of the more environmentally enlightened and culturally attuned developers have finally grasped the popularity of hiking and what an attractive "neighborhood amenity" a hiking trail can be and have actually built footpaths in the Simi Hills. Rancho Simi Recreation and Park District along with local trails groups have worked hard to establish and maintain trails.

Most hikers say the rocks are the most picturesque feature of the hills. Severely tilted (about 35 to 40 degrees) tan-hued sandstone outcroppings lunge out of the hilltops and are quite photogenic.

And the rocks are more than just a pretty face. Scientists say the Las Llajas Formation, deposited some 45 million years ago when this area was under a tropical ocean is one of North America's most important geological formations because it holds such a diversity of both marine and terrestrial fossils.

SIMI PEAK

China Flat Trail
5 mile loop with 1,000-foot elevation gain

China Flat Trail is an excellent (but not easy) introduction to the Simi Hills. It leads to China Flat, perched on the wild west side of the National Park Service's Cheeseboro Canyon Site. The trail's return loop contours high over the shoulder of 2,403-foot Simi Peak, highest summit in the Simi Hills.

Ambitious hikers will enjoy China Flat Trail as a backdoor entry along the ridgecrest to Cheeseboro and Palo Comado canyons, part of the Santa Monica Mountains National Recreation Area. Expect a 10- or 12-mile hike (or more), as well as a measure of solitude on this lightly traveled route.

China Flat Trail is a bit of a misnomer; the trail is anything but flat. And China Flat itself, while of more level relief than surrounding Simi peaks, will never be confused with one of those truly flat Flats found in other mountain ranges.

Still, China Flat Trail is a most enjoyable loop, requiring only a one-block neighborhood stroll to connect trail's end with the trailhead.

Directions to trailhead: From the Ventura Freeway (101) in Westlake Village, exit on Lindero Canyon Road and head north 4 miles. A few blocks from the trailhead, Lindero Canyon Road bends east. Look for the signed trailhead on the left (north) side of the road between King James Court and Wembly Avenue. Park on Lindero Canyon Road.

The trail: Follow the trail north up a short, steep hill. Here a connector trail rising from King James Court meets the path. Continue on the main (China Flat) trail as it ascends past a sandstone formation. After climbing some more, the path gentles a bit and contours east to an unsigned junction. Keep to the left (north) and begin a stiff climb toward the ridgeline.

Finally the trail gains the ridge and you encounter another unsigned junction. Bear left and continue an ascent along the ridge to a saddle and yet another trail junction. (Ambitious trekkers bound for Cheeseboro Canyon will take the right fork.)

This hike uses the left fork and begins a moderate descent. Views from the shoulder of Simi Peak include Westlake Village, Agoura Hills and other communities clustered on the Ventura-Los Angeles County line, as well as the peaks of the Santa Monica Mountains.

The trail ends at a gate on King James Court. Follow this short street one block down to Lindero Canyon Road and your vehicle.

CHEESEBORO CANYON

Cheeseboro Canyon Trail
From NPS Parking Lot to Sulfur Springs is 6 miles round trip
with 100-foot elevation gain; to Sheep Corral
is 9.5 miles round trip with 200-foot elevation gain

It's the old California of the ranchos: Oak-studded potreros, rolling foothills that glow amber in the dry months, emerald green in springtime. It's easy to imagine vaqueros rounding up tough Mexican range cattle.

For years this last vestige of old California faced an uncertain future, but thanks to the efforts of conservationists it was saved from golf course and suburban development in 1991.

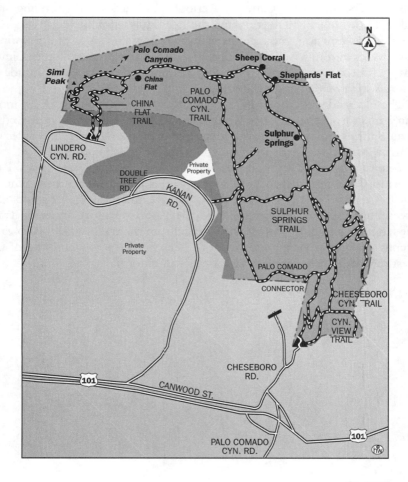

From the days of the ranchos to 1985, Cheeseboro Canyon was heavily grazed by cattle. Grazing altered canyon ecology by displacing native flora and allowing opportunistic plants such as mustard and thistle to invade. As you walk through the canyon, you'll see signs indicating research areas. The National Park Service is attempting to re-colonize native flora and eradicate nonnatives.

Directions to trailhead: From the Ventura Freeway (101) in Agoura, exit on Chesebro Road. Loop inland very briefly on Palo Comado Canyon Road, then turn right on Chesebro Road, which leads to the National Park Service's gravel entrance road and parking lot.

The trail: Note your return route, Modello Trail, snaking north up the wall of the canyon, but follow the fire road east into Cheeseboro Canyon. The fire road soon swings north and dips into the canyon. You'll pass a signed intersection with Canyon Overlook Trail, a less-than-thrilling side trail that leads to a knoll overlooking the Lost Hills landfill.

After this junction, the main canyon trail, now known as Sulfur Springs Trail, winds through valley oak-dotted grassland and coast live oak-lined canyon. Watch for mule deer browsing in the meadows and a multitude of squirrels scurrying amongst the oaks.

The old road crisscrosses an (usually) all-but-dry streambed. A bit more than 3 miles from the trailhead, your nose will tell you that you've arrived at Sulfur Springs. You can turn around here or continue another 1.75 miles up a narrowing trail and narrowing canyon to an old sheep corral.

You can continue a bit farther on the trail to a junction with Palo Comado Canyon Trail and head south on this path back to the trailhead. Ranch Center Trail, a 1.1 mile long path, connects Palo Comado and Cheeseboro canyons, as does the 1.5 mile Palo Comado Connector Trail. The latter path leads to a junction 0.7 mile from the trailhead. Modelo Trail ascends a ridgetop for a good view of Cheeseboro Canyon and one of the finest remaining oak woodlands in Southern California.

Ahmanson Ranch

East Las Virgenes Canyon Trail
From Las Virgenes Road to Laskey Mesa is 5.5 miles round trip with 500-foot elevation gain; many shorter and longer hikes possible

From atop the ridge on the southeastern corner of Ahmanson Ranch, commanding vistas of two competing visions of 21st-century Southern California are revealed to the hiker. Eastward and southward the San Fernando Valley suburbanopolis sprawls across Los Angeles County. Westward beckons a magnificent, nearly untouched landscape of rolling grassland, oak dotted slopes and the dramatic summits of the Simi Hills, miles of wildland extending across Ventura County.

The preservationist vision prevailed after a decade-long battle that pitted conservationists and celebrity allies such as Rob Reiner and Martin Sheen against Washington Mutual with a $2 billion plan that called for construction of 3,000 homes, a golf course and a shopping mall on the ranch land. The enormous savings institution agreed to sell the land to the Santa Monica Mountains Conservancy in 2003.

Ahmanson Ranch's natural resources include some 4,000 valley and coastal live oak trees, as well as the ultra-rare San Fernando Valley spine flower, recently rediscovered after botanists believed it extinct for 70 years. The ranch is one of the state's prime raptor habitats and is home to Southern California's last viable population of the red-legged frog.

The rolling hills and broad mesas of Ahmanson Ranch have been a favorite location for filmmakers since the silent movie era. The Lasky Company owned the ranch, which boasted both a close proximity to studios and an almost complete lack of development. Among the movies filmed at Laskey Mesa, as it was then known, were *The Charge of the Light Brigade, They Died with Their Boots On,* and *Gone with the Wind.*

Few improvements are planned for Ahmanson Ranch, which will be preserved in an unaltered state as wildlife habitat and a nature park. Hikers can explore the 2,900-acre park on some 15 miles of trails and dirt roads.

More than one great ranch trail awaits the hiker, so I've suggested four possible routes for your wanderings.

Directions to trailhead: From Highway 101 in Calabasas, exit on Las Virgenes Canyon Road and drive north 1.5 miles to road's end. Park on either side of the road. At road's end, you'll find the start of the main trail that leads into Ahmanson Ranch.

You can also enter Ahmanson Ranch from undeveloped trailheads located near the ends of Victory Boulevard and Van Owen Street.

The hike: One good introduction to the ranch's charms is the hike to

Laskey Mesa. Head out along the park's main dirt entry road, branch right on East Virgenes Canyon Road and, about 1.75 miles from the trailhead, veer southward on the path to Laskey Mesa. Hike a mile loop around the 1,391-foot mesa and then return the way you came.

For a west-to-east traverse of the ranch, follow the entirety of East Las Virgenes Canyon Road from the trailhead to a pending trailhead near the end of Victory Boulevard. This route is a 6-mile round trip with modest elevation gain.

For a short (2 miles round trip), but nevertheless rewarding loop, walk a short way up the access road to the first intersection and bear left (northwest) up the main branch of Las Virgenes Canyon. After a mile, you'll intersect a footpath on your left. Return south on this trail, which travels the canyon west wall back to a trailhead located very close to the main trailhead.

Gung-ho hikers will ascend the road through Las Virgenes Canyon to wildland known as Upper Las Virgenes Canyon Open Space. About three miles from the trailhead, the road crosses the creek for a final time and arcs west. The ambitious can continue to the upper reaches of Cheeseboro Canyon and connect with many miles of national parkland trails.

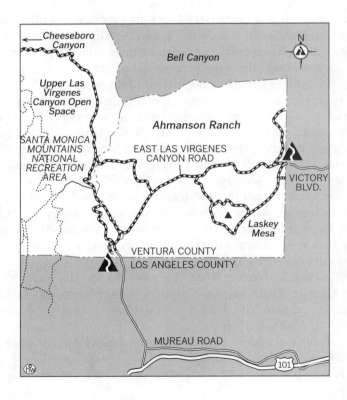

CORRIGANVILLE PARK

Corriganville Loop, Rocky Peak Connector Trails
Park loop is 2 miles round trip; to Rocky Peak Fire Road
is 5 miles round trip with 600 foot elevation gain

Some Hollywood historians claim this picturesque locale in the Simi Hills was the most extensively used film location outside a major studio. About a thousand Western and adventure movies were filmed at the Corriganville Movie Ranch from 1937 to 1965. Now the old movie ranch where the Lone Ranger rode, the Fugitive fled and Lassie came home is a new park that offers the hiker the chance to step back into film history.

Corriganville was founded by Raymond Bernard who changed his name to Ray "Crash Corrigan," the name of a character he played in *Undersea Kingdom*, a 1930s movie serial. Corrigan broke into the biz as a stuntman, and as a body double for *Tarzan* (Johnny Weismuller), then starred in two Western serials. In 1938 he purchased 2,000 acres of land he was certain would be an ideal Western movie backdrop.

Among the memorable Westerns filmed in Corriganville were *Duel in the Sun, Streets of Laredo, Fort Apache* and *How the West was Won*. Noted TV horse operas lensed here included "Gunsmoke," "Have Gun, Will Travel" and "The Cisco Kid." In 1948 Corriganville was opened to the public as a Wild West-flavored amusement park, complete with a rodeo and stagecoach rides.

Today, Corriganville Park plays a dual role as nature preserve and nostalgia. A family-friendly, 20-stop interpretive trail explores the terrain's natural and cinematic highlights. Between stops, even more plaques and signs delve deeper into this land's movie history.

A trail and tunnel connect Corriganville with Rocky Peak and the rugged hills located on the other side of 118. The tunnel and trails north and south of the freeway form a "wildlife corridor" designed to allow animals to migrate across the Simi Hills without becoming road kill. The corridor appears to be working: I've seen coyotes on both sides of the freeway.

Directions to trailhead: From the Ronald Reagan Freeway (118) in Simi Valley, exit on Kuehner Road and drive south a mile to Smith Road. Turn left and proceed a short distance to road's end and plenty of parking in Corriganville Park.

The trail: From the east end of the parking lot, follow the dirt road east past some coast live oaks and you'll soon join the park's signed nature trail. Your route parallels railroad tracks which seem to disappear up ahead into the mountains; the "disappearance" is actually a 1.5 mile long tunnel connecting Simi Valley with Chatsworth.

At Sherwood Forest, the oaks featured in *Robin Hood* now shade an inviting picnic ground. Here the trail splits. Those wishing to continue Nature Trail's exercise in nostalgia need only follow the numbered signs.

(Hardier hikers will walk to the far end of the picnic area and a shade ramada, and join the unsigned trail leading northeast. As this path ascends it morphs into a crumbling asphalt road, then an Appian Way-like path.

A short but steep climb brings you to the 118 freeway and the mouth of the tunnel leading under it. Walk through the graffiti-marred tunnel and emerge to join a footpath that briefly heads west above and parallel to the freeway, then swings northeast. What seems like a very long mile of hiking brings you to a junction with Rocky Peak Fire Road. Reward yourself by walking 100 yards south down the fire road to a bench and viewpoint of Corriganville and the Simi Valley.

From Sherwood Forest, cross a bridge over the creek that cuts through Corriganville. Note the concrete pool created by moviemakers, who filmed underwater scenes through portholes.

The path turns back west and soon passes the rocky hideouts used by many a movie bad guy. Hike the 75-yard side trail to a cave featured in episodes of "The Fugitive" television series.

The nature trail becomes just that again briefly with ecological explanations about lichen and sandstone formations. For Western movie fans, the trail saves the best for last as it visits the site of the John Ford-directed 1948 Western *Fort Apache* starring John Wayne and Henry Fonda.

The path skirts the scant remains of Silvertown, Corriganville's movie set town, then returns to the parking area.

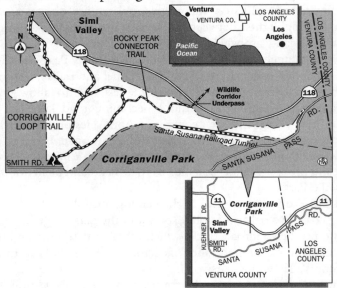

ROCKY PEAK

Rocky Peak, Chumash Trails
To Rocky Peak via Rocky Peak Trail is 6 miles round trip
with 1,200 foot elevation gain; to Rocky Peak via Chumash Trail
is 7 miles round trip with 1,400-foot gain

One conservation success story is the preservation of Runkle Ranch, now Rocky Peak Park. The park, which straddles the Los Angeles-Ventura county line, sets aside some much-needed parkland for fast-growing Simi Valley.

The rocks of Rocky Peak are sandstone outcroppings that geologists say were formed some 65 million years ago during the Cretaceous Period of the Mesozoic Era. Besides its namesake promontory, 4,369-acre Rocky Peak Park includes Las Llajas and Blind canyons. These canyons have two of the most pleasant seasonal streams in the mountains. After a good rain, waterfalls cascade down the canyons. Until purchased by the Santa Monica Mountains Conservancy in 1991, the Rocky Peak area was owned by entertainer Bob Hope.

Chumash Trail begins in Chumash Park on the outskirts of Simi Valley and leads 2.5 miles to a junction with Rocky Peak Trail, which leads to the peak. Park trails provide access to Blind Canyon and the rolling meadowlands of the Santa Susana Mountains to the north. This hike is a good introduction to the charms of the Santa Susanas.

Directions to trailhead: To reach the Rocky Peak trailhead, take Highway 118 through the Simi Valley and exit on Rocky Peak Road (that's

Rocky Peak area, Santa Susana Mountains.

one exit west of Topanga Canyon Boulevard). The trailhead is immediately opposite the end of the freeway offramp. Caution: You can exit on Rocky Peak Road only by traveling west on Highway 118.

To Chumash trailhead: From Highway 118 (Simi Valley-San Fernando Valley Freeway) in Simi Valley, exit on Yosemite Avenue. Head north 0.5 mile to Flanagan Drive, turn right, and drive 0.75 mile to road's end and Chumash Park.

The trail: (Via Rocky Peak Trail) Begin at the locked gate of the fire road (closed to vehicles) and begin the ascent. Soon you'll get grand view (if you turn around, that is) across the freeway to the historic Santa Susana Pass, once crossed by stagecoaches.

The fire road continues up and up, with only a lone oak along the trail for shade. Rocky Peak is off to the right (east) of the trail. From the peak and related smaller peaks, you'll get vistas of the San Fernando Valley, Simi Valley, high peaks of Los Padres National Forest, Anacapa Island and the Santa Barbara Channel. Way off to the right (west) is the Ronald Reagan Presidential Library.

From Chumash Park, Chumash trailheads north from the end of Flanagan Drive: The path soon parallels a creek, makes a half-circle around a minor hill, then begins climbing in earnest high above Blind Canyon.

Some 2.5 miles of steady ascent brings you to an intersection with Rocky Peak Trail. If you turn right (south) on this trail, it's about a mile's walk to Rocky Peak. A left turn leads 2.5 miles to the park boundary and a large oak savanna.

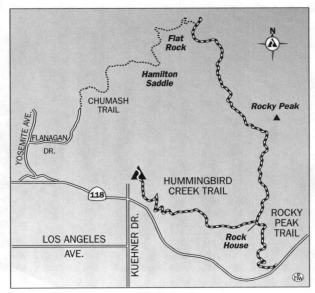

4. SANTA MONICA MOUNTAINS

THE SANTA MONICAS ARE the only relatively undeveloped mountain range in the U.S. that bisects a major metropolitan area. A near-wilderness within reach of sixteen million people, they stretch all the way from Griffith Park in the heart of Los Angeles to Point Mugu, 50 miles away. The mountains, which include the civilized Hollywood Hills and the oh-so-civilized Beverly Hills, extend westward to the steep wildlands above Malibu.

The range is 12 miles wide at its broadest point, and it reaches an elevation of a little over 3,000 feet. Large stretches are open and natural, covered with chaparral and oak trees, bright in spring with wildflowers. Water from winter rains runs down steep slopes and fosters a wide variety of life on the canyon floors. Oak woodland and fern glens shade gentle seasonal streams.

Ancestors of the Chumash lived in the mountains as early as 7,000 years ago. Abundant food sources helped the Chumash become the largest native group in California at the time of Juan Cabrillo's arrival in 1542. The highly developed Chumash culture included ocean-going plank canoes called tomols, and a system of astronomy that was both mystical and practical.

Spanish missionaries, soldiers and settlers displaced the Chumash. During the nineteenth century, the Santa Monicas were controlled by a few large holdings—including the Rancho Topanga-Malibu-Sequit and Rancho Guadalasca—and used primarily for cattle raising. As these holdings were broken up, ranchers supplemented their modest living by renting space to visiting horsemen and vacationers.

At the turn of the century, eccentric oilman Colonel Griffith J. Griffith gave 3,000 acres of his ostrich farm to Los Angeles on the condition that it be forever maintained as a park. Thus Griffith Park was formed on the eastern terminus of the Santa Monicas. Throughout the past four decades, conservationists have made inch-by-inch progress to secure park lands.

The largest areas of open space are in the western part of the mountains. Point Mugu State Park holds the finest native tall grass prairie and the best sycamore grove in the state. The gorge cut by Malibu Creek is an unforgettable sight.

In the eastern part of the mountains, open space is harder to find, but those little pockets that do exist are all the more valuable for being so close to the metropolis. Canyons such as Los Liones, Caballero, and Franklin are precious resources for the park-poor Los Angeles Basin.

Nicholas Flat, Santa Monica Mountains.

Southern California nature lovers put on their hiking boots and jumped for joy in 1978 when the bill creating the Santa Monica Mountains National Recreation Area was approved by Congress. Allocations are slowly being made by the state and federal government to fund purchase of private land to supplement the four major holdings: Will Rogers, Topanga, Malibu Creek and Point Mugu State Parks. The Santa Monica Mountains Conservancy, a state agency has been particularly effective in acquiring parkland.

The National Recreation Area is not one large area, but a patchwork of state parks, county parks, and private property still to be acquired. Currently, some 65,000 acres is the public domain.

The network of trails through the Santa Monicas is a rich pastiche of nature walks, scenic overlooks, fire roads and horse trails, leading through diverse ecosystems: meadowlands, savannas, yucca-covered slopes, handsome sandstone formations, and springs surrounded by lush ferns. The Backbone Trail, extending from Will Rogers State Historic Park to Point Mugu State Park, is nearly completed and, when finished, will literally and symbolically link the scattered beauties of the Santa Monicas.

LA JOLLA VALLEY

La Jolla Valley Loop Trail

From Ray Miller Trailhead to La Jolla Valley is 7 miles round trip with 700-foot elevation gain; return via Overlook Trail, Ray Miller Trail is 7 miles round trip with 800-foot gain

Ringed by ridges, the native grassland of La Jolla Valley welcomes the walker with its drifts of oak and peaceful pond. This pastoral upland in the heart of Point Mugu State Park is unique: it has resisted the invasion of non-native vegetation. It's rare to find native grassland in Southern California because the Spanish introduced oats and a host of other foreign grasses for pasture for their cattle. In most cases, the imported grasses squeezed out the natives; but not in La Jolla Valley.

La Jolla Valley Loop Trail passes a small waterfall and tours the beautiful grasslands of the valley. This is a fine pathway to follow during the spring when wildflowers and numerous coastal shrubs are in bloom; this is a trail that smells as good as it looks.

Another way to loop through the park is to make use of Ray Miller Trail. Sometimes called Overlook Fire Road, this trail is the beginning (or the end, depending on how you view the mountains) of the Backbone Trail. The path offers terrific coastal views and nicely complements the park's interior trails.

The trailhead was named the Ray Miller Trailhead in 1986, a tribute to volunteer ranger Ray Miller. The first official camp host in the state park system, Miller spent his retirement years, from 1972 until his death in 1989, welcoming visitors to Pt. Mugu State Park.

Directions to trailhead: Drive up the coast on Pacific Coast Highway from Santa Monica (21 miles up from Malibu Canyon Road if you're coming from the Ventura Freeway and the San Fernando Valley). The turnoff is 1.5 miles north of Big Sycamore Canyon Trailhead, which is also part of Point Mugu State Park. From the turnoff, bear right to the parking area. The signed trailhead, near an interpretive display, is at a fire road that leads into the canyon.

The hike: The fire road leads north up the canyon along the stream bed. As the canyon narrows, some tiny waterfalls come into view. Past the falls, the trail passes some giant coreopsis plants. In early spring the coreopsis, also known as the tree sunflower, sprouts large blossoms. Springtime travel on this trail takes the hiker past the dainty blue and white blossoms of the ceanothus and the snowy white blossoms of the chamise. Pause to take in the sight (and pungent aroma!) of the black sage with its light-blue flowers and hummingbird sage with its crimson flowers.

At the first trail junction, bear right on the La Jolla Valley Loop Trail. In a little less than a half mile, you'll arrive at another junction. Leave the main trail and you will descend the short distance to a lovely cattail pond. The pond is a nesting place for a variety of birds including the redwing blackbird. Ducks and coots paddle the perimeter.

Returning to the main trail, you'll skirt the east end of La Jolla Valley, enjoy an overview of waving grasses and intersect a "T" junction. To the right 0.7 mile away, is Deer Camp Junction, which provides access to trails leading to Sycamore Canyon and numerous other destinations in the state park.(To return via Overlook and Ray Miller Trails, bear right toward Deer Camp Junction. See instructions below.)

To continue with La Jolla Valley Loop Trail, bear left and in half a mile you'll arrive at La Jolla Valley Camp. The camp, sheltered by oaks and equipped with piped water and tables, is an ideal picnic spot. The valley is a nice place to spend a day. You can snooze in the sun, watch for deer, or perhaps stalk the rare and elusive chocolate lily, known as the Cleopatra of the lily family— the darkest and the loveliest.

After leaving the camp, you could turn left on a short connector trail that skirts the pond and takes you back to La Jolla Valley Loop Trail, where you retrace your steps on that trail and La Jolla Canyon Trail.

To complete the circle on La Jolla Valley Loop Trail, however, continue a half mile past the campground to the signed junction, where you'll bear left and follow a connector trail back to La Jolla Canyon Trail.

Those returning via Overlook and Ray Miller Trails will find that bearing right (west) at the above-described junction will soon bring you to Overlook Trail, a dirt road. Bear right (south) here, descending south along the ridge that separates Big Sycamore Canyon to the east from La Jolla Canyon to the west.

At a fork, bear right, continuing your descent to a junction with Ray Miller Trail. Join this trail, which descends over some red rock, then parallels the coast and coast highway.

Listen carefully and you can hear the distant booming of the surf. Enjoy the stunning ocean views. The Channel Islands—particularly Anacapa and Santa Cruz—are prominent to the northwest. Farther south is Catalina Island. During the winter months, you might sight a migrating California gray whale on the horizon.

The path crosses slopes burned in an 1989 brushfire and works its way west, squeezing through a draw dotted with prickly pear cactus. The path marches down a brushy hill past a group camp and returns you to the trailhead.

SYCAMORE CANYON

Sycamore Canyon Trail
From Big Sycamore Canyon to Deer Camp Junction is 6.5 miles round trip
with 200-foot elevation gain; return via Overlook Trail is 10 miles round trip
with 700-foot gain

Every fall, millions of monarch butterflies migrate south to the forests of Mexico's Transvolcanic Range and to the damp coastal woodlands of Central and Southern California. The monarch's awe-inspiring migration and formation of what entomologists call over-wintering colonies are two of nature's most colorful autumn events.

All monarch butterflies west of the Rockies head for California in the fall; one of the best places in Southern California to observe the arriving monarchs is the campground in Big Sycamore Canyon at Point Mugu State Park.

The monarch's evolutionary success lies not only in its unique ability to migrate to warmer climes, but in its mastery of chemical warfare. The butterfly feeds on milkweed—the favored poison of assassins during the Roman Empire. This milkweed diet makes the monarch toxic to birds; after munching a monarch or two and becoming sick, they learn to leave the butterflies alone.

The butterflies advertise their poisonous nature with their conspicuous coloring. They have brownish-red wings with black veins. The outer edge of the wings are dark brown with white and yellow spots. While one might assume the monarch's startling coloration would make them easy prey for predators, just the opposite is true; bright colors in nature are often a warning that a creature is toxic or distasteful.

Sycamore Canyon Trail takes you through a peaceful wooded canyon, where a multitude of monarchs dwell, and past some magnificent sycamores. The sycamores that shade the canyon bearing their name are incomparable. The lower branches, stout and crooked, are a delight for tree-climbers. Hawks and owls roost in the upper branches.

The trail follows the canyon on a gentle northern traverse across Point Mugu State Park, the largest preserved area in the Santa Monica Mountains. This trail, combined with Overlook Trail, gives the hiker quite a tour of the park. During October and November, Sycamore Canyon offers the twin delights of falling autumn leaves and

Monarch butterfly

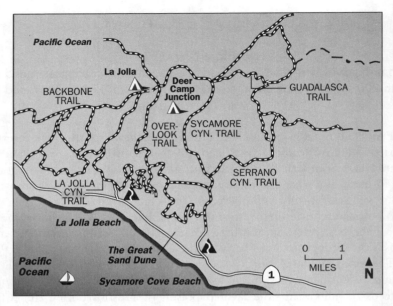

fluttering butterflies. (Ask park rangers where the monarchs cluster in large numbers.)

Directions to trailhead: Drive up-coast on Highway 1, 32 miles from Santa Monica, to Big Sycamore Canyon Campground in Point Mugu State Park (day-use fee). Walk past the campground entrance through the campground to a locked gate. The trail begins on the other side of the gate.

The hike: Take the trail up-canyon, following the creek. Winter rains cause the creek to rise, and sometimes keeping your feet dry while crossing is difficult. Underground water keeps much of the creekside vegetation green year-round—so this is fine hike in any season.

One-half mile from the campground you'll spot Overlook Trail, which switchbacks to the west up a ridge and then heads north toward the native tall grass prairie in La Jolla Valley. Make note of this trail, an optional return route.

A second half-mile of nearly level canyon walking brings you to another major hiking trail that branches right—Serrano Canyon Trail, an absolute gem. (See Serrano Canyon hike description on page 68.)

Another easy mile of walking beneath the sycamores brings you to a picnic table shaded by a grove of large oak trees. The oaks might be a good turnaround spot for a family with small children. The total round trip distance would be a little over 4 miles.

Continuing up the canyon you'll pass beneath more of the giant sycamores and soon arrive at Wood Canyon Junction, the hub of six trails which lead to all corners of the park. Bear left on signed Wood Canyon Trail

Sycamore Canyon, gem of the Santa Monica Mountains.

and in a short while you'll reach Deer Camp Junction. Drinking water and picnic tables suggest a lunch stop. Oak trees predominate over the sycamores along Wood Canyon Creek; however, the romantic prefer the sycamores, some of which have large clumps of mistletoe in the upper branches.

You can call it a day here and return the way you came. As you hike down the canyon back to the campground, the large and cranky scrub jay population will scold you, but don't let the squawking birds stop you from enjoying one of California's finest sycamore savannas.

To return via Overlook Trail: Continue past the junction with Wood Canyon Trail and Deer Camp Junction on the Wood Canyon Trail, which becomes Pumphouse Road. You'll climb over the divide between Sycamore Canyon and La Jolla Valley. Upon reaching a junction, you'll head south on the Overlook Trail, staying on the La Jolla Canyon side of the ridge. True to its name, Overlook Trail offers good views of grassy mountainsides, Boney Peak and Big Sycamore Canyon.

You'll pass an intersection with Scenic Trail, a rough path that hugs the ridge separating La Jolla and Big Sycamore Canyon, where you'll bear right and follow the fire road one-half mile back to the trailhead.

SERRANO CANYON

Serrano Canyon Trail
8.5 mile loop through Point Mugu State Park with 1,100 foot elevation gain

"When the trail had climbed to a height of fifteen hundred feet, there opened a still more striking landscape. Near by to the north rose the fine shape of Boney Mountain, its highest crags hidden in dragging mists. . . ."

Trail writer/rider Joseph Smeaton Chase (*California Coast Trails*, 1913) was inspired by the rough, brushy, tumbled-up country around Boney Mountain, though he got a bit lost. Fortunately for Chase, he spotted a small farm belonging to Jesus Serrano and his son Francisco. The dirt-poor Serranos offered Chase all they had—a bed in their tiny cabin, one of their fine homemade Spanish cheeses and directions for getting back on the right trail.

The climb through Serrano Canyon and the trek across Serrano Valley is a memorable sampling of the state park's Boney Mountain Wilderness. Trails and signage can be mediocre to poor on this route. Check on current conditions with the park.

Directions to trailhead: See previous hike.

The hike: Walk through the campground and hike the fire road that leads into Sycamore Canyon for 1.5 nearly level miles to a signed junction with Serrano Canyon Trail. Join this trail, which soon enters its namesake canyon, a dramatic, water-cut, high-walled gorge. The trail is narrow and lightly traveled. The trail climbs moderately through coastal sage and eventually works its way down to a creek at the bottom of the oak- and sycamore-lined canyon. Some railroad-tie-stairsteps on the creek banks help you across the creek. The creek is sprightly, with pretty pools in winter and spring. (Keep alert for abundant poison oak.)

The trail continues for more than a mile through the fern-filled canyon bottom, then ascends a canyon wall and arrives at an unsigned junction in a shallow gully. Take the right fork, uphill, about 50 yards to an old fence line separating the chaparral community from the sweeping grasslands of Serrano Valley. Park trail markers keep you on the path, which passes a solitary sumac and an abandoned aluminum and wood shed that houses an old pump.

The path cuts across grasslands and reaches a signed junction. Serrano Valley Loop Trail veers right, but you continue straight on the path signed "To Old Boney Trail." You'll reach an unsigned junction with Old Boney Trail, turn left, and soon reach another unsigned trail that leads left. You can see Big Sycamore Canyon below. Join this trail, which plunges down the steep canyon wall.

The very steep trail drops to the floor of Big Sycamore Canyon. Turn left on the fire road, Big Sycamore Canyon Trail, and travel a bit more than three miles down-canyon back to the trailhead.

Rancho Sierra Vista/Satwiwa

Satwiwa Loop Trail
Loop Trail is 1.5 miles round trip with 200-foot elevation gain; to Waterfall is 5.6 miles round trip From parking area, add 0.5 mile round trip to all hikes

Satwiwa Native American Natural Area offers a chance to explore a place where Chumash walked for thousands of years before Europeans arrived on the scene. A visitor center helps moderns learn the habits of birds and animals, the changes the seasons bring, and gain insight into the ceremonies that kept—and still keep—the Chumash bonded to the earth.

For hunter-gatherers, as anthropologists call them, this land on the wild west end of the Santa Monica Mountains was truly bountiful with seeds, roots, bulbs, berries, acorns and black walnuts. Birds, deer and squirrel were plentiful, as were fish and shellfish from nearby Mugu Lagoon. It was this abundant food supply that helped the Chumash become the largest tribal group in California at the time of Cabrillo's arrival in 1542.

Chumash territory ranged from Topanga Canyon near the east end of the Santa Monica Mountains all the way up the coast to San Luis Obispo and out to the Channel Islands. Satwiwa means "The Bluffs" and was the name of a Chumash settlement located at this end of the Santa Monica Mountains.

The name of this park site, Rancho Sierra Vista/Satwiwa reflects its history as both a longtime (1870s to 1970s) horse and cattle ranch and ancestral land of the Chumash. Many visitors are surprised to learn of the extent of Chumash settlement and even more surprised to be greeted by a living Chumash and find out they're not just museum relics.

The National Park Service prefers to call Satwiwa a culture center rather than a museum in order to keep the emphasis on living Native Americans. The park service decided not to interpret the loop trail through Satwiwa with plant ID plaques and brochures; instead of the usual natural history lessons, it's hoped that hikers will come away with a more spiritual experience of the land.

Directions to trailhead: From Highway 101 in Newbury Park, exit on Wendy Drive and head south a short mile to Borchard Road. Turn right and travel 0.5 mile to Reino Road. Turn left and proceed 1.2 miles to Lynn Road, turn right and continue another 1.2 miles to the park entrance road (Via Goleta) on the south side of the road opposite the new Dos Vienta housing development.

The paved park road passes an equestrian parking area on the right and a small day use parking lot on the left before it dead-ends at a large parking lot 0.7 miles from Lynn Road.

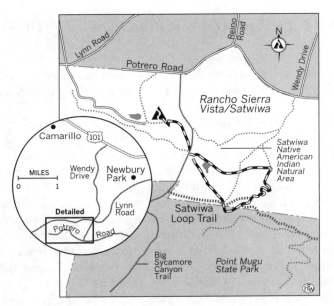

The hike: From the parking lot, follow the signed footpath a short quarter-mile to the Satwiwa Native American Indian Culture Center. Signed Satwiwa Loop Trail begins its clockwise journey by leading past an old cattle pond, now a haven for waterfowl and wildlife.

The path then crosses a landscape in transition—from grazing land back to native grasses and wildflowers. You'll pass a junction with Wendy Trail, a pathway that connects the Satwiwa area with Wendy Drive.

Next the trail traverses a narrow, oak-filled ravine, then ascends to an old windmill. From the trail's high point near the windmill, the hiker gains excellent vistas to the north of Conejo Valley and scattered suburbs. To the west lies a landmark, cone-shaped prominence, 1,814-foot Conejo Mountain.

Dominating the view to the south is Boney Mountain, a series of sheer cliffs and some of the highest peaks in the Santa Monica Mountains. Shamans gathered some of their power from Boney Mountain, still considered a sanctuary by the Chumash..

Satwiwa Loop Trail descends to a junction with Hidden Valley Connector Trail (an opportunity to extend your hike to a waterfall or other destinations in Pt. Mugu State Park). The loop trail descends back to the culture center.

SANDSTONE PEAK

Mishe Mokwa Trail
From Circle X Ranch to Sandstone Peak is 5 miles round trip
with 1,100-foot elevation gain

Sandstone Peak, highest peak in the Santa Monica Mountains, is one of the highlights of a visit to Circle X Ranch, 1,655 acres of National Park Service land on the border of Los Angeles and Ventura counties. The park boasts more than 30 miles of trail plus a much-needed public campground.

Half a century ago the land belonged to a number of gentlemen ranchers, including movie actor Donald Crisp, who starred in *How Green Was My Valley*. Members of the Exchange Club purchased the nucleus of the park in 1949 for $25,000 and gave it to the Boy Scouts. The emblem for the Exchange Club was a circled X—hence the name of the ranch.

During the 1960s, in an attempt to honor Circle X benefactor Herbert Allen, the Scouts petitioned the United States Department of the Interior to rename Sandstone Peak. The request for "Mt. Allen" was denied because of a long-standing policy that prohibited naming geographical features after living persons. Nevertheless, the Scouts held an "unofficial" dedication ceremony in 1969 to honor their leader.

Sandstone Peak—or Mt. Allen if you prefer—offers outstanding views from its 3,111-foot summit. If the five-mile up-and-back hike to the peak isn't sufficiently taxing, park rangers can suggest some terrific extensions.

Directions to trailhead: Drive up-coast on Pacific Coast Highway past the outer reaches of Malibu, a mile past the Los Angeles County line. Turn inland on Yerba Buena Road and proceed five miles to Circle X Ranch. You'll pass the park's tiny headquarters building and continue one more mile to the signed trailhead on your left. There's plenty of parking.

The hike: From the signed trailhead, walk up the fire road. A short quarter-mile of travel brings you to a signed junction with Mishe Mokwa Trail. Leave the fire road here and join the trail, which climbs and contours over the brushy slopes of Boney Mountain.

Breaks in the brush offer good views to the right of historic Triunfo Pass, which was used by the Chumash to travel inland to coastal areas. Mishe Mokwa Trail levels for a time and tunnels beneath some handsome red shanks.

The trail then descends into Carlisle Canyon. Across the canyon are some striking red volcanic formations, among them well-named Balanced Rock. The path, shaded by oak and laurel, drops into the canyon at another aptly named rock formation—Split Rock.

Split Rock is the locale of a trail camp, shaded by oak and sycamore. An

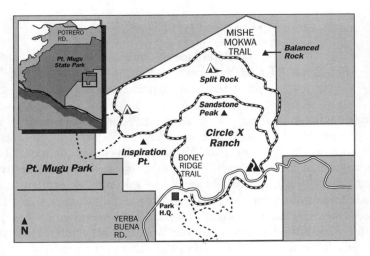

all-year creek and a spring add to the camp's charm. It's a fine place for a picnic.

From Split Rock bear right past an old outhouse—"the historic four-holer" as it is known—and begin your ascent out of Carlisle Canyon on an old ranch road. From the road's high point, look straight ahead up at a pyramid-like volcanic rock formation the Boy Scouts call Egyptian Rock. To the northwest is Point Mugu State Park. You are walking on the Backbone Trail.

The fire road turns south and you'll pass a trail camp located amidst some cottonwoods. Past the camp, the fire road angles east. Look sharply to the right for a short, unsigned trail that leads to Inspiration Point. Mt. Baldy and Catalina are among the inspiring sights pointed out by a geographical locator monument.

Continue east on the fire road and you'll soon pass the signed intersection with Boney Peak Trail. This trail descends precipitously to park headquarters. If for some reason you're in a hurry to get down, this bone-jarring route is for you.

Continue ascending on the fire road. After a few switchbacks look for a steep trail on the right. Follow this trail to the top of Sandstone Peak. "Sandstone" is certainly a misnomer; the peak is one of the largest masses of volcanic rock in the Santa Monica Mountains. Sign the summit register and enjoy commanding, clear-day views: the Topatopa Mountains, haunt of the condors, the Oxnard Plain, the Channel Islands, and the wide blue Pacific.

After you've enjoyed the view, you'll descend a bit more than a mile on the fire road back to the trailhead.

Nicholas Flat

Nicholas Flat Trail
From Leo Carrillo State Beach to Nicholas Flat is 7 miles round trip with 1,600-foot elevation gain

Leo Carrillo State Beach has always been a popular surfing spot. Surfers tackle the well-shaped south swell, while battling the submerged rocks and kelp beds. In recent years, the state added a large chunk of Santa Monica Mountains parkland, prompting a name change to Leo Carrillo State Park.

The park's Nicholas Flat area is one of the best spots in the Santa Monica Mountains for spring wildflowers because it's a meeting place for four different plant communities. Chaparral, grassland, coastal scrub and oak woodland all converge near the flat. Another reason for the remarkable plant diversity is Leo Carrillo's elevation, which varies from sea level to nearly 2,000 feet.

Along park trails, look for shooting star, hedge nettle, sugar bush, hollyleaf redberry, purple sage, chamise, blue dick, deer weed, burr clover, bush lupine, golden yarrow, fuschia-flowered gooseberry, and many more flowering plants. Around Nicholas Pond, keep an eye out for wishbone bush, encelia, chia, Parry's phacelia, ground-pink, California poppy, scarlet bugler and goldfields.

Even when the wildflowers fade away, Nicholas Flat is worth a visit. Its charms include a big meadow and a pond patrolled by coots. Atop grand boulders you can enjoy a picnic and savor Malibu coast views.

The park is named after Angeline Leo Carrillo, famous for his television role as Pancho, the Cisco Kid's sidekick. Carrillo, the son of Santa Monica's first mayor, was also quite active in recreation and civic affairs.

Nicholas Flat Trail can also be savored for one more reason: In Southern California, very few trails connect the mountains with the sea. Get an early start. Until you arrive at oak-dotted Nicholas Flat itself, there's not much shade en route.

Directions to trailhead: From the west end of the Santa Monica Freeway in Santa Monica, head up-coast on Pacific Coast Highway about 25 miles to Leo Carrillo State Beach. There's free parking along Coast Highway, and fee parking in the park's day use area. Signed Nicholas Flat trailhead is located a short distance past the park entry kiosk, opposite the day use parking area.

The hike: Soon the trail splits. The right branch circles the hill, climbs above Willow Creek, and after a mile, rejoins the main Nicholas Flat Trail. Enjoy this interesting option on your return from Nicholas Flat.

Take the left branch, which immediately begins a moderate to steep ascent of the grassy slopes above the park campground. The trail switchbacks through a coastal scrub community up to a saddle on the ridgeline.

Here you'll meet the alternate branch of Nicholas Flat Trail. From the saddle, a short side trail leads south to a hilltop, where there's a fine coastal view. From the viewpoint, you can see Point Dume and the Malibu coastline. During the winter, it's a good place to bring your binoculars and scout the Pacific horizon for migrating whales.

Following the ridgeline, Nicholas Flat Trail climbs inland over chaparral-covered slopes. Keep glancing over your right shoulder at the increasingly grand coastal views, and over your left at the open slopes browsed by the park's nimble deer.

After a good deal of climbing, the trail levels atop the ridgeline and you get your first glimpse of grassy, inviting Nicholas Flat. The trail descends past a line of fire-blackened, but unbowed, old oaks and joins an old ranch road that skirts the Nicholas Flat meadows. Picnickers may unpack lunch beneath the shady oaks or out in the sunny meadow. The trail angles southeast across the meadow to a small pond. The man-made pond, used by cattle during the region's ranching days, is backed by some handsome boulders.

Return the way you came until you reach the junction located 0.75 mile from the trailhead. Bear left at the fork and enjoy this alternate trail as it descends into the canyon cut by Willow Creek, contours around an ocean-facing slope, and returns you to the trailhead.

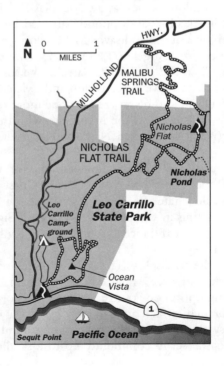

Charmlee Park

Ocean Vista Trail
3-mile loop

Charmlee, perched on the blufftops above Malibu, often has outstanding spring wildflower displays. Most of the park is a large open meadow; the flower display, given timely rainfall, can be quite colorful. Lupine, paintbrush, larkspur, mariposa lily, penstemon and California peony bust out all over.

Stop at Charmlee's small nature center and inquire about what's blooming where. Also pick up a copy of a brochure that interprets the park's Fire Ecology Trail. This nature trail interprets the important role of fire in Southern California's chaparral communities.

Good views are another reason to visit Charmlee. The Santa Monica Mountains spread east to west, with the Simi Hills and Santa Susana Mountains rising to the north. Down-coast you can see Zuma Beach and Point Dume and up-coast Sequit Point in Leo Carrillo State Park. Offshore, Catalina, Anacapa and Santa Cruz islands can be seen on clear days.

Beginning in the early 1800s this Malibu meadowland was part of Rancho Topanga-Malibu-Sequit and was used to pasture cattle. For a century and a

Golden Stars bloom throughout the Santa Monica Mountains in the spring.

half, various ranchers held the property. The last of these private land-holders—Charmain and Leonard Swartz—combined their first names to give Charmlee its euphonious name. Los Angeles County acquired the Charmlee property in the late 1960s and eventually opened the 460-acre park in 1981.

For the hiker, Charmlee is one of the few parks, perhaps even the only park, that actually seems to have a surplus of trails. Quite a few paths and old ranch roads wind through the park, which is shaped like a big grassy bowl.

Because the park is mostly one big meadow fringed with oak trees, it's easy to see where you're going and improvise your own circle tour of Charmlee. Bring a kite and a picnic to this undiscovered park and take it easy for an afternoon.

Directions to trailhead: From Pacific Coast Highway, about 12 miles up-coast from the community of Malibu, head into the mountains on Encinal Canyon Road 4.5 miles to Charmlee Park.

The hike: Walk through the park's picnic area on a dirt road, which travels under the shade of coast live oaks. The trail crests a low rise, offers a couple of side trails to the left to explore, and soon arrives at a more distinct junction with a fire road leading downhill along the eastern edge of the meadow. This is a good route to take because it leads to fine ocean views.

Follow the road as it skirts the eastern edge of the meadow and heads south. Several ocean overlooks are encountered but the official Ocean Overlook is a rocky outcropping positioned on the far southern edge of the park. Contemplate the coast, then head west to the old ranch reservoir. A few hundred yards away is an oak grove, one of the park's many picturesque picnic spots.

You may follow any of several trails back to the trailhead or join Fire Ecology Trail for a close-up look at how Southern California's Mediterranean flora rises phoenix-like from the ashes.

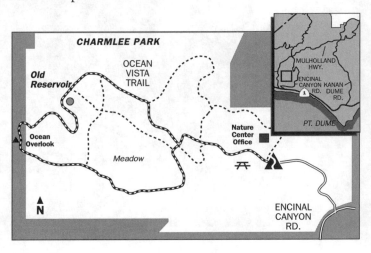

Solstice Canyon Park

Solstice Canyon Trail
3 miles round trip

Solstice Canyon Trail leads visitors along a year-around creek and introduces them to the flora and history of the Santa Monica Mountains. The path is a narrow country road—suitable for strollers and wheelchairs—which offers an easy family hike in the shade of grand old oaks and towering sycamores.

Solstice Canyon in the Santa Monica Mountains is enjoyable year-round, but autumn and winter are particularly fine times to ramble through the quiet canyon. In autumn, enjoy the fall color display of the sycamores and in winter, from the park's upper slopes, look for gray whales migrating past Point Dume.

Solstice Canyon Park opened on summer solstice, 1988. The Santa Monica Mountains Conservancy purchased the land from the Roberts family and transformed the 550-acre Roberts Ranch into a park. Ranch roads became foot trails. Milk thistle, castor bean and other assorted nonnative plants were almost eliminated (but since returned); picnic areas and a visitor contact station were built. Today National Park Service rangers are the stewards of Solstice Canyon.

Solstice Canyon's strangest structure resembles a futurist farm house with a silo attached, and really defies architectural categorization. Bauhaus, maybe. Or perhaps Grain Elevator Modern. From 1961 to 1973 Space Tech Labs, a subsidiary of TRW used the building to conduct tests to determine the magnetic sensitivity of satellite instrumentation. The Santa Monica Mountains Conservancy was headquartered here for many years.

Directions to trailhead: From Pacific Coast Highway, about 17 miles up-coast from Santa Monica and 3.5 miles up-coast from Malibu Canyon Road, turn inland on Corral Canyon Road. At the first bend in the road, you'll leave the road and proceed straight to the very small Solstice Canyon

parking lot.

The trail: Stop at the bulletin board, pick up a trail brochure.

About halfway along, you'll pass the 1865 Mathew Keller House and in a few more minutes—Fern Grotto. The road travels under the shade of oak and sycamore to its end at

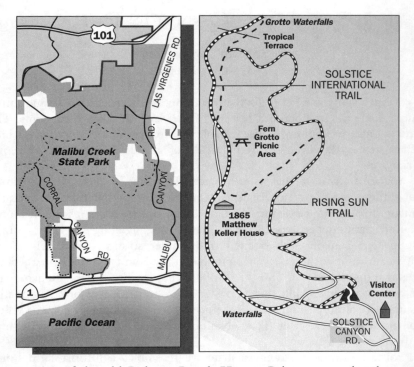

the remains of the old Roberts Ranch House. Palms, agave, bamboo and bird of paradise and many more tropical plants thrive in the Roberts' family garden gone wild. A waterfall, fountain and an old dam are some of the other special features found in this paradisiacal setting known as Tropical Terrace.

Across the creek from Tropical Terrace is signed Rising Sun Trail, which climbs a ridge for rewarding canyon and ocean views. The two-mile trail offers an excellent, but more difficult return route.

Zuma Canyon

Zuma Loop, Zuma Ridge Trails
Around Zuma Canyon is 2-mile loop; via Zuma Ridge Trail is 9.8-mile loop with 1,700-foot elevation

At first, when you turn inland off Pacific Coast Highway onto Bonsall Drive and enter Zuma Canyon, the canyon looks like many others in the Santa Monica Mountains: huge haciendas perched on precipitous slopes, accompanied by lots of lots for sale. But the road ends and only footpaths enter Zuma Canyon.

Malibu, Topanga, Temescal and Santa Ynez—perhaps these canyons and others in the Santa Monica Mountains looked like Zuma a century ago: a creek cascading over magnificent sandstone boulders, a jungle of willow and lush streamside flora, fern-fringed pools and towering rock walls.

Hikers can partake of Zuma Canyon's grandeur via three routes: For an easy family walk join 2-mile Zuma Loop Trail, which explores the canyon mouth; hardy hikers will relish the challenge of the gorge—two miles of trail-less creek-crossing and boulder-hopping—one of the most difficult hikes in the Santa Monicas; Zuma Ridge Trail, lives up to the promise of its name. Hikers ascend Zuma Canyon's west ridge for grand ocean and mountain views, then follow a series of fire roads and footpaths to circle back to the trailhead.

This loop around Zuma Canyon's walls is a great workout and conditioning hike because of two major ascents and descents en route. Bring lots of water. Water is available at the Bonsall Drive trailhead but nowhere else on the hike.

Directions to trailhead: From Pacific Coast Highway in Malibu, head up-coast one mile past an intersection with Kanan-Dume Road and turn right on Bonsall Drive (this turn is just before the turnoff for Zuma Beach). Drive a mile (the last hundred yards on dirt road) to road's end at a parking lot.

To start the hike on Zuma Ridge Trail, continue very briefly up-coast past the Bonsall Drive turnoff on Pacific Coast Highway to the next major right turn—Busch Drive. Travel a bit over a mile to the small dirt parking lot and signed trail.

The trail: Just before you join Zuma Ridge Trail (a dirt road, gated to prevent vehicle entry) note the signed footpath (Ridge Canyon Access Trail) just to the east. This path will return you to the trailhead on the very last leg of your long loop.

Begin your shadeless ascent, following the dirt road below some water tanks. Up, up, up you go along the ridge between Zuma Canyon on your

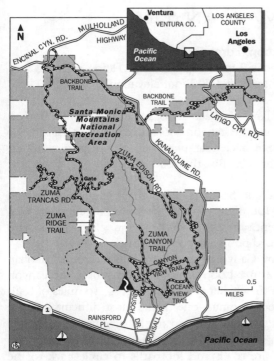

right and Trancas Canyon on your left. Look behind you at the sparkling blue Pacific and the Malibu Riviera.

Three miles of vigorous ascent brings you to a junction with the right-forking Zuma Edison Road. What goes up must come down, and down east you go toward the floor of Zuma Canyon. After a mile's descent you'll pass a horse guzzler, then continue the steep descent another mile or so to the sycamore-shaded canyon bottom. By all means take a break here and marshal your energy for this hike's second major climb.

The road climbs southeasterly out of the canyon. Far below is Kanan-Dume Road, about a mile to the east. Zuma Edison Road bends north for 0.25 mile to intersect Zuma Canyon Connector Trail, a footpath that turns south to travel along a knifeedge ridge. This engaging path takes you 0.7 mile down to meet Kanan-Edison Road. Coast coastward as you descend this dirt fire road 1.3 miles to a junction with Canyon View Trail, a path that descends into the heart of Zuma Canyon. You could branch off on this pleasant trail, but in keeping with the ridge-route theme of this walk I prefer to continue on Kanan-Edison Road just 0.1 mile more to meet Ocean View Trail. This path descends westward 1.1 miles to the canyon bottom while serving up fine ocean views.

When you meet Zuma Canyon Trail, go left about 100 feet to meet Ridge-Canyon Access Trail. Join this 0.7 mile long footpath on a climb from the canyon bottom up and over a low hill to return to the Busch Drive trailhead.

CASTRO CREST

Backbone Trail
From Malibu Canyon Road to Castro Crest is 7 miles one way
with 2,000 foot gain; return via Bulldog Motorway and
Twentieth Century Road is 14 miles round trip

The Backbone Trail route through Malibu Creek State Park has been finished for quite some time and has proved very popular. Both a primary and alternate route lead through the state park. The high "primary" route follows a dramatic ridgetop toward Castro Crest while the "alternate" route meanders along with Malibu Creek through the heart of the state park.

This day hike connects the two branches of the Backbone Trail and provides a grand tour of Malibu Creek State Park. Fine ocean and island views are offered along the first half of the hike and a chance to explore geologically and ecologically unique Malibu Creek Canyon on the second half.

Directions to trailhead: From Pacific Coast Highway, turn inland on Malibu Canyon Road and proceed 5 miles to the signed trailhead, located a short mile south of the main part of Malibu Creek State Park. Formerly Tapia County Park, the land hereabouts is now officially known as the Tapia Subunit of Malibu Creek State Park.

The hike: Mesa Peak Motorway, as this dirt road is known, ascends steeply at first, gaining 1,500 feet in 2.5 miles. With the elevation gain comes sweeping panoramic views of Point Dume, Santa Monica Bay, and Palos Verdes Peninsula. On clear days, Catalina, Anacapa and Santa Cruz Islands float upon the horizon.

The trail veers left toward Mesa Peak (1,844 feet) and continues climbing in a northwesterly direction through an area rich in fossilized shells. Hillside roadcuts betray the Santa Monica Mountains' oceanic heritage. As you hike the spine of the range, a good view to the north is yours: the volcanic rocks of Goat Butte tower above Malibu Creek gorge and the path of Triunfo Canyon can be traced.

The road passes through an area of interesting sandstone formations and intersects paved Corral Canyon Road, which is termed Castro Motorway from this point. Continue west on Castro Motorway for one mile, reaching the intersection with Bulldog Motorway.

Clinging to life in the Castro Crest area is the humble Santa Susana tarweed, a plant only a botanist could love—or even find. *Heminzonia minthornii*, a low mass of woody stems and dull green herbage, was believed to exist only in the Santa Susana Mountains before its discovery in the late 1970s atop Castro Crest and in other isolated locales high in the Santa Monica Mountains.

Castro Crest: Stalk the rare Santa Susana tarweed, enjoy the terrific views.

Backbone Trail continues west toward the forest of antennae atop Castro Peak (2,824 feet).

Return via Bulldog Motorway: For a nice loop trip back through Malibu Creek State Park, bear right on Bulldog Motorway. Descend steeply under transmission lines, veering east and dropping into Triunfo Canyon. In 3.5 miles, you reach Crags Road. Turn right and soon pass what was once the location of the exterior sets used by the "M*A*S*H" TV series. (The set is now on display in the Smithsonian.) The prominent Goat Buttes that tower above Malibu Creek are featured in the opening shot of each episode.

The road passes Century Lake, crosses a ridge, then drops down to Malibu Creek and comes to a fork in the road. Take either the left (high road) or continue straight ahead over the bridge on the low road; the roads meet again downstream, so you may select either one. One-half mile after the roads rejoin, you approach the park's day use parking area.

Follow a dirt road that skirts this parking area, leads past a giant valley oak and approaches the state park's campground. Bear right on a dirt road that leads a short distance through meadowland to the park's new Group Camp. Here you'll join a connector trail, signed with the international hiking symbol, that will take you a mile up and over a low brushy ridge to Tapia Park. Walk through the park back to your car.

MALIBU CREEK

Malibu Creek Trail
To Rock Pool is 3.5 miles round trip with 150-foot elevation gain; to Century Lake is 4.5 miles round trip with 200-foot elevation gain

Before land for Malibu Creek State Park was acquired in 1974, it was divided into three parcels belonging to Bob Hope, Ronald Reagan, and 20th Century Fox. Although the park is still used for moviemaking, it's primarily a haven for day hikers and picnickers.

Today the state park preserves more than 7,000 acres of rugged country in the middle of the Santa Monica Mountains. Malibu Creek winds through the park. The creek was dammed at the turn of the century to form little Century Lake.

The trail along Malibu Creek explores the heart of the State Park. It's an easy, nearly level walk that visits a dramatic rock gorge, Century Lake and several locales popular with moviemakers.

Directions to trailhead: From Pacific Coast Highway, turn inland on Malibu Canyon Road and proceed 6.5 miles to the park entrance, 0.25 mile south of Mulholland Highway. If you're coming from the San Fernando Valley, exit the Ventura Freeway (101) on Las Virgenes Road and continue four miles to the park entrance.

The hike: From the parking area, follow the wide fire road. You'll cross the all-but-dry creek. The road soon forks into a high road and a low road. Go right and walk along the oak-shaded high road, which makes a long, lazy left arc as it follows the north bank of Malibu Creek. You'll reach an intersection and turn left on a short road that crosses a bridge over Malibu Creek.

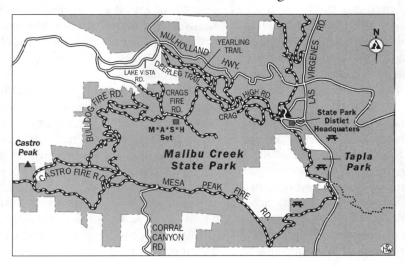

The gorge of Malibu Creek.

You'll spot the Gorge Trail and follow it upstream a short distance to the gorge, one of the most dramatic sights in the Santa Monica Mountains. Malibu Creek makes a hairpin turn through 400-foot volcanic rock cliffs and cascades into aptly named Rock Pool. The "Swiss Family Robinson" television series and some Tarzan movies were filmed here.

Return to the trailhead or retrace your steps back to the high road and bear left toward Century Lake. As the road ascends you'll be treated to a fine view of Las Virgenes Valley. When you gain the crest of the hill, you'll look down on Century Lake. Near the lake are hills of porous lava and topsy-turvy sedimentary rock layers that tell of the violent geologic upheaval that formed Malibu Canyon. The lake was scooped out by members of Crag's Country Club, a group of wealthy, turn-of-the-century businessmen who had a nearby lodge.

You can call it a day here, or continue on the fire road past Century Lake. You'll pass the location of the now-removed set for the "M*A*S*H" television series. The prominent Goat Buttes that tower above Malibu Creek were featured in the opening shot of each episode.

TOPANGA STATE PARK

Eagle Rock Loop Trail (Backbone Trail)

To Eagle Rock via Eagle Rock/Eagle Springs Loop is 6.5 miles round trip
with 800-foot elevation gain; to Will Rogers SHP via Eagle Rock, Fire Road
30, and Rogers Road is 10.5 miles one way with a 1,800-foot loss

Topanga Canyon is a quiet retreat, surrounded by L.A. sprawl but retaining its rural character. The state park is sometimes billed as "the largest state park within a city limit in the U.S."

The name Topanga is from the Shoshonean Indian dialect. These Indians and their ancestors occupied the canyon on and off for several thousand years until the Spanish evicted them and forced them to settle at the San Fernando Mission.

Until the 1880s, there was little permanent habitation in the canyon. Early settlers tended vineyards, orchards, and cattle ranches. In the 1920s, the canyon became a popular weekend destination for Los Angeles residents. Summer cabins were built along Topanga Creek and in subdivisions in the surrounding hills. For $1 round-trip fare, tourists could board a Packard auto stage in Santa Monica and be driven up Pacific Coast Highway and Topanga Canyon Road to the Topanga Post Office and other, more scenic spots.

Most Topanga trails are good fire roads. On a blustery winter day, city and canyon views are superb.

In the heart of the park, the walker will discover Eagle Rock, Eagle Spring and get topographically oriented to Topanga. The energetic will enjoy the one-way journey from Topanga to Will Rogers State Historic Park.

The Topanga State Park to Will Rogers Park section of the Backbone Trail is a popular route. The lower reaches of the trail offer a fine tour of the wild side of Topanga Canyon while the ridgetop sections offer far-reaching inland and ocean views.

Directions to trailhead: From Topanga Canyon Boulevard, turn east on Entrada Road; that's to the right if you're coming from Pacific Coast Highway. Follow Entrada Road by turning left at every opportunity until you arrive at Topanga State Park. The trailhead is at the end of the parking lot.

(For information about the end of this walk, consult the Will Rogers State Historic Park write-up and directions to the trailhead on page 89 of this guide.)

The hike: From the Topanga State Park parking lot, follow the distinct trail eastward to a signed junction, where you'll begin hiking on Eagle Springs Road. You'll pass through an oak woodland and through chaparral country. The trail slowly and steadily gains about 800 feet in elevation on the way to Eagle Rock. When you reach a junction, bear left on the north loop of Eagle Springs Road to Eagle Rock. A short detour will bring you to the top of the rock.

To complete the loop, bear sharply right (southwest) at the next junction, following the fire road as it winds down to Eagle Spring. Past the spring, return to Eagle Spring Road and retrace your steps to the trailhead.

Three-mile long Musch Ranch Trail, which passes from hot chaparral to shady oak woodland, crosses a bridge and passes the park pond, is another fine way to return to the trailhead.

To Will Rogers State Historic Park: Follow the loop trip directions to the northeast end of Eagle Rock/Eagle Spring Loop, where you bear right on Fire Road 30. In one-half mile you reach the intersection with Rogers Road. Turn left and follow the dirt road (really a trail) for 3.5 miles, where the road ends and meets Rogers Trail. Here a level area and solitary oak suggest a lunch stop. On clear days enjoy the spectacular views in every direction: To the left is Rustic Canyon and the crest of the mountains near Mulholland Drive. To the right, Rivas Canyon descends toward the sea.

Stay on Rogers Trail, which marches up and down steep hills, for about two more miles, until it enters Will Rogers Park near Inspiration Point.

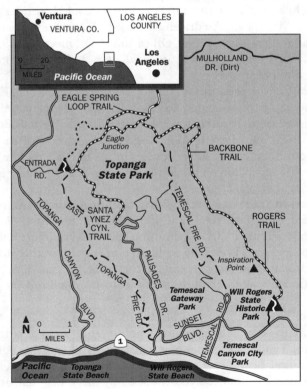

Temescal Canyon

Sunset, Temescal Canyon, Temescal Ridge Trails
Canyon loop is 4.4 miles round trip with 700-foot gain; to Skull Rock is 5.4 miles round trip

Park agencies in the Santa Monica Mountains have combined forces to open a number of "gateways" to the mountains. For hikers (particularly those of us accustomed to beginning hikes at the end of dirt roads greeted by trail signs nailed to trees), these gateways are deluxe trailheads indeed: restrooms, picnic grounds, water fountains, native plant gardens and more.

I have a particular fondness for Temescal Gateway Park in Pacific Palisades. Not only does this park have it all, park pathways quickly leave it all behind.

Temescal Canyon is an ideal Santa Monica Mountains sampler. You get an oak- and sycamore-shaded canyon, a seasonal waterfall and terrific views from the ridge crest.

Skull Rock

Temescal has long been a canyon that inspired nature lovers and enlightenment-seekers. During the 1920s and 1930s, the canyon hosted Chatauqua assemblies—large educational and recreational gatherings that featured lectures, concerts and stage performances. The canyon was purchased by the Presbyterian Synod in 1943 and used as a retreat center until 1995 when the Santa Monica Mountains Conservancy purchased the property.

Directions to trailhead: From Los Angeles, head west on the Santa Monica Freeway (10) to its end and continue up-coast on Pacific Coast Highway. Turn north (right) on Temescal Canyon Road and drive 1.1 miles. Just after the intersection with Sunset Boulevard, turn left into the parking area for Temescal Gateway Park.

(Sidewalks, picnic grounds, and an intermittent greenbelt along Temescal Canyon Road might tempt intrepid hikers to stride the mile from the beach to the trailhead.)

The hike: Walk up canyon on the landscaped path past the restrooms. The footpath takes on a wilder appearance and soon crosses a branch of Temescal Creek via a wooden footbridge.

At a signed junction, save Temescal Ridge Trail for your return route and continue through the canyon on Temescal Canyon Trail. Travel among graceful old oaks, maples and sycamores to the "doggie turnaround" (no dogs beyond this point) and enter Topanga State Park.

The path ascends moderately to another footbridge and a close-up view of the small waterfall, tumbling over some large boulders. Leaving the canyon behind, the path steepens and climbs westward up Temescal Ridge to a signed junction with Temescal Ridge Trail.

I always enjoy heading uphill on this trail a half mile or so to distinctly shaped Skull Rock. The rock is a good place to rest, cool off, and admire the view.

As you return down Temescal Ridge Trail, you'll get excellent views of Santa Monica Bay, Palos Verdes Peninsula, Catalina Island, and downtown Los Angeles. The view to the southwest down at the housing developments isn't too inspiring, but the view of the rough, unaltered northern part of Temescal Canyon is.

After serving up fine views, the path descends rather steeply and tunnels into tall chaparral. Continue past junctions with Bienveneda and Leacock trails and follow the narrow ridgeline back to a junction with Temescal Canyon Trail. Retrace your steps on Sunset Trail back to the trailhead.

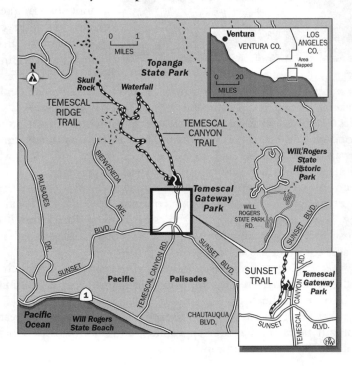

WILL ROGERS STATE HISTORIC PARK

Will Rogers Trail
To Inspiration Point is 2 miles round trip with a 300-foot elevation gain

Will Rogers, often called the "Cowboy Philosopher," bought a spread in the Santa Monica Mountains in 1922. He and his family enlarged their weekend cottage to 31 rooms.

The Oklahoma-born Rogers toured the country as a trick roper, punctuating his act with humorous comments on the news of the day. His roping act led the humorist to later fame as a newspaper columnist, radio commentator and movie star.

Today, the ranch and grounds of the Rogers Ranch is maintained as Will Rogers State Historic Park, set aside in 1944. You can see a short film on Rogers's life at the park visitor center and tour the ranch house, still filled with his prized possessions.

Rogers himself designed the riding trails that wind into the hills behind his ranch. The path to Inspiration Point is an easy walk for the whole family.

Directions to trailhead: From Sunset Boulevard in Pacific Palisades, 4.5 miles inland from Sunset's junction with Pacific Coast Highway, turn inland on the access road leading to Will Rogers State Historic Park. Park your car near the polo field or near Rogers' house.

The hike: Join the path near the tennis courts west of park headquarters and begin ascending north into the mountains. (You'll see a couple of different trails; you want to join the main, wide bridle path.)

Rogers Trail ascends a ridge overlooking nearby Rivas Canyon and leads to a junction, where you take the turnoff for Inspiration Point. Not really a point at all, it's actually more of a flat-topped knoll; nevertheless, clear-day views are inspiring: the Santa Monica Bay, the metropolis, the San Gabriel Mountains, and even Catalina Island.

Snow-capped San Gabriel Montains tower above the Los Angeles Basin.

5. San Gabriel Mountains

OST OF THE SAN GABRIEL MOUNTAINS are included within the 700,000 acres of the Angeles National Forest, one of the most heavily used national forests in America. For more than a century the range has delighted Southland residents seeking quiet retreats and tranquil trails.

The San Gabriels twist atop the San Andreas Fault. Geologists claim these mountains are among the most fractured and shattered in California. The range consists of crystalline metamorphic and granitic blocks, sixty miles long and twenty miles wide, extending from Soledad Canyon on the west to Cajon Pass on the east. The mountains bless Los Angeles by keeping out hot desert winds, and curse it by keeping in the smog.

The San Gabriels are the only major mountain range in California that is considered a Transverse Range; that is, extending east-west across the state. Once the mountains formed a nearly impassable barrier to travel and blocked the northward expansion of Los Angeles into the Mojave Desert. A glance at a modern map attests to the fact that the San Gabriels are no longer a barrier to transportation and settlement.

The range is young (less than a million years in its present location), dynamic (it moves and grooves with the San Andreas Earthquake Fault), and complex; geologists claim the fractured and shattered mountains are composed of many different kinds of rocks of diverse ages.

The San Gabriels are divided lengthwise into a steeper southern front range and a taller northern range by a series of east-west trending canyons. They vary extensively in temperature. Along the northern rim at the edge of the Antelope Valley, the mountains seem an extension of the Mojave Desert. However, some alpine areas with peaks near 10,000 feet know snow from one winter to the next.

John Muir found it tough going in the San Gabriels: "The slopes are exceptionally steep and insecure to the foot and they are covered with thorny bushes from five to ten feet high." Muir was referring to the dominant plant community of the San Gabriels—the chaparral—that elfin forest of burrs and brambles which covers much of the sun-drenched lower slopes of the mountains. Higher elevations bring easier traveling and a wealth of taller trees: mountain laurel, oaks, pines, cedar. The arroyos are another special feature of the San Gabriels. These boulder-strewn washes seem dry and lifeless in the bottomland; however, as hikers follow their course upward, they'll soon find the arroyo's banks are verdant and graceful with a tangle of ferns and wildflowers.

As early as the 1880s, it became obvious to Southern Californians the mountains should be protected from the destruction of indiscriminate logging and other ventures. In 1892, the San Gabriel Timberland Reserve was proclaimed by President Harrison. It was the first forest reserve in California, and the second in the U.S. (The first was Yellowstone.)

One of the first trail construction projects in the San Gabriels began in 1864 when Benjamin Wilson revamped an old Indian path to his timbering venture on the mountain that now bears his name. Later, other Indian trails were improved. William Sturtevant, who came to California from Colorado in the early 1880s and became a premier packhorseman and trail guide, linked and improved several Indian trails and made it possible to cross the mountains from west to east. Until Sturtevant figured out a route, most people did not know that a network of Indian trails reached from the desert to the L.A. Basin.

More trails were built around the turn of the century when Southern California's "Great Hiking Era" began. With Rough Rider Teddy Roosevelt urging Americans to lead "the strenuous life," Southlanders challenged the nearby San Gabriels. Mountain farmers and ranchers, fighting against the odds of fire, flood and distance to market, began capitalizing on the prevailing interest in the great outdoors. As more and more hikers headed into the backcountry, the settlers began to offer food and accommodations. Soon every major canyon on the south side of the mountains had its resort or trail camp, and many had several.

Most resorts were not big business, with the exception of the Mt. Wilson and Echo Mountain complexes which featured luxury hotels and observatories. The majority were run by rugged entrepreneurs who offered rustic accommodations, hearty meals, and good fellowship. Visitors thronged to the resorts on weekends and holidays. Many stayed all summer.

Depression-era public works projects of the 1930s brought about a golden age of public campground construction. These camps, tied to an ever-increasing network of highways, eventually doomed the private resorts and trail camps. Angeles Crest Highway, built between 1929 and 1956 by a motley assortment of Depression laborers, prison road gangs and various construction crews, linked many of the best high mountain picnic and camping areas.

Today, only a few stone foundations and scattered resort ruins remind the hiker of the "Great Hiking and Resort Era." Though the modern mountaineer will not be greeted with tea, lemonade or something stronger, or a hearty welcome from a trail camp proprietor, the mountains still beckon. That bygone era left us a superb network of trails—more than 500 miles of paths linking all major peaks, camps and streams.

Rising above the smog and din of the Big Basin, the San Gabriels still delight. A second "Great Hiking Era" is already be underway.

Placerita Canyon

Placerita Canyon Trail
From Nature Center to Walker Ranch Picnic Area is 4 miles round trip with 300-foot elevation gain

Placerita Canyon has a gentleness that is rare in the steep, severely fault-ed San Gabriel Mountains. A superb nature center, plus a walk through the oak- and sycamore-shaded canyons adds up to a nice outing for the whole family.

In 1842, seven years before the '49ers rushed to Sutter's Mill, California's first gold rush occurred in Placerita Canyon. Legend has it that herdsman Francisco Lopez awoke from his nap beneath a large shady oak tree, during which he had dreamed of gold and wealth. During the more mundane routine of fixing his evening meal, he dug up some onions to spice his supper and there, clinging to the roots, were small gold nuggets. Miners from all over California, the San Fernando Placers, as they became known, poured into Placerita Canyon. The prospecting was good, though not exceptional, for several years. The spot where Lopez made his discovery is now called the Oak of the Golden Dream. A plaque marks his find.

Placerita Canyon has been the outdoor set for many a Western movie and 1950s television series, including "The Cisco Kid" and "Hopalong Cassidy." Movie companies often used the cabin built in 1920 by Frank Walker. Walker, his wife, Hortense, and their 12 children had a rough time earning a living in what was then a wilderness. The family raised cows and pigs, gathered and sold leaf mold (fertilizer), panned for gold, and hosted movie companies. The family cabin, modified by moviemakers, stands by the park's nature center.

Placerita Canyon's nature center has some very well done natural history exhibits and live animal displays. Pamphlets, available at the center, help visitors enjoy park nature trails including: Ecology Trail, which interprets the canyon bottom and chaparral communities; Hillside Trail which offers a view of Placerita Canyon; Heritage Trail, which leads to the Oak of the Golden Dream.

Directions to trailhead: From Highway 14 (Antelope Valley Freeway) in Newhall, exit on Placerita Canyon Road and turn right (east) two miles to Placerita Canyon County Park. Park in the large lot near the Nature Center.

The hike: From the parking lot, walk up-canyon, following the stream and enjoying the shade of oaks and sycamores. A 1979 fire scorched brush within a hundred feet of the nature center, but remarkably spared the oak woodland on the canyon bottom. Nature regenerates quickly in a chaparral community; some of the chamise on the slopes may be a hundred years old and veterans of dozens of fires.

The canyon narrows and after a mile the trail splits. Take your pick: the right branch stays on the south side of the canyon while the left branch joins the north side trail. The two intersect in a half-mile, a little short of the Walker Ranch Group Campground. Here you'll find a picnic ground with tables, water and restrooms.

From the campground, Waterfall Trail (1.5 miles round trip with 300-foot gain) ascends along Los Pinetos Canyon's west wall, then drops into the canyon for an up-close look at a fall.

Big cone spruce and live oak, plus a few stray big leaf maple shade the canyon walls. The waterfall, sometimes an impressive flow after a good rain, splashes into a grotto at trail's end.

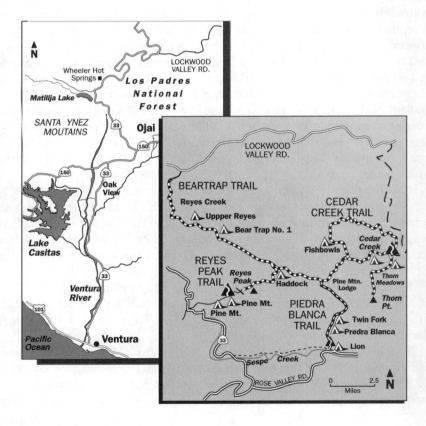

Mt. Lukens

Stone Canyon Trail
From Vogel Flats to Mt. Lukens is 8 miles round trip
with 3,200-foot elevation gain

Mt. Lukens, a gray whale of a mountain beached on the eastern boundary of Los Angeles, is the highest peak within the city limits. A hike up this mile-high mountain offers a great aerobic workout and terrific clear-day views of the metropolis.

Theodore P. Lukens, for whom the mountain is named, was a Pasadena civic and business leader, and an early supporter of the first scientific reforestation effort in California. A self-taught botanist, Lukens believed that burnt-over mountainsides could be successfully replanted. During 1899 alone, Lukens and fellow mountaineers planted some 65,000 seeds in the mountains above Pasadena.

After the death of Lukens in 1918, a 5,074-foot peak was named to honor the one-time Angeles National Forest Supervisor and Southern California's "Father of Forestry."

Stone Canyon Trail is by far the nicest way to ascend Mt. Lukens. (Other routes are via long wearisome fire roads.) The trail climbs very steeply from Big Tujunga Canyon over the north slope of Lukens to the peak.

Carry plenty of water on this trail; none is available en route. It's fun to unfold a city map on the summit to help you identify natural and man-made points of interest.

One warning: In order to reach the beginning of the Stone Canyon Trail, you must cross the creek flowing through Big Tujunga Canyon. During times of high water, this creek crossing can be difficult and dangerous—even impossible. Use care and your very best judgement when approaching this creek.

Directions to trailhead: From Foothill Boulevard in Sunland, turn north on Mt. Gleason Avenue and drive 1.5 miles to Big Tujunga Canyon Road. Turn right and proceed 5 miles to Wildwood Picnic Area. Stone Canyon Trail begins at the back end of the parking lot.

The hike: After you've signed the trail registry, begin the vigorous ascent, which first parallels Stone Canyon, then switchbacks to the east above it. Pausing now and then to catch your breath, you'll enjoy the view of Big Tujunga Canyon.

The trail leads through chamise, ceanothus and high chaparral. The 1975 Big Tujunga Fire scorched the slopes of Mt. Lukens. Stone Canyon Trail could use a few more shady big cone spruce and a little less brush. Theodore Lukens and his band of tree planters would today be most welcome on the mountain's north slopes!

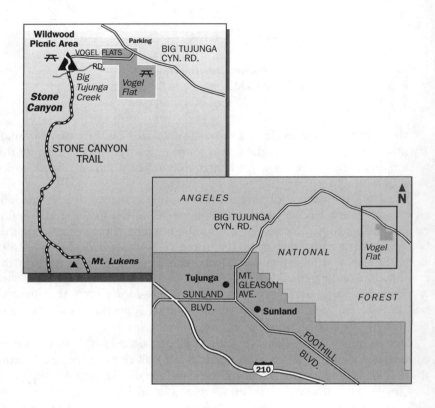

Three-and-a-half miles from the trailhead, you'll intersect an old fire road and bear left toward the summit. Atop the peak is a forest of radio antennae.

Old maps call the summit "Sister Elsie." Before the peak was renamed for Lukens, Sister Elsie Peak honored a beloved Roman Catholic nun who was in charge of an orphanage for Native American children located in the La Crescenta area.

Enjoy the sweeping panorama of the Santa Monica and Verdugo Mountains, Santa Monica Bay and the Palos Verdes Peninsula, and the huge city spreading from the San Gabriel Mountains to the sea.

Lower Arroyo Seco

Arroyo Seco Trail (Gabrielino National Recreation Trail)

From Windsor Avenue to Teddy's Outpost is 3 miles round trip; to Gould Mesa Campground is 4 miles round trip; to Paul Little Picnic Area is 6.5 miles round trip with a 400-foot elevation gain; to Oakwilde Trail Camp is 10 miles round trip with a 900-foot gain

During the early decades of this century, Arroyo Seco was an extremely popular place for a weekend outing. About halfway up the wild section of the canyon stood Camp Oak Wilde, a rustic resort constructed in 1911. Hikers and horsemen stayed a night or two or used the hostelry as a rest stop on the way up to Mt. Wilson. During the 1920s, a road was constructed and automobilists traveled the Arroyo to Camp Oak Wilde.

Southern California's "flood of the century" wiped out Oak Wilde in 1938. The awesome torrent also washed away the road and many vacation cabins. A few stone steps and foundations, ivy-covered walls and bridges give today's hiker hints of a time gone by.

Besides the Southern California history lesson, oak, sycamore and bay-filled Arroyo Seco has much to offer. The modern day traveler can walk the old 1920s auto road and newer Forest Service trails to quiet picnic areas. Because the path up the Arroyo Seco is officially part of the Gabrielino National Recreation Trail, it's usually kept in very good condition.

This is a great morning walk. On hot afternoons, however, you might want to exercise elsewhere; smog fills the Arroyo Seco.

Directions to trailhead: From the Foothill Freeway (210) in Pasadena, take the Arroyo Boulevard/ Windsor Avenue exit. Head north on Arroyo, which almost immediately becomes Windsor, and travel 0.75 mile. Just before Windsor's intersection with Ventura Street, turn into the parking lot on your left. From the small lot you can look down into the bottom of the Arroyo Seco and see the Jet Propulsion Laboratory.

The hike: As you walk up Windsor you'll spot two roads. The leftward road descends to JPL. You head right on a narrow asphalt road, closed to vehicle traffic. You'll pass some fenced-off areas and facilities belonging to the Pasadena Water Department and a junction with Lower Brown Mountain Road. A short mile from the trailhead are some Forest Service residences.

The road, dirt now, penetrates the arroyo and enters a more sylvan scene, shaded by oaks and sycamores. Often you can't help but chuckle at the "No Fishing" signs posted next to the creekbed; most of the time the arroyo is quite "seco" and if there are any fish around, they must've walked here.

Teddy's Outpost Picnic Area is your first destination. In 1915 Theodore

Syvertson had a tiny roadside hostelry at this site. A half-mile beyond Teddy's is large Gould Mesa Campground, with plenty of picnic tables. Next stop, a short distance past the campground is a small picnic area called Nino. A mile beyond Gould Mesa Campground is Paul Little Picnic Area.

Now you leave the bottom of the arroyo and climb moderately to steeply up the east wall of the canyon. After curving along high on the wall, the trail then drops back to the canyon floor, where oak-shaded Oakwilde Trail Camp offers a tranquil rest stop. A few stone foundations remind the walker that Arroyo Seco was once Pasadena's most popular place for a weekend outing.

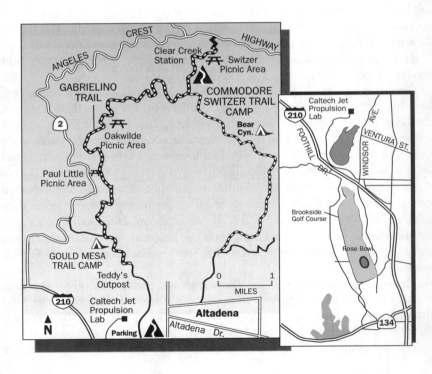

Upper Arroyo Seco

Gabrielino National Recreation Trail

From Switzer Picnic Area to Switzer Falls is 4 miles round trip with 600-foot elevation loss; to Bear Canyon is 8 miles round trip with 1,000-foot gain; to Oakwilde is 9 miles round trip with 1,400-foot loss

Arroyo Seco is undoubtedly the best-known canyon in Southern California. It's the site of the Rose Bowl and has the dubious distinction of hosting California's first freeway, the Pasadena. But the ten miles of canyon dominated by the freeway bear little resemblance to the ten miles of wild and rugged arroyo spilling from the shoulder of Mt. Wilson.

And the arroyo is rugged. A quiet stream—lined with colonnades of alder, live oak and mountain lilac clinging to the narrow sides of the gorge—cascades over boulders of big gray granite. A walk through the wildest part of Arroyo Seco and a visit to Switzer Falls is a jaunt to remember.

Perry Switzer, a carpenter who regained his health in the invigorating San Gabriels, built a trail up the Arroyo Seco and decided to build a trail resort. He put up some rough log cabins, despite arguments that "no one would want to pay for a bed up among the grizzlies, mountain lions and bobcats." He earned the nickname "Commodore" because of his skill in navigating his squadron of burros as they forded the Arroyo Seco. His hospitality made Switzer's the most popular trail camp in the San Gabriels.

The resort passed into the hands of Lloyd Austin, who added a tennis court, chapel and dance floor. A sign across from the resort greeted visitors: "Leave your cars and animals this side of the stream." Switzer-land was popular with hikers well into the 1930s, until Angeles Crest Highway rendered the peaceful camp "obsolete."

During the Great Hiking Era, a hiker could venture up the Arroyo Seco and within an hour lose all signs of civilization. Amazingly, you still can today. This hike takes you past the site of Switzer's retreat and visits Switzer Falls. Further exploration of the Arroyo Seco country is possible by taking one of the optional trails to Oakwilde and Bear Canyon. (See previous hike description of the Lower Arroyo Seco on page 97.)

Directions to trailhead: Take Angeles Crest Highway (2) north from La Canada for 10 miles. A short way past the junction of Angeles Crest and Angeles Forest (N3) Highways, you'll see the Angeles National Forest Clear Creek Information Station on your right. Inquire here about trails or road conditions.

A half-mile past the information station, park in the Forest Service Lot on the right side of the highway. Walk down the paved road 0.25 mile to Switzer Picnic Area. The trail begins across the bridge at the lower end of the picnic grounds.

The hike: Cross the bridge and follow the trail into the canyon. The pathway meanders with the stream under oak, alder and spruce. You'll cross and recross the stream several times and do some easy boulder-hopping. Plan to get wet. In some places, stream crossing is quite difficult in the spring. In a mile, you'll reach Commodore Switzer Trail Camp. Perched on a bench just above the falls, it's an inviting place complete with picnic tables. The creek trail below the camp dead-ends above the falls.

From the camp, cross the stream and follow the trail on the west slope. You'll soon get a nice view of the falls. A signed junction soon appears. To the right (southwest) is the main trail down to Oakwilde and Pasadena. Bear left here and hike down into the gorge of the Arroyo Seco below the falls. When you reach the creek, turn upstream 0.25 mile to the falls. Heed the warning signs and don't try to climb the falls; it's very dangerous.

To Bear Canyon Trail Camp: Continue down the Arroyo gorge on a mediocre trail. This path is slowly being restored, thanks to the efforts of the Sierra Club, the Forest Service and the San Gabriel Mountain Trail Builders.

After 0.75 mile, the trail reaches Bear Canyon and heads east up the canyon, crossing and re-crossing the creek. Along the way are many nice pools. In spring, the water is cold from snowmelt and little sun reaches the canyon floor. The trail, shaded by big cone spruce, closely parallels the creek.

When you look at an Angeles Forest map, you'll discover that Bear Canyon is surrounded on all sides by highways, dams and development. The canyon has no right to be so quiet, so pristine, but it is. As you boulder-hop from bank to bank, the only sound you'll hear is that of water cascading over granite and clear pools. Give thanks that there is at least one spot in the front range of the San Gabriels that is untouched wilderness, and continue to Bear Canyon Camp, two miles up the canyon.

To Oakwilde: From the signed junction above Commodore Switzer Trail Camp, continue right on the Gabrielino National Recreation Trail. The trail leaves the main Arroyo Seco canyon, crosses a chaparral ridge, then drops into Long Canyon. It then descends to Arroyo Seco creek bottom and follows the creek an easy mile to Oakwilde Trail Camp. In this canyon, yuccas and a variety of wildflowers bloom seasonally.

"Oak Wylde," as it was known during the Great Hiking Era, was a jumping-off place for trips farther up the Arroyo Seco. Pack burro trains connected Oak Wylde with the stage station in Pasadena. The trail camp is located among the crumbling stone foundation of a resort. Alder and oak shade a pleasant campground and picnic area.

Return the same way, or continue down the Arroyo Seco. (See Lower Arroyo Seco trail description on page 97.)

Millard Canyon, Dawn Mine

Millard Canyon Trail
From Sunset Ridge to Millard Canyon Falls is 1 mile round trip; to Dawn Mine is 5 miles round trip with 800-foot elevation gain

Hidden from the metropolis by Sunset Ridge, lush Millard Canyon is one of the more secluded spots in the front range of the San Gabriels. A cold stream tumbling over handsome boulders, a trail meandering beneath a canopy of alder, oak and sycamore, a waterfall and a historic mine, are a few of Millard's many attractions.

Millard Canyon is best-known as the site of the Dawn Mine which, unfortunately for its investors, produced more stories than gold. The mine was worked off and on from 1895, when gold was first discovered, until the 1950s. Enough gold was mined to keep ever-optimistic prospectors certain that they would soon strike a rich ore-bearing vein, but the big bonzana was never found.

You can explore Millard Canyon by two different routes, which lack an official name, but are often referred to as Millard Canyon Trail. An easy half-mile path meanders along the canyon floor to 50-foot Millard Falls. This is a pleasant walk, suitable for the whole family.

More experienced hikers will enjoy the challenge of following an abandoned trail through Millard Canyon to the site of the Dawn Mine. Enough of the old trail remains to keep you on track, but it's slow going with many stream crossings en route.

Directions to trailhead: From the Foothill Freeway (210) in Pasadena, exit on Lake Avenue. Drive north four miles, at which point Lake veers left

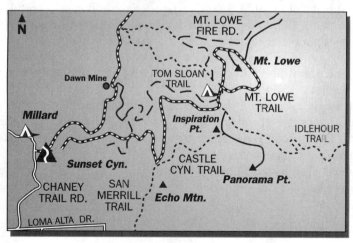

and becomes Loma Alta Drive. Continue a mile to Chaney Trail and turn right. Proceed another mile to a junction atop Sunset Ridge. If you're hiking to Dawn Mine, you'll bear right at this junction and park just outside the gate blocking Sunset Ridge Fire Road. If you're bound for Millard Canyon Falls, you'll stay left at the junction and descend to a parking lot at the bottom of the canyon.

The hike: (To Millard Canyon Falls) From the parking area at the bottom of Millard Canyon, you'll walk a hundred yards up a fire road to Millard Canyon Campground. Walk through the campground and pick up the signed trail leading to the falls. The trailheads east along the woodsy canyon bottom, crosses the stream a couple times, and arrives at the base of the waterfall. Don't try to climb up, over, or around the falls; people have been injured attempting this foolhardy ascent.

(To Dawn Mine) From the Sunset Ridge parking area, head up the fire road. Enjoy the clear-day ridgetop views of the metropolis. You'll soon pass a junction on your left with a trail leading down to Millard Canyon Campground.

A short 0.25 mile from the trailhead, you'll spot signed Sunset Ridge Trail, which you'll join and begin descending into Millard Canyon. A few minutes of walking down the well-graded path will reward you with an eagle's-eye view of Millard Canyon Falls.

Near the canyon bottom, you'll meet a trail junction. Sunset Ridge Trail continues along the canyon wall, but you bear left and descend past a cabin to the canyon floor. As you begin hiking up-canyon, turn around and take a mental photograph of the trail that brought you down to the canyon; it's easy to miss on your return trip.

As you pick your way stream-side amongst the boulders and fallen trees on the canyon floor, you'll follow vestiges of the old trail. Typically, you'll follow a fifty- or hundred-yard stretch of trail, boulder-hop for a bit, cross the stream, then pick up another length of trail.

The canyon floor is strewn with lengths of rusting pipe and assorted mining machinery. Several pools, cascades, and flat rocks suggest a stream-side picnic.

After hiking a bit more than a mile up-canyon, you'll find that Millard Canyon turns north. From this turn, it's a bit less than a mile to the Dawn Mine site. Don't go into the mine shaft. Darkness and deep holes filled with water make it very dangerous.

Return the same way, and remember to keep a sharp lookout for the trail that leads out of the canyon back to the trailhead.

MT. LOWE

Mt. Lowe Railway Trail

From Sunset Ridge to Mt. Lowe Trail Camp is 10 miles round trip with 2,700-foot gain; to Inspiration Point is 11 miles round trip.

Professor Thaddeus Lowe, Civil War balloonist, man of fame and fortune, was the quintessential California dreamer. His dream was to build a railway into—and a resort complex atop—the San Gabriel Mountains high above Pasadena. In the 1890s, his dream became a reality.

During the height of its popularity, millions took Professor Lowe's "Railway to the Clouds" to fine hotels and spectacular views of Southern California. Until it was abandoned in the 1930s, it was the Southland's most popular tourist attraction.

From Pasadena, visitors rode a trolley up Rubio Canyon, where a pavilion and hotel were located. After taking refreshments, they boarded the "airships" of the great cable incline, which carried them 3,000 feet (gaining 1,300 feet) straight up to the Echo Mountain Resort Area. "Breathtaking" and "hair-raising" were the most frequent descriptions of this thrilling ride. Atop Echo Mountain was the White City, with a hotel, observatory, and a magnificent searchlight purchased from the Chicago World's Fair. When the searchlight swept the mountaintop, the white buildings of the resort were visible from all over Los Angeles. From Echo Mountain, tourists could board a trolley and ride another few miles to Mt. Lowe Tavern at the end of the line.

This historic walk follows the old railway bed, visits the ruins of the White City and Mt. Lowe Tavern, and concludes with some fine views of Los Angeles from Inspiration Point. The old railway bed with its gentle seven percent grade makes for easy walking.

Directions to trailhead: Exit the Foothill Freeway (210) at Lake Avenue and follow it north to its end. Turn left on Loma Alta Drive. Go one mile to Chaney Trail Road and turn right. At a "Y" in the road, take the right fork to the Sunset Ridge parking area. The trailhead is located at the locked gate, which bars vehicles from Sunset Ridge Fire Road.

The hike: The trail begins just past the locked gate. Follow paved Sunset Ridge Fire Road. You may follow the fire road two miles to the junction with Echo Mountain Trail, but a more attractive alternative is described below.

Follow the road 0.25 mile to the signed Sunset Ridge Trail on your left. Join this trail which, for the most part, parallels the fire road and leads into peaceful Millard Canyon. Near the canyon bottom, the trail forks at a signed junction. Bear right and ascend back up to Sunset Ridge Fire Road. Follow the fire road about 75 yards, and on your right you'll spot the signed junction with Echo Mountain Trail.

Mt. Lowe "Railway to the Clouds."

To Echo Mountain: Bear right on Echo Mountain Trail, which leads one-half mile over the old railway bed to Echo Mountain. Echo Mountain takes its name from an echo that bounces around the semicircle of mountain walls.

On Echo Mountain are the foundations of Echo Mountain House and the chalet. The most prominent ruin is the large iron bull wheel that pulled the cars up the steep incline fromm Rubio Canyon. A fire swept Echo Mountain in 1900, leveling all of the White City except the observatory. Picnic tables suggest a lunch stop among the ruins. Leave behind the ruins of the White City, return to Sunset Ridge Fire Road and bear right.

The paved road soon becomes dirt and an interpretive sign at "Cape of Good Hope" lets you know you've joined the Mt. Lowe Railway tour. Continue along the railway bed, passing the tourist attractions that impressed an earlier generation of travelers: Granite Gate, Horseshoe Curve, and the site of the Great Circular Bridge.

Near the top, you'll come to the site of Mt. Lowe Tavern, which burned in 1936. Almost all signs of the tavern are gone, but this peaceful spot under oaks and big cone spruce still extends its hospitality. On the old tavern site is Mt. Lowe Trail Camp, which welcomes day hikers with its shade, water, restrooms and picnic tables.

Before heading down, follow the fire road east and then south for 0.5-mile to Inspiration Point. Where the fire road makes a hairpin left to Mt. Wilson, go right. At Inspiration Point, you can gaze through several tele-scope-like sighting tubes aimed at Santa Monica, Hollywood and the Rose Bowl. After you've found a sight that inspires you, return the same way.

Henninger Flats

Mt. Wilson Toll Road
From Altadena to Henninger Flats is 6 miles round trip with
1,400-foot elevation gain.

Consider the conifers: A wind-bowed limber pine clinging to a rocky
summit. A sweet-smelling grove of incense cedar. The deep shade and
primeval gloom of a spruce forest.

Where do trees come from?

I know, I know. "Only God can make a tree."

Keep your Joyce Kilmer. Hold the metaphysical questions. Our inquiry
here is limited to what happens in the aftermath of a fire or flood, when
great numbers of trees lie dead or dying.

Fortunately for California's cone-bearing tree population—and tree
lovers—there is a place where trees, more than 120,000 a year, are grown to
replace those lost to the capriciousness of nature and the carelessness of
humans. That place is Henninger Flats, home of the Los Angeles County
Experimental Nursery.

Perched halfway between Altadena and Mt. Wilson, Henninger Flats is
the site of Southern California's finest tree plantation. On the flats you'll be
able to view trees in all shapes and sizes, from seedlings to mature stands. A
museum with reforestation exhibits, a nature trail, and the Los Angeles
County foresters on duty will help you understand where trees come from.

The Flats have a colorful history. After careers as a gold miner, Indian
fighter and first Sheriff of Santa Clara County, Captain William Henninger
came to Los Angeles to retire in the early 1880s. While doing a little prospecting, Henninger discovered the little mesa that one day would bear his
name. He constructed a trail over which he could lead his burros.

Atop the flats he built a cabin, planted fruit trees, raised hay and corn.
His solitude ended in 1890 when the Mt. Wilson Toll Road was constructed
for the purpose of carrying the great telescope up to the new observatory.
Captain Henninger's Flats soon became a water and rest stop for hikers, riders and fishermen who trooped into the mountains.

After Henninger's death in 1895, the flats were used by the U.S. Forest
Service as a tree nursery. Foresters emphasized the nurturing of fire- and
drought-resistant varieties of conifers. Many thousands of seedlings were
transplanted to fire- and flood-ravaged slopes all over the Southland. Since
1928, Los Angeles County foresters have continued the good work.

The Pasadena and Mt. Wilson Toll Road Company in 1891 fashioned a
trail to the summit of Mt. Wilson. Fees were 50 cents per rider, 25 cents per
hiker. A 12-foot wide road followed two decades later.

During the 1920s, the road was the scene of an annual auto race, similar to the Pikes Peak hillclimb. In 1936 the Angeles Crest Highway opened and rendered the toll road obsolete. Since then the toll road has been closed to public traffic and maintained as a fire road.

A moderate outing of just under six miles, on good fire road, the trail up to Henninger Flats is suitable for the whole family. The Flats offer a large picnic area and fine clear day city views.

Directions to trailhead: From the Foothill Freeway (210) in Pasadena, exit on Lake Avenue. Turn north and continue to Altadena Drive. Make a right, continue about ten blocks, and look closely to your left. Turn left on Pinecrest Drive and wind a few blocks through a residential area to the trailhead. The trailhead is found in the 2200 block of Pinecrest. You'll spot a locked gate across the fire road that leads down into Eaton Canyon.

The hike: Proceed down the fire road to the bottom of Eaton Canyon. After crossing a bridge, the road begins a series of switchbacks up chaparral-covered slopes. Occasional painted pipes mark your progress.

Henninger Flats welcomes the hiker with water, shade, and two campgrounds where you may enjoy a lunch stop. Growing on the flats are some of the more common cone-bearing trees of the California mountains including knobcone, Coulter, sugar, digger and Jeffrey pine, as well as such exotics as Japanese black pine and Himalayan white pine.

After your tree tour, return the same way. Ultra-energetic hikers will continue up the old toll road to Mt. Wilson; the journey from Altadena to the summit is 9 miles one-way with an elevation gain of 4,500 feet.

Trees are grown at Henninger Flats for replanting in the San Gabriels.

MT. WILSON

Mt. Wilson Trail

From Sierra Madre to Orchard Camp is 9 miles round trip with a 2,000-foot elevation gain; to Mt. Wilson is 15 miles round trip with a 4,500-foot gain

The Mt. Wilson Trail up Little Santa Anita Canyon is the oldest pioneer's trail into the San Gabriels. It was built in 1864 by Benjamin Wilson, who overhauled a Gabrielino Indian path in order to log the stands of incense cedar and sugar pine on the mountain that now bears his name.

The first telescope was carried up this trail to Mt. Wilson in 1904. During the Great Hiking Era, thousands of hikers rode the Red Cars to Sierra Madre, disembarked, and hiked up this path to the popular trail resort to Orchard Camp. Forty thousand hikers and horseback riders passed over the trail in 1911, its peak year.

After the passing of the Great Hiking Era in the 1930s, the trail was all but abandoned until the late 1950s when rebuilding efforts began. Sierra Madre citizens, aided by Boy Scout troops, rebuilt the trail all the way up canyon to its junction with the old Mt. Wilson Toll Road.

Sierra Madre citizens also prevented county flood control engineers from bulldozing and check-damming Little Santa Anita Canyon. The aroused citizenry established Sierra Madre Historical Wilderness Area to preserve the canyon. This area is patterned after federal Wilderness Areas; that is, the land is to be preserved forever without development or mechanized use.

Benjamin Wilson

This hike takes you up Little Santa Anita Canyon, visits Orchard Camp, and climbs to the top of Mt. Wilson. It's a classic climb, one of the nicest all-day hikes in the Southland.

Directions to trailhead: From the Foothill Freeway (210) in Arcadia, exit on Baldwin Avenue and head north. Turn right on Miramonte Avenue near the junction of Mt. Wilson Trail Road, which is on your left. The trail begins 150 yards up this road and is marked by a large wooden sign. After passing some homes, the trail shortly intersects the main trail.

The hike: After trudging 1.5 miles up Santa Anita Canyon you reach a junction with a side trail, which leads to the nearby canyon bottom. Here you can lean against an old oak, cool your heels in the rushing water, relax and watch the river flow.

Continue hiking on the ridge trail as it climbs higher and higher above the

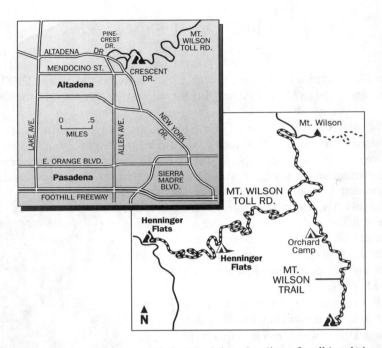

canyon floor onto sunny, exposed slopes. A hot 3 miles of walking brings you to Decker Spring and another 0.5 mile to Orchard Camp, a shady glen dotted with oak and spruce trees. When Wilson was building his trail, a construction camp called Halfway House was built here. Later homesteaders tried their hand planting apple and cherry trees—hence the name Orchard Camp.

During the Great Hiking Era, a succession of entrepreneurs utilized Orchard Camp as a trail resort and welcomed thousands of hikers. Hikers traveling through the canyon in the 1920s reported seeing "The Nature Man of Mt. Wilson," a tall bronzed hermit who looked like he stepped out of the pages of the Old Testament. The nature man carried a stone axe and worked on the trail for his keep. Some say he's still around, protecting the canyon—though he no longer springs out of the brush and greets every hiker who passes.

Orchard Camp is a nice place to picnic. You might want to call it a day here and return the same way.

The trail continues through thick chaparral up Santa Anita Canyon to its head. It contours on the shelf-like trail, heads east on a firebreak and crosses over a steep manzanita-covered ridge. At the intersection with Winter Creek Trail, turn left (west) and ascend steeply to Mt. Wilson Toll Road, 2 miles from Orchard Camp.

Turn right on the Toll Road and follow it a mile as it ascends through well-spaced spruce to Mt. Wilson Road, just outside Skyline Park.

BIG SANTA ANITA CANYON

Gabrielino National Recreation Trail

From Chantry Flat to Sturtevant Falls is 3.5 miles round trip with 500-foot gain; to Spruce Grove Camp is 8 miles round trip with 1,400-foot gain; to Mt. Wilson is 8 miles one-way with 4,000-foot gain

Cascades, a waterfall and giant woodwardia ferns are a few of the many delights of historic Big Santa Anita Canyon. The bucolic canyon has been popular with Southern California hikers for a hundred years.

William Sturtevant, known to his friends as "Sturde," pioneered many miles of San Gabriel Mountains trails. He traveled from California to Colorado in the early 1880s with forty burros. A packer par excellence, he soon found his services to be in great demand in the San Gabriels.

Sturtevant hewed out a trail over the ridge from Winter Creek to the top of the canyon and in 1898 opened Sturtevant Camp. The rustic resort consisted of a dining hall, tents, and a store and was a popular trail resort well into the 1930s.

In Santa Anita Canyon today some eighty-odd cabins are serviced by a burro train from Chantry Flats, named for another early packer, Charlie Chantry. One of the more colorful sights in the local mountains—and a look backward into a bygone era—is a glimpse at the pack animals plodding up the trail to Sturtevant Camp, now a Methodist Church retreat.

Sturtevant's trail is now a section of the 28-mile long Gabrielino National Recreation Trail. The trail to Sturtevant Falls is very popular on weekends—but not as popular as it was on Fourth of July weekend 1919 when 5,000 people tramped into the canyon and signed the trail register! The ambitious hiker may continue past the falls to Spruce Grove Camp and even as far as the top of Mt. Wilson.

Directions to trailhead: From the Foothill Freeway (210) in Arcadia, exit on Santa Anita Avenue and drive six miles north to its end at Chantry Flat. The trail begins across the road from the parking area. A tiny store at the edge of the parking lot sells maps and refreshments.

The hike: Descend on the paved fire road, part of the Gabrielino Trail, into Big Santa Anita Canyon. At the bottom of the canyon you'll cross a footbridge near the confluence of Big Santa Anita and Winter Creeks. Here a small sign commemorates Roberts Camp, a resort camp founded in 1912. Owner Otto Roberts and other canyon boosters really "sold" the charms of the canyon to Southern Californians in need of a quiet weekend. As you follow the path up-canyon along the oak and alder-shaded creek, you'll soon determine that the canyon "sells" itself.

The only blemish on the pristine scene is a series of check-dams

Sturtevant Falls

constructed of giant cement "Lincoln logs," by the Los Angeles County Flood Control District and the Forest Service in the early 1960s. In their zeal to tame Big Santa Anita Creek, engineers apparently forgot that fast-moving water is supposed to erode canyon bottoms; floods are what originally sculpted this beautiful canyon. Today, thanks to the check-dams, the creek flows in well-organized fashion, lingering in tranquil pools, then spilling over the dams in fifteen-foot cascades. Over the years, moss, ferns, alders and other creekside flora have softened the appearance of the dams and they now fit much better into the lovely surroundings.

The trail passes some private cabins and reaches a three-way trail junction. To visit Sturtevant Falls, continue straight ahead. You'll cross Big Santa Anita Creek, then re-cross where the creek veers leftward. Pick your way along the boulder-strewn creek bank a final hundred yards to the falls. The falls drops in a silver stream fifty feet to a natural rock bowl. (Caution:

Climbing the wet rocks near the falls can be extremely hazardous to your health. Stay off.)

Return the same way, or hike onward and upward to Spruce Grove Trail Camp. Two signed trails lead toward Spruce Grove. The leftward one zigzags high up on the canyon wall while the other passes above the falls. The left trail is easier hiking while the right trailheads through the heart of the canyon and is prettier. Either trail is good walking and they rejoin in a mile.

After the trails rejoin, continue along the spruce-shaded path to Cascade Picnic Area. Call it a day here or ascend another mile to Spruce Grove Trail Camp. Both locales have plenty of tables and shade.

Still feeling frisky? Hikers in top condition will charge up the trail to Mt. Wilson—an 8-mile (one way) journey from Chantry Flat. Continue on the trail up-canyon a short distance, cross the creek and you'll find a trail junction. A left brings you to historic Sturtevant Camp, now owned by the Methodist Church. The trail to Mt. Wilson soon departs Big Santa Anita Canyon and travels many a switchback through the thick forest to Mt. Wilson Skyline Park.

Early hiker,
Big Santa Anita Canyon

WINTER CREEK

Winter Creek Trail

From Chantry Flat to Hoegees Camp is 6 miles round trip with 300-foot elevation gain; return via Mt. Zion Trail, Gabrielino Trails is 9 miles round trip with 1,500-foot gain

Before the turn of the 20th century, packer/entrepreneur William Sturtevant set up a trail camp in one of the woodsy canyons on the south-facing slope of Mt. Wilson. This peaceful creekside refuge from city life was called Sturtevant's Winter Camp. In later years the name Winter was given to the creek whose headwaters arise from the shoulder of Mt. Wilson and tumble southeasterly into Big Santa Anita Canyon.

In 1908, Arie Hoegee and his family built a resort here that soon became a popular destination for Mt. Wilson-bound hikers; it remained so until it was battered by the great flood of 1938. A trail camp named for the Hoegees now stands on the site of the old resort and offers the modern-day hiker a tranquil picnic site or rest stop.

A hike along Winter Creek is a fine way to greet the arrival of winter. One of a half-dozen trails accessible from the popular Chantry Flat trailhead located just above Altadena in the Angeles National Forest, Winter Creek Trail offers a pleasant family hike in the front range of the San Gabriel Mountains. The trail provides a good close-to-town opportunity to exercise those out-of-town guests or to work off those huge holiday meals.

Directions to trailhead: From the Foothill Freeway (210) in Arcadia, exit on Santa Anita Avenue and drive six miles north to its end at Chantry Flat. The trail begins across the road from the parking area. A tiny store at the edge of the parking lot sells maps and refreshments.

The hike: Descend 0.75-mile on the paved fire road, part of the signed Gabrielino Trail, into Big Santa Anita Canyon. At the bottom of the canyon, you'll cross a footbridge near the confluence of Big Santa Anita and Winter Creeks.

After crossing the bridge, look leftward for the signed Lower Winter Creek Trail. Following the bubbling creek, the trail tunnels beneath the boughs of oak and alder, willow and bay. The only blemish on the pristine scene is a series of check dams constructed of giant cement "Lincoln logs" by the Los Angeles County Flood Control District and Forest Service in the early 1960s. Fortunately, during the last quarter-century, moss, ferns and other creekside flora have softened the appearance of the dams and they now fit much better into the lovely surroundings.

You'll pass some cabins, built just after the turn of the century and reached only by trail. For more than eight decades, the needs of the cabin owners have been supplied by pack train.

After crossing Winter Creek, you'll arrive at Hoegees Camp. A dozen or so tables beneath the big cone spruce offer fine picnicking. Almost all signs of the original Hoegees Camp are gone, with the exception of flourishing patches of ivy. (In later years, Hoegees was renamed Camp Ivy.)

Walk through the campground until you spot a tiny tombstone-shaped trail sign. Cross Winter Creek here and bear left on the trail. In a short while you'll pass a junction with Mt. Zion Trail, a steep trail that climbs over the mountain to Sturtevant Camp and Big Santa Anita Canyon.

After recrossing the creek, you'll pass a junction with a trail leading to Mt. Wilson and join the Upper Winter Creek Trail. This trail contours around a ridge onto open chaparral-covered slopes. This stretch of trail offers fine clear-day views of Sierra Madre and Arcadia. The trail joins a fire road just above Chantry Flat and you follow this road through the picnic area back to the parking lot where you left your car.

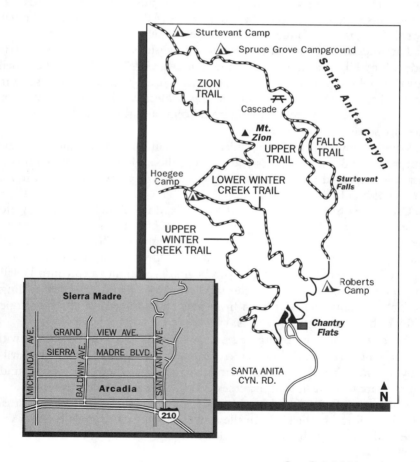

SAN GABRIEL WILDERNESS

Devil's Canyon Trail
From Chilao to Devil's Canyon Trail Camp is 7 miles round trip with 1,500-foot elevation loss; to Devil's Canyon Waterfall is 11 miles round trip with 2,300-foot loss

Los Angeles residents, while inching along on some crowded interchange, may be comforted by knowing that no other metropolis has a wilderness area so close. When you hike the primeval canyons of the San Gabriel Wilderness Area, you won't believe you're only eighteen as-the-crow-flies miles from downtown L.A.

The 36,137-acre wilderness is rough and rugged country, the bulk of which is contained in two canyons, Devil's and Bear. Chaparral coats the sunny canyon slopes while pine and fir reach from the ridges to the sky. In spring, this is color country: the laurels glow yellow with flowers, the willows fluff up, the ceanothus blossoms blue and white.

The wilderness area is surrounded on three sides by roads: on the north and west by Highway 2, on the east by Highway 39. Picnickers and campers crowd its edges, skiers peer down at it from nearby ridges. But despite its accessibility, most people only look at this wilderness. The view down from the brink of Devil's Canyon, the sharp descent, and the thought of the walk back up, scare off casual walkers.

Devil's Canyon Trail, from Chilao to the trail camp, is the most pleasant path in the wilderness. It takes you through the middle third of the canyon, past willow-shaded pools and dancing cascades, to spots that make the Big City seem hundreds of miles away.

Directions to trailhead: From La Canada, drive 27 miles up the Angeles Crest Highway, 0.25 mile past the entrance to Upper Chilao Campground. Look for a parking lot on the left side of the highway. The signed trailhead, which is usually below snowline, is across the highway from the parking lot.

The hike: Remind yourself, as you begin descending steeply into Devil's Canyon, that the tough part of this trip comes last. Pace yourself accordingly. The trail steps back and forth from pine and spruce on the shady slopes to thick chaparral on sunny slopes.

After two miles, the trail meets a pleasant little creek and descends with its bubbling waterway down into the canyon. At trail's end is Devil's Canyon Trail Camp, a primitive creekside retreat, where the only sounds you hear are the murmur of the creek and the rustling of alder leaves.

You can bushwhack and boulder-hop a mile upstream before the brush gets uncomfortably thick. From the trail camp, you can return the way you came or do some further exploring downstream.

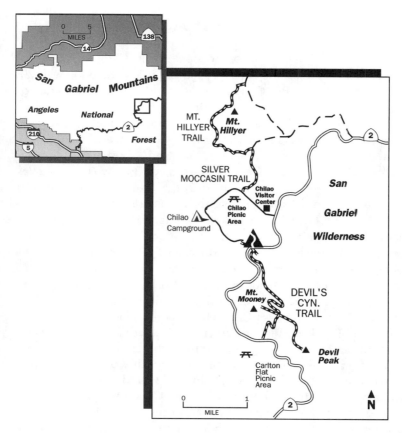

Below the trail camp, a path follows Devil's Creek for a time, but soon ends. Pick your way across rock islands in the creek. The walls of Devil's Canyon close in and you find yourself in trackless boulder-hopping country; pleasant, but slow-going. You continually cross the creek, decipher routes around deep pools and descend gingerly down misty boulders.

Blackened alder leaves cover the surface of still eddies, where pan-sized trout may lurk. The canyon narrows, its steep rock walls pinching Devil's Creek into a series of cascades. As the canyon narrows further, the cascades grow more spectacular and waterfalls occur. The first falls come from side creeks and 0.25 mile farther down-creek you arrive at the first mainstream falls, which plunge 20 feet to a bubbling pool.

Expert mountaineers sometimes continue downstream from the falls, but it's a precarious route and is recommended only for the very skilled. Your return to Devil's Canyon Trail Camp may be faster than your descent, because it's easier to pick routes and climb up rocks, than down them. Your climb from the trail camp to the highway will, of course, be slower.

CHILAO

Silver Moccasin Trail

From Chilao to Horse Flats Campground is 2 miles round trip with 200-foot elevation gain; to Mt. Hillyer is 6 miles round trip with 1,000-foot gain

Even on the Angeles National Forest map, the trail looks intriguing: a red dashed line zigs and zags through the heart of the San Gabriel Mountains and connects Chantry Flat and Shortcut Station, Chilao, Cloudburst and Cooper Canyon. Designed by the Los Angeles Area Council of the Boy Scouts of America, the 53-mile long Silver Moccasin Trail, extends from Charlton Flat to the mountain named for the founder of the Boy Scouts, Lord Baden-Powell. Scouts who complete the week-long trek earn the prized Silver Moccasin award.

One pretty stretch of the Silver Moccasin Trail tours the Chilao country, a region of giant boulders and gentle, Jeffrey pine-covered slopes. Another path—Mt. Hillyer Trail—leads to the top of 6,162-foot Mt. Hillyer. From the top, you'll get great views to the north of the desert side of the San Gabriels.

Located just off Angeles Crest Highway near the trailhead, the Angeles National Forest Chilao Visitor Center is well worth a visit. Exhibits interpret flora, fauna and forest history. Behind the station is a short nature trail.

Directions to trailhead: From the Foothill Freeway (210) in La Canada, exit on Angeles Crest Highway (2) and wind 27 miles up the mountain road to the signed turnoff for the Chilao Visitor Center. Turn left and follow the paved road past the visitor center a half-mile to signed Silver Moccasin Trail on your right. Parking at the trailhead is limited to a few cars, but there's a wide turnout located just up the road.

The hike: The trail ascends a manzanita- and yucca-covered slope to the top of a minor ridge. A mile from the trailhead, the trail widens and you reach a signed junction. Here Silver Moccasin Trail swings southeast toward Angeles Crest Highway and Cooper Canyon, but you go right with a retiring dirt road one hundred yards to Horse Flat Campground. The Camp, with plenty of pine-shaded picnic tables, is a good rest stop.

Just as you reach the gravel campground road, you head left with the signed Mt. Hillyer Trail. The path switchbacks up pine, incense cedar- and scrub oak-covered slopes.

Up top, Mt. Hillyer may remind you of what Gertrude Stein said of Oakland: "There's no there there." The summit is not a commanding pinnacle, but a forested flat. With all those trees in the way, you'll have to walk a few hundred yards along the ridgeline to get your view of green Chilao country to the south and the brown, wrinkled desert side of the San Gabriels to the north.

MT. WILLIAMSON

Mt. Williamson Trail
From Islip Saddle to Mt. Williamson is 5 miles round trip with 1,600-foot elevation gain Season: April-November

Mt. Williamson stands head and shoulders above other crests along Angeles Crest Highway. The 8,214-foot peak offers grand views of earthquake country—the Devil's Punchbowl, San Andreas Fault and the fractured northern edges of the San Gabriel Mountains.

Desert views this peak may offer, but Mt. Williamson is anything but a desert peak. It's plenty green and bristling with pine and fir.

The summit of Mt. Williamson is the high point and culmination of well-named Pleasant View Ridge, a chain of peaks that rises from the desert floor to Angeles Crest Highway. It's quite a contrast to stand atop the piney peak, which is snow-covered in winter, and look down upon Joshua trees and the vast sandscape of the Mojave Desert.

Hot and cold, desert and alpine environments—these are the contrasts that make hiking in Southern California so very special.

The mountain's namesake is Major Robert Stockton Williamson, who first explored the desert side of the San Gabriels in 1853. Williamson, a U.S. Army mapmaker led an expedition in search of a railroad route over or through the mountains. Certainly Williamson found no passable route through the Mt. Williamson area or any other place in the San Gabriel Mountains high country, but the Major did find a way around the mountains, so his mission was definitely a success. Williamson's Pacific Railroad Survey report to Congress detailed two railroad routes: Cajon Pass on the east end of the San Gabriels and Soledad Canyon on northwest.

Two fine trails ascend Mt. Williamson from Angeles Crest Highway. One trail leads from Islip Saddle, the other from another (unnamed) saddle 1.5 miles farther west. Both are well-graded, well maintained routes.

Possibly, after a glance at a map, the idea of linking the east and west Mt. Williamson trails with a walk along Angeles Crest Highway, in order to make a loop trip, will occur to you. Don't be tempted. The problem is that between the two trails, Angeles Crest Highway passes through a couple of tunnels—a definite no-no for pedestrians. Both Mt. Williamson trails are winners; you can't go wrong. Mt. Williamson is a great place to beat the heat, and offers fine hiking in all seasons but winter, when snow covers the trail.

Directions to trailhead: From the Foothill Freeway (210) in La Canada, exit on Angeles Crest Highway (2) and drive about 38 miles, or 2.5 miles past (east of) the Krakta Ridge Ski Area. Look for the (sometimes) signed trail to Mt. Williamson on the left (north) side of the highway.

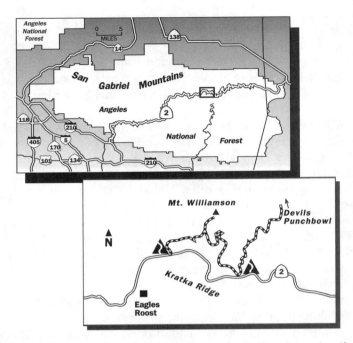

The Mt. Williamson east trail is easier to find. Continue 4 mile east of the Krakta Ridge Ski Area, and after you pass through the highway tunnels, you'll see the parking area at Islip Saddle on the left (north) side of the highway.

The hike: At Islip Saddle, you'll spot South Fork Trail (remember this fine trail for another day) heading northeast down to South Fork Camp near Devil's Punchbowl County Park. But you'll join the trail to Mt. Williamson and begin ascending through a forest of Jeffrey and ponderosa pine.

Two miles of steep, but not brutal, climbing brings you to a junction with the Mt. Williamson West trail. The two trails continue as one, passing scattered white fir (more numerous as you near 8,000 feet in elevation). You'll enjoy over-the shoulder views south of Bear Creek Canyon and the heart of the rugged San Gabriel Wilderness.

Keep hiking north on the trail, which gets a little fainter as it nears the summit of Mt. Williamson. From the peak, enjoy the dramatic views of the desert below. If you have a good map along, you can pick out the many playas (dry lake beds), buttes and mountain ridges of the dry lands below. At the base of Mt. Williamson is that greatest of earthquake faults—the San Andreas Rift Zone. Most striking of all is the view of Devil's Punchbowl and its jumbled sedimentary strata.

Remember that this isn't a loop hike; return the way you came.

Big Rock Canyon

South Fork Trail
From South Fork Campground to Islip Saddle is 10.4 miles round trip
with 2,100-foot elevation gain

For purposes of geographical orientation, Southland hikers often divide the San Gabriel Mountains into a front country, backcountry, foothills, high country, east end, west end, urban interface and alpine wilderness. Rarely, however, does the north (desert) side of the range come up for discussion.

The San Gabriels thrust abruptly up from the desert floor, stopping much of the Mojave's heat and hot air from reaching the Los Angeles Basin. (Thank you San Gabriel Mountains!) From vista points near the crest of Angeles Crest Highway at Dawson Saddle (7,901 feet) travelers get grand panoramas of the Mojave Desert which, from this vantage point, seems mighty close to the metropolis. Clear-day vistas are quintessential West Mojave features—dry lakebeds and isolated buttes.

At the base of the mountains lie the communities of Pearblossom and Little Rock. In earlier times, farmers tapped the intermittent creeks cascading from the north shoulders of the range and planted orchards of pears, peaches, cherries and almonds. A limited amount of agriculture continues today and the traveler can stop at fruit stands to purchase some of the local offerings.

The desert side of the San Gabriels is characterized by deep V-shaped gorges. Perhaps the most dramatic of these gorges is the South Fork of Big Rock Creek, a steep canyon that extends from the northern crest of the range down to the San Andreas Fault Zone and the intensively fractured Devil's Punchbowl.

South Fork Trail climbs from the high desert to the highway, from pinyon pine to ponderosa pine. With changes in elevation come changes in vegetation—from sage and cactus to manzanita and ceanothus to incense cedar and spruce. The path traces the South Fork of Big Rock Creek Canyon adjacent to Devil's Punchbowl and ascends to Islip Saddle (6,685 feet), located on Angeles Crest Highway.

Long ago, before Angeles Crest Highway was constructed and the San Gabriel Mountains became easy to cross by car, South Fork Trail was a major passageway into the mountains. These days the path is little used, and you might just find yourself the only one enjoying this connection between desert and alpine environments.

Directions to trailhead: From Highway 14 (Antelope Valley Freeway) a bit south of Palmdale, take the Pearblossom Highway exit and drive 5 miles east to Highway 138, and continuing another 8.5 miles east on 138 to

Long View Road. Turn south (signed for Devil's Punchbowl County Park) and travel 2.2 miles to Fort Tejon Road. Signs point to the Devil's Punchbowl, but you follow the signs briefly left toward Valyermo and join Valyermo Road for 3.5 miles to signed Big Rock Creek Road. Turn right and travel 3 miles to the signed turnoff for South Fork Campground and proceed one mile on the dirt road to the special day use/hiker's parking lot below the campground. The signed trail departs from the parking area.

Those hikers wishing to make a one-way descent on South Fork Trail will find the upper trailhead at Islip Saddle parking area, located at mile 64.1 on Angeles Crest Highway. Winter storms and icy conditions often keep this stretch of highway closed until well into spring.

The hike: From the parking area below South Fork Campground, join the signed trailheading south. Almost immediately, you'll reach a trail junction with the path leading to Devil's Punchbowl. Stay left and you'll soon pass South Fork Campground on your left.

After 0.25 mile, cross to the other side of Big Rock Creek and switchback up the canyon wall. The trail continues its ascent, sometimes at quite a height above Big Rock Creek. With your ascent the environment changes from desert to forest, though not all at once, and the hiker will note some intriguing combinations of desert and woodland plant life in the transition zone.

South Fork Trail meets Angeles Crest Highway at a point where the Pacific Crest Trail climbs northward toward Mt. Williamson.

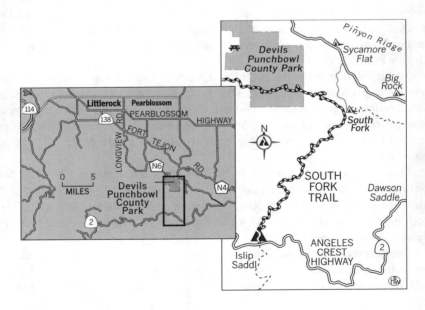

MT. ISLIP

Mt. Islip Trail
From Angeles Crest Highway to Little Jimmy Trail Camp is 3 miles round trip
with 500-foot elevation gain; to Mt. Islip is 5 miles round trip
with 1,100-foot gain; Season: April-November

Mt. Islip, (pronounced eye-slip) is not named, as you might guess, for a clumsy mountaineer, but for Canadian George Islip, who homesteaded in San Gabriel Canyon a century ago. The mountain is not one of the tallest San Gabriel Mountains peaks, but its isolated position on the spine of the range makes its stand out. The summit offers the hiker fine views of the middle portion of the Angeles National Forest high country and of the metropolis.

Mt. Islip has long been a popular destination for hikers. The mountain was particularly popular with Occidental College students who in 1909 built a huge cairn (heap of boulders), dubbed the "Occidental Monument" atop the summit. The monument, which had the name Occidental on top, stood about two decades, until the Forest Service cleared the summit of Mt. Islip to make room for a fire lookout tower. The monument and the fire lookout are long gone, but the stone foundation of the fire lookout's living quarters remains.

One early visitor to the slopes of Mt. Islip was popular newspaper cartoonist Jimmy Swinnerton (1875-1974), well known in the early years of this century for his comic strip "Little Jimmy." By the time he was in his thirties, hard-working, hard-drinking Swinnerton was suffering from the effects of exhaustion, booze, and tuberculosis. His employer and benefactor William Randolph Hearst sent Swinnerton to the desert to dry out. Swinnerton, however, found the summer heat oppressive so, loading his paintbrushes onto a burro, he headed into the San Gabriel Mountains.

Swinnerton spent the summers of 1908 and 1909 at Camp Coldbrook on the banks of the north fork of the San Gabriel River. Often he would set up camp high on the shoulder of Mt. Islip near a place called Gooseberry Spring, which soon became known as Little Jimmy Spring. During the two summers Swinnerton was encamped in the San Gabriels, he entertained passing hikers with sketches of his Little Jimmy character. His campsite, once known as Swinnerton Camp, is now called Little Jimmy Trail Camp.

You can reach Mt. Islip from the south side of the mountains, the way Jimmy Swinnerton did, or start from the north side from Angeles Crest Highway. This hike follows the latter route, which is a bit easier than coming up from Crystal Lake.

Directions to trailhead: From the Foothill Freeway (210) in La Canada, exit on Angeles Crest Highway (2) and proceed to signed Islip Saddle. (At the saddle, on the north side of the highway, is a large parking area. If you want,

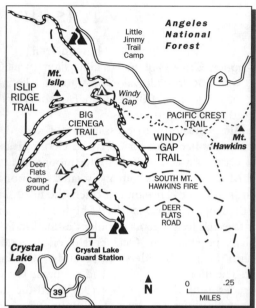

you can start your hike to Mt. Islip at the trailhead across the road from the parking area. An old trailheads west, paralleling the highway for a mile, then veers upward to meet the trail leading to Little Jimmy Trail Camp.)

From Islip Saddle, a 1.5-mile drive east on Angeles Crest Highway brings you to the signed trailhead for Little Jimmy Trail Camp on the right (south) side of the road. There's parking on both sides of the highway.

The hike: Your trail, at first, is a dirt road (closed to all but Forest Service vehicles). Jeffrey and sugar pine shade the route. A half-mile ascent brings you to a three-way junction. To your right is the old crest trail coming up from Islip Sadddle. The forest road you've been following continues to Little Jimmy Trail Camp.

Bear left on the signed trail to Little Jimmy. The trail stays just below and parallel to the road as it ascends a mile over forested slopes to Little Jimmy Trail Camp. The camp has tables, stoves and restrooms. A side trail leads 0.25 mile southeast to all-year Little Jimmy Spring.

At the west end of camp, pick up the signed trail to Mt. Islip. A half-mile of switchbacks through piney woods brings you up to a sharp ridgeline. From atop the ridge, you'll enjoy great views of Crystal Lake, the San Gabriel Wilderness, and the canyons cut by Bear Creek and the San Gabriel River. The trail turns east and follows the ridge for another half-mile to the 8,250-foot peak. Summit views include the ski areas of Krakta Ridge and Mt. Waterman to the west and Mt. Baden-Powell to the east.

MT. BADEN-POWELL

Mt. Baden-Powell Trail
From Vincent Gap to summit is 8 miles round trip with 2,800-foot elevation gain; Season: May-October

This trail and peak honor Lord Baden-Powell, a British Army officer who founded the Boy Scout movement in 1907. The well-engineered trail, grooved into the side of the mountain by the Civilian Conservation Corps in the mid-1930s, switchbacks up the northeast ridge to the peak.

The peak was once known as North Baldy, before Southern California Boy Scouts lobbied the Forest Service for a name change. Mt. Baden-Powell is the terminus of the scouts' 53-mile Silver Moccasin Trail, a rugged week-long backpack through the San Gabriels. Scouts who complete the long trail earn the Silver Moccasin Award.

The trail follows a moderate, steady grade to the top of the mountain, where there's a monument honoring Lord Baden-Powell. On the summit, you'll meet those ancient survivors, the limber pines, and be treated to superb views across the Mojave Desert and down into the Iron Fork of the San Gabriel River.

Limber Pines cling to the summit of Mt. Baden-Powell.

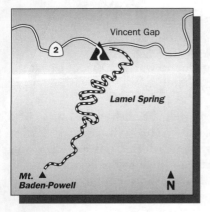

Directions to trailhead: Take the Angeles Crest Highway (2) for 53 miles from La Canada to the Vincent Gap Parking Area. The signed trailhead is at the northwest edge of the parking area.

If you're coming from the east, take Interstate 15 to the Wrightwood exit, three miles south of Cajon Pass. Proceed 8 miles west on Highway 138 to its intersection with Highway 2. Turn left on Highway 2 and follow it for 14 miles to the trailhead.

The hike: The trail immediately begins ascending from Vincent Gulch Divide, a gap which separates the upper tributaries of the San Gabriel River to the south from Big Rock Creek to the northwest. You begin switchbacking southwest through Jeffrey pine and fir. The trail numbers more than three dozen of these switchbacks, but so many beautiful attractions compete for the hiker's attention that it's hard to get an accurate count.

In 1.5 miles, a side trail (unmarked) leads a hundred yards to Lamel Spring, an inviting resting place and the only dependable water en route.

With increased elevation, the switchbacks grow shorter and steeper and the vegetation changes from fir to lodgepole pine. Soon, even the altitude-loving lodgepoles give way to the heartiest of pines, the limber pine. A half-mile from the summit, around 9,000 feet in elevation, the first of these squat, thick-trunked limber pines come into view. Shortly, you'll intersect a side trail to the limber pine forest.

To Limber Pine Forest: A tiny sign points right (southwest) to the limber pine stand, 0.125 mile. These wind-loving, subalpine dwellers are one of the few living things that can cope with the rarefied atmosphere. *Pinus flexilis,* botanists call the species, for its long, droopy, flexible branches. They bow and scrape like hyperextended dancers and appear to gather all their nourishment from the wind.

Back on the main trail, a few more switchbacks bring you atop the ridge where Mt. Baldy can be glimpsed. You walk along the barren crest and intersect the Pacific Crest Trail. PCT swoops off to Little Jimmy Spring.

You continue past the limber pines to the summit. A concrete monument pays homage to Lord Baden-Powell. Enjoy the superb view out across the Mojave to the southern Sierra and east to Baldy, San Gorgonio and San Jacinto.

CRYSTAL LAKE

Windy Gap, Big Cienega, Islip Ridge Trails
From Crystal Lake to Mt. Islip is 9 miles round trip with 2,200-foot gain;
Season: April-November. (See map page 122)

Just below the crest of the Angeles Crest is a well-watered, cedar and pine-forested basin. This basin has no outlet and thus gathers rainwater and snowmelt from the San Gabriel Mountains above. A happy result of this geographical happenstance is Crystal Lake, the only natural lake in the San Gabriel Mountains.

During the 19th century, the lake was known as Sycamore Lake; that is, until Pasadena Judge Benjamin Eaton visited in 1887 and proclaimed: "The water is clear as a crystal and the party found it good to drink." Crystal Lake is has remained ever since.

Today, the Forest Service, along with dedicated volunteers, have made Crystal Lake Recreation Area an attractive destination, complete with nature trails, a pleasant campground and a visitors information center.

Trail connoisseurs will appreciate the look—and feel—of handbuilt Islip Ridge Trail. The moderate grade, well-engineered switchbacks, the rock work and the way the path gently crosses the land are due to the skill and hard work of many dedicated volunteers, particularly the San Gabriel Mountains Trail Builders.

This trail to Mt. Islip climbs the forested shoulder of the mountain, and intersects a summit trail which leads to the peak.

Directions to trailhead: From the Foothill Freeway (210) in Azusa, take the Highway 39/Azusa Avenue exit. Drive north on Highway 39 for 24 miles to the turnoff for Crystal Lake Recreation Area. After a mile you'll reach the Forest Service entry station.

Continue another mile to Crystal Lake Visitor Center, which is open on the weekends, then another 0.5 mile to a large dirt parking lot on your right and signed Windy Gap Trail on your left.

The hike: Ascend moderately on Windy Gap Trail, which passes near a campground and heads into the cool of the forest. The trail crosses a forest service road leading to Deer Flat Campground, ascends some more and reaches the dirt South Mt. Hawkins Truck Road. Cross the road and look left for the beginning of Big Cienega Trail.

Enjoy the pleasant trail as it ascends moderately more or less west through pine, spruce and cedar forest. A bit more than a mile from the top, Islip Ridge Trail turns sharply north into a more sparse alpine forest.

The trail intersects the path coming from Windy Gap. Turn left and walk a short, but steep distance to the top of 8,250-foot Mt. Islip.

San Gabriel River's East Fork

East Fork Trail
From East Fork Station to the "Bridge to Nowhere," is 9 miles round trip
with 1,000-foot elevation gain; to Iron Fork is 12 miles round trip
with 1,400-foot gain

Sometimes you'll see a weekend gold miner find a flash in the pan, but the real treasure of this section of the San Gabriel River lies in its beauty, its alders and tumbling waters. It's wet going; you'll be doing a lot of wading as well as walking, but you'll be well rewarded for all your boulder-hopping and stream crossing.

This day hike takes you through the monumental middle section of the East Fork of the San Gabriel River, into the Sheep Mountain Wilderness. The dizzy chasm of the Narrows is awesome, the steepest river gorge in Southern California.

Road builders of the 1930s envisioned a highway through the East Fork to connect the San Gabriel Valley with Wrightwood and the desert beyond. The great flood of 1938 interrupted these plans, leaving a handsome highway bridge stranded far up-river, the so-called "Bridge to Nowhere." You'll pass the cracked asphalt remains of the old East Fork Road and gain access to the well named Narrows. Expect to get wet at numerous river crossings. High water during winter or spring means these crossings will likely be unsafe.

In the early years of this century, at the junction of Iron Fork with the main river, miner George Trogden had a home and angler's headquarters, where miners and intrepid fishermen gathered to swap tales. Up-river from Iron Fork is Fish Fork, whose waters cascade from the shoulders of Mt. Baldy. It, too, has been a popular fishing spot for generations of anglers.

Directions to trailhead: From Interstate 10 (San Bernardino Freeway)

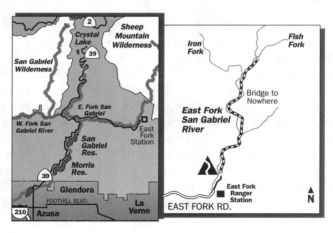

"The Bridge to Nowhere," East Fork of San Gabriel River.

exit on Azusa Avenue (Highway 39) and head north. You'll need to pick up a parking permit on weekends en route from the ranger station on 39. Ten miles up Highway 39, turn right (east) on East Fork Road and continue eight more miles to the East Fork Ranger Station. You'll need a second permit—a wilderness permit—which you can fill out at the self-service dispenser at the base of the ranger station road.

The hike: Follow the service road above the east side of the river 0.5 mile to Heaton Flat Campground. The trail descends to the canyon floor and begins crossing and re-crossing the river (more than a dozen times). A bit more than two miles from the trailhead is Swan Rock, a mighty wall west of the river with the faint outline of a gargantuan swan.

As the canyon floor widens and twists northward, you'll climb up the right side of the canyon and continue up-river on the remains of East Fork Road, high above the rushing water. After ascending north a ways, you'll reach the "Bridge to Nowhere." No road meets this bridge at either end; the highway washed away in the flood of '38.

Cross the bridge and join a slim trail that soon drops you into The Narrows. A quarter-mile from the bridge is the site of former Narrows Trail Camp, now a fine place to picnic and view the handsome gorge. A rough trail—made by use not design—leads a bit more than a mile through The Narrows.

You, like the river, squeeze your way between towering granite walls. Iron Fork joins the river from the left, six miles from the trailhead.

Yet another mile up-river is Fish Fork, where another abandoned camp offers good picnicking. You can slosh up Fish Fork for another mile before a falls and the sheer canyon walls halt your progress.

Icehouse Canyon

Icehouse Canyon Trail

From Icehouse Canyon to Icehouse Saddle is 8 miles round trip with 2,600-foot elevation gain. Season: May-October

Icehouse Canyon Trail, leading from Icehouse Canyon to several 8,000-foot peaks, is an ideal introduction to the high country delights of the Cucamonga Wilderness. The precipitous subalpine slopes of the wilderness, thickly forested with sugar pine, ponderosa pine and incense cedar, offer fresh mountain air and a network of good footpaths. The 4,400-acre wilderness, set aside by Congress in 1984, includes the Three T's—Timber Mountain, Telegraph Peak and Thunder Mountain—as well as 8,859-foot Cucamonga Peak, easternmost sentinel of the San Gabriel Mountains.

Located at the far eastern end of the San Gabriel Mountains, the Cucamonga Wilderness sprawls across the boundaries of both the San Bernardino and Angeles National Forests, and a wilderness permit can be obtained from either agency.

Icehouse Canyon is the hiker's only easy entry into the Cucamonga high country. The saddle and nearby peaks offer fine views to the hiker. Sierra Club peak-baggers like this trail because several peaks are within "bagging distance" of Icehouse Saddle, an important trail junction.

Icehouse Canyon was for many years known as Cedar Canyon because, as the story goes, the great cedar beams for Mission San Gabriel were logged here. The name Icehouse originated in the 1860s when ice was cut in the lower canyon and shipped to San Gabriel Valley residents.

The Chapman Trail, constructed in 1980, was named for the family that built the Icehouse Canyon resort and numerous cabins in the 1920s. The well-constructed trailheads up Cedar Canyon to Cedar Glen. The cedars were severely scorched by the 1980 Thunder Mountain fire, but the canyon flora is slowly recovering. The trail climbs out of Cedar Canyon, then contours on a steady grade back over to Icehouse Canyon.

Another Chapman—no relation to the family whose name is found on the trail—figured in the history of Icehouse Canyon. Yankee Joseph Chapman arrived in Monterey in 1818, was accused of insurgency by the Spanish governor of California, and soon shipped to Los Angeles as a prisoner. Los Angeles, then a remote outpost, lacked lumber and when authorities learned that the New Englander was a master woodsman, they put him in charge of timber operations in the San Gabriel Mountains. The Spaniards and their Indian helpers thought that Chapman's ability to chop a tree down—and make it fall whichever way he wanted—was nothing less than magical. Some of the more superstitious called him "Diablo Chapman."

"Old Baldy"

The cedar beams, hewed square up in the mountains, were dragged out of the canyon by oxen. Chapman's logging operations here and in other parts of Southern California earned him amnesty from the governor. Some historians believe Chapman to be the third Anglo resident of California, and the first to reside in Los Angeles.

Directions to trailhead: From the San Bernardino Freeway (10) in Upland, exit on Mountain Avenue. Head north on Mountain, which joins Mt. Baldy Road in San Antonio Canyon and winds its way to Mt. Baldy Village. Go 1.5 miles past the village to Icehouse Canyon Resort. Park in the dirt lot. The trail starts just to the right of the resort.

The hike: The trail leads east along the floor of the canyon. The path stays close to the oak- and spruce-shaded creek and passes some cabins. Brick chimneys and stone foundations are all that remain of other cabins, swept away during the great flood of 1938. After 1.5 miles, the trail forks. You may take the "high route," the Chapman Trail, one mile to Cedar Flats and then three miles up to Icehouse Saddle, or continue straight ahead on the shorter and steeper Icehouse Canyon Trail directly up the canyon.

If you decided to continue on the Icehouse Canyon Trail, you'll pass a few more cabins. The trail climbs up the north slope of the canyon, before dropping down again and crossing the creek. The trail switchbacks steeply through pine and spruce. The tall trees frame a nice picture of Old Baldy. Chapman Trail and Icehouse Canyon Trail intersect and a single trail ascends a steep 0.75 mile to the top of Icehouse Saddle.

You can enjoy the view and return the same way, or pick one of the fine trails that lead from Icehouse Saddle and add to your day hike. You can continue eastward and drop down the Middle Fork Trail to Lytle Creek. A right (southeast) turn puts you on a trail that climbs two miles to Cucamonga Peak. A sharp right (southwest) leads 2.5 miles to Kelly's Camp and Ontario Peak. And a left on the Three T's Trail takes you past Timber Mountain, Telegraph Peak and Thunder Mountain, then drops to Baldy Notch.

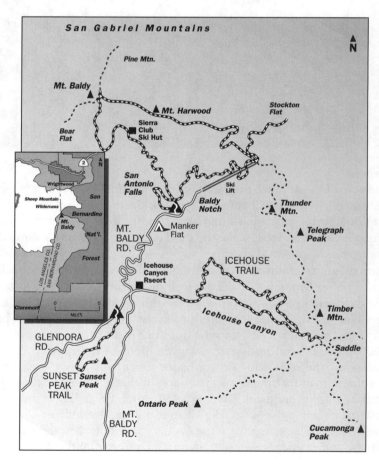

SAN ANTONIO CANYON

Ski Hut Trail

To San Antonio Falls is 2.5 miles round trip with 200-foot elevation gain;
to San Antonio Canyon Overlook is 6.5 miles round trip with 2,600-foot
gain; to Mt. Baldy summit is 8.5 miles round trip with 3,800-foot gain;
Season: May-October

This day hike utilizes an attractive, but not-so-well-known trail that leads up San Antonio Canyon to the top of Baldy. Locals call it the Ski Hut Trail because the Sierra Club maintains a hut halfway up the path.

Hikers of all ages and abilities will enjoy the 0.5-mile walk to San Antonio Falls. After a little rain, the three-tiered, 60-foot waterfall is an impressive sight.

Beyond the falls, the hiking is strenuous. Hikers who want more than the "leg stretcher" walk to the falls but aren't quite up for an assault on the peak can choose two intermediate destinations: the Sierra Club ski hut, where there's a cool spring, or a high ridge overlooking San Antonio Canyon.

Hikers in top form, with good trail sense (the last mile of trail is rough and tentative), will relish the challenge of the summit climb. A clear-day view from the top offers a panorama of desert and ocean, the sprawling Southland and the southern High Sierra.

Directions to trailhead: From the San Bernardino Freeway in Claremont, exit on Mountain Avenue and head north, joining Mt. Baldy Road in San Antonio Canyon and winding about 11 miles to Manker Campground. About 0.3 mile past the campground entrance, look to the left for an unsigned paved road with a vehicle barrier across it. Park in the dirt lot just below the beginning of the road.

The hike: Walk up the fire road, which is closed to all motor vehicles except those belonging to ski-lift maintenance workers. After a modest ascent, you will hear the sound of falling water and soon behold San Antonio Falls. If you decide to hike down to the base of the falls, watch for loose rock and use caution on the rough trail.

Resume walking along the road (unpaved beyond the falls). After about ten minutes of walking at a moderate pace, look sharply left for an unsigned trail.

The no-nonsense trail ascends very steeply along the side of San Antonio Canyon. Enjoy great over-the-shoulder views of the canyon bottom and of Mt. Baldy Village. Trail connoisseurs will appreciate this path which, despite its steepness, has a hand-hewn, unobtrusive look and follows the natural contours of the land. Jeffrey pine, ponderosa pine and fir shade the path.

From the ski lift road it's 1.75 miles by trail to Sierra Club ski hut. Near the hut, constructed in 1935, is a cool and refreshing spring.

Just past the ski hut the trail crosses a tiny creek, then snakes through a boulder field. Beyond the boulders the trail ascends via a 0.5-mile series of

For more than a century, San Antonio Canyon has lured admiring hikers.

steep switchbacks to a ridgetop overlooking the headwaters of San Antonio Canyon. There's a great view from the tree-shaded ridgetop and, if you aren't up for a summit climb, this is a good picnic spot or turnaround point.

Peak-baggers will continue up the extremely rugged trail for another mile to the summit. The trail is rough and tentative in places, but rocks piled in cairns help you stay on course. You'll get a good view of Devil's Backbone, the sharp ridge connecting Mt. Harwood to Mt. Baldy.

Boulders are scattered atop Baldy's crown. Some rock windbreaks offer shelter. Enjoy the view of an assortment of San Gabriel and San Bernardino mountain range peaks, the Mojave and the metropolis.

Depending on energy or inclination, you can either return the same way or take Devil's Backbone Trail to Mt. Baldy Notch. From the Notch, follow the fire road down Manker Canyon back to the trailhead or ride down the ski lift.

MT. BALDY

Devil's Backbone Trail
From Baldy Notch to Mt. Baldy summit is 7 miles round trip with 2,200-foot gain; Season: May-October

Three saintly mountains—San Gorgonio, San Jacinto and San Antonio—tower over the City of the Angels. Lowest of the three, but by far the best-known is Mt. San Antonio, more commonly known as Mt. Baldy. The 10,064-foot peak, highest in the San Gabriel Mountains, is visible from much of the Southland. Its summit gleams white in winter and early spring, gray in summer and fall. Old Baldy is so big and bare that it seems to be snow-covered even when it's not.

Legend has it, the padres of Mission San Gabriel, circa 1790, named the massive stone bulwark after Saint Anthony of Padua, Italy. The 13th-century Franciscan friar was evidently a favorite of California missionaries; a number of geographical features, both in Monterey County and around Southern California, honor San Antonio. In the 1870s, San Antonio Canyon and the nearby high country swarmed with gold-seekers, who dubbed the massive peak a more earthly "Old Baldy."

Surely one of the most unique resorts in the San Gabriels was the Baldy Summit Inn, perched just below the summit of the great mountain. Gale-force winds battered the above-timberline camp, which consisted of two stone buildings and a cluster of tents. William Dewey, the owner/guide, and Mrs. Dewey, the chef, welcomed guests to their resort during the summers of 1910 through 1912. Advertised rates were $1 a meal, $1 a bed. The camp burned in 1913 and never reopened.

A moderate (compared to other routes up Baldy), but certainly not easy, ascent follows the Devil's Backbone Trail from Baldy Notch to the summit. This is a very popular trail and the one most hikers associate with Mt. Baldy. A clear-day view from the top offers a panorama of desert and ocean, the sprawling Southland and the southern High Sierras.

Baldy is a bit austere from afar, but up-close, the white granite shoulders of the mountain are softened by a forest of pine and fir. Dress warmly for this trip and keep an eye out for rapidly changing weather conditions.

Directions to trailhead: From the San Bernardino Freeway (10), exit on Mountain Avenue. Head north on Mountain, which joins Mt. Baldy Road in San Antonio Canyon and winds 12 miles to road's end just beyond Manker Campground. (You can also exit the freeway on Monte Vista Avenue and drive north to intersect Mt. Baldy Road.) Park in the ski lift parking area.

Purchase a ticket and ride the ski lift up to Baldy Notch. The lift is operated weekends and holidays all year.

An alternative is to walk up a fire road to Baldy Notch. This option adds three miles each way and a 1,300-foot gain to the walk. The fire road switchbacks up the west side of the steep San Antonio Canyon, offers a good view of San Antonio Falls, then climbs northward to the top.

The hike: From Baldy Notch, a wide gravel path leads to a commanding view of the desert. You then join a chair lift access/fire road, and ascend a broad slope forested in Jeffrey pine and incense cedar. The road ends in about 1.25 miles at the top of a ski lift.

From the top of the ski lift, a trail leads out onto a sharp ridge known as the Devil's Backbone. To the north, you can look down into the deep gorge of Lytle Creek, and to the south into San Antonio Canyon. You'll then pass around the south side of Mt. Harwood, "Little Baldy," and up through scattered stands of lodgepole pine.

The trail reaches a tempestuous saddle. (Hold onto your hat!) From the saddle, a steep rock-strewn pathway zigzags past a few wind-bowed limber pine to the summit.

Boulders are scattered atop Baldy's crown. A couple of rock windbreaks offer some shelter. Enjoy the view of San Gabriel and San Bernardino mountain peaks, the Mojave and the metropolis, and return the same way.

6. Orange County

Orange County shares its coastline and coastal plain with neighboring Los Angeles County, but has a distinct geographical identity. This geography, which in the decades since World War II has been almost unbelievably altered, nevertheless still holds some intrigue for the lover of wild places.

The orchards that gave Orange County its name are nearly gone, but the mountains occupying half the County still afford invigorating vistas. This guide seeks out what remains of the pastoral in the County's hills and canyons.

San Mateo Point is the northernmost boundary of San Diego County, the southern boundary of Orange County. When the original counties of Los Angeles and San Diego were set up in 1850, the line that separated them began on the coast at San Mateo Point. When Orange County was formed from southern Los Angeles County in 1889, San Mateo Point was established as the southern point of the new county. The northern boundary is Seal Beach. Riverside County and the Santa Ana Mountains form the eastern boundary.

During the last decade of the 19th century and the first few decades of the 20th, the County was known for its fruited plain watered by the Santa

O.C.'s diverse park system includes Barbara's Lake in James Dilley Preserve.

Ana River (although for most of its length it is now a cement-lined flood control channel, it was once a substantial river). Citrus and other fruits, flowers and vegetables were grown on the fertile coastal plain. Valencia orange groves, protected from the wind by rows of eucalyptus, stretched across the plain to the foothills.

Today the coastal plain has been almost completely covered by residential and commercial development. Once huge farms and ranches such as Laguna Niguel, Moulton, Mission Viejo and Irvine are now suburbs. Although 782-square mile Orange is not one of California's larger counties, it is the state's second most populous, right behind Los Angeles County.

In a county with more than two million residents and with most of its flatland developed, hikers must head for the hills to find untouched or less-touched places. In the backcountry, where level land and water are scant, there has been little settlement.

Protecting the last of Orange County's ecological heritage are Crystal Cove State Park and many county parks. Oak woodland, chaparral slopes and grassy meadows are among the natural communities found in these parks.

Hiking this land is a good way to shed some stereotypes about Southern California in general, and Orange County in particular. One stereotype—that Orange County is nothing more than a monotonous urban-suburban sprawl—vanishes when you witness firsthand the ecological diversity of the backcountry. Another stereotype—that Orange County's history is all Anglo—disappears when you walk into the land's Spanish, Indian, German, Polish and Japanese heritage. The names on the land—from Flores to Modjeska to Anaheim—speak of this rich tapestry of cultures.

Carbon Canyon

Carbon Canyon Nature Trail
2 miles round trip

Carbon Canyon Regional Park offers some much-needed "breathing room" for fast-growing northeastern Orange County. The park has both a natural area with trails that connect to nearby Chino Hills State Park, and a more developed part with wide lawns, tennis courts, ball fields, picnic grounds and a lake.

The park spreads up-canyon behind Carbon Canyon dam. As Orange County grew, so did the need for flood control, and in 1959, a dam was built at the mouth of the canyon. If, as a result of winter storms, the Santa Ana River rises too high, the dam's floodgates will be closed, thus sparing communities downstream of the dam, but flooding the park.

A century ago, the arrival of the Santa Fe Railroad precipitated a minor land boom. Farmers and ranchers rushed to the area. Cattle and sheep were pastured in the canyon now called Carbon.

But it was another boom—an oil boom—that put Carbon Canyon on the map. E.L. Doheny, soon to become one of L.A.'s leading boosters, discovered oil in the area in 1896. His company and several others drilled the foothills of Orange County. The name Carbon was applied to the canyon because of the many dried-up oil seeps in evidence.

A century ago, it was oil—not scenery—that was the attraction in Carbon Canyon.

Santa Fe Railroad tracks were extended to the mouth of Carbon Canyon in order to haul out the oil. At the end of the tracks was the oil town of Olinda, boyhood home of the great baseball pitcher Walter Johnson. "Big Train," as the hurler was known, pitched for the Washington Senators, and led the American League in strikeouts each year from 1912 to 1919. Olinda boomed until the 1940s when the oil fields began to play out.

The undeveloped part of Carbon Canyon Regional Park is a narrow corridor along Carbon Canyon Creek. A one-mile nature trail leads creek-side through an interesting mixture of native and foreign flora. At the park entrance station, ask for an interpretive pamphlet, which is keyed to numbered posts along the nature trail, and details points and plants of interest. Rewarding the hiker at trail's end is a small, shady redwood grove.

Directions to trailhead: From the Orange Freeway (57) in Brea, exit on Lambert Road. Drive 4 miles east on Lambert (which changes to Carbon Canyon Road east of Valencia Avenue) to the park entrance. There's a vehicle entry fee.

The hike: From the parking area, walk back to the entrance station, and you'll spot the signed trail in a stand of pine, just east of the park entrance. On closer inspection, you'll discover that the pines are Monterey pines, native to California but not to this area. This stand is a holdover from a Christmas tree farm that was operated before the park opened in 1975.

From the pines, the nature trail descends to the Carbon Canyon creekbed. After crossing the creek, the trail forks. (The path to the left leads toward Telegraph Canyon and to a network of hiking trails that crisscross Chino Hills State Park. The 8-mile length of Telegraph Canyon, home of native walnut groves, is well worth exploring.) Carbon Canyon Nature trailheads right with the creekbed. Creek-side vegetation is dominated by mustard, castor bean and hemlock. You'll also find two exotic imports—the California pepper tree, actually a native of Peru, and some giant reeds, bamboo-like plants that harm the native plant community because they take a great deal of the scarce water supply.

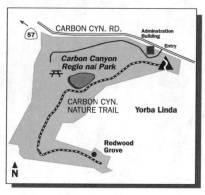

At the trail's mid-point, there's a distinct, but unmarked, side trail that angles across the creekbed to the developed part of the park. If for some reason you want to call it a day, here's your exit point.

As you near trail's end you'll get brush-framed glimpses of Carbon Canyon Dam. The trail ascends out of the creekbed to the park's redwood grove. The redwoods, planted in 1975, have a lot of growing to do before they rival their majestic cousins to the north.

Anaheim Hills

Anaheim Hills Trail
From Santiago Oaks Regional Park to Robbers Roost is 3.5 miles round trip
with 700-foot elevation gain

"Who determines the names of natural features? Fundamentally, names
are a part of language, and the eventual power rests with the people."
—GEORGE STEWART, *Names on the Land*

Housing developments often take the name of the natural features
around them, but in one O.C. suburb the naming process is reversed.

Geologists and mapmakers have long referred to the long, low ridge
extending west from the Santa Ana Mountains and rising above Santa Ana
Canyon as the Peralta Hills, but almost no one uses that name anymore.
Today the hills are known as the Anaheim Hills.

The hills honor, or did honor, Juan Pablo Peralta and his family, original
owners of the huge Rancho Santiago de Santa Ana. Peralta is an excellent
name, historic and euphonious. It recalls the Latin expression per alta,
"through the high things." Sounds like a university motto, doesn't it?

Anaheim, which German settlers in 1858 named after the river Santa Ana
plus the suffix (home), already names a city, a boulevard, a bay, a stadium and
much more. Perhaps it's time for concerned day hikers and Orange Countians
to rally to save the Peralta Hills. (Alas, it is not merely the name of the hills, but
the hills themselves that are fast-disappearing beneath the suburban sprawl.)

Other names from the past still remain. Santiago Oaks Regional Park,
Santiago Creek and Santiago Canyon are derived from the old Rancho
Santiago de Santa Ana. One intriguing name for a rocky knob overlooking
the regional park is Robber's Roost. From this lookout, such infamous 19th
century outlaws as Joaquin Murietta and Three-Finger Jack kept watch over
rural Orange County. The outlaws would ride down from the hills to rob
the Butterfield Stagecoach or ride into the hills to escape the sheriff's posse.

Santiago Oaks Regional Park preserves 125 acres of pastoral Orange
County, including an oak woodland that attracts many species of birds. A
checklist of commonly sighted birds is available at park headquarters.

You can sample the park's ecosystem with Windes Nature Trail. The
0.75-mile trail and its Pacifica Loop offer a glimpse of the county's coastline. A nature center, located near the trailhead, is well-worth a visit.

A network of fire roads and equestrian trail crisscross the park and extend
into the Anaheim Hills. While the hills seem destined for suburban development, for now, at least, you can enjoy a ramble up to Robber's Roost and
steal a last look at fast-vanishing rural Orange County.

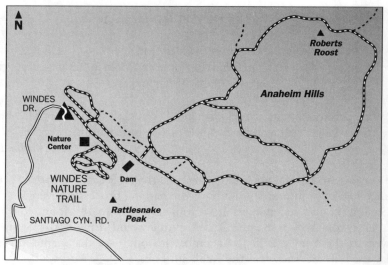

Directions to trailhead: From the Newport Freeway (55) in Orange, exit on Katella. Turn east on Katella, which undergoes a name change in a half-mile to Villa Park Road, then a second name change to Santiago Canyon Road. A bit more than two miles from the freeway, turn left on Windes Drive and drive a mile to Santiago Oaks Regional Park.

The hike: From the end of the parking area, you'll spot Windes Nature Trail on your right, then swing left and cross Santiago Creek on some man-made stepping-stones. You'll pass a number of trails leading left into the woods, but for now stay with the main trail along the creek. Along with the native oaks, you might spot some more uncommon flora, including eucalyptus and pepper trees, and even a small grove of Valencia oranges.

Soon you'll see an old dam. With the aid of Chinese laborers, the Serrano and Carpenter Water Company built a clay dam here in 1879. This dam was destroyed by floods, and replaced in 1892 with a more substantial structure of river rock and cement. The dam looks particularly tiny when compared to the huge Villa Park Flood Control dam a short distance upstream.

Bear left, uphill, and ascend steeply up a dirt road to the park's north boundary gate. Beyond the gate you'll ascend to an unsigned junction and bear left, then ascend a prickly pear cactus-dotted slope to a junction signed with an equestrian symbol and turn right. After passing under some transmission lines, the equestrian trail reaches Robber's Roost.

From the 1,152-foot peak, you can look over the Peralta Hills and trace the path of Santiago Creek. Not so long ago, the view would have taken in hundreds of cattle, orange groves, and barley fields. Nowadays the panorama is considerably less pastoral.

WEIR CANYON WILDERNESS PARK

Weir Canyon Loop Trail
From Hidden Canyon—a 4-mile loop with 300-foot elevation gain.

From the trail high on the west wall of Weir Canyon, the hiker gets a view of Orange County that's both stereotypical and surprising. The view westward is that of Orange County to the max: houses perched everywhere on the slopes of the Anaheim Hills, several freeways, the city of Anaheim, plus many more cities sprawling toward the coast. In contrast to this 21st century vista, the view east is minimalist Orange County; that is to say, mostly parkland, a pastoral landscape of hills and canyons that in the right light looks like a plein-air painting made during the late 19th century.

Weir Canyon Wilderness Park (the name wilderness might be stretching the definition a bit, but it's certainly a wilderness compared to the developed areas of the Anaheim Hills) is one of those great so-near-yet-so-far-away places in Orange County to take a hike. It's a pleasure to report it's the park—not nearby subdivisions—that's been extending its boundaries farther into the hills toward the toll road (Highway 241).

Geographers say the Anaheim Hills comprise a long, low ridge extending west from the Santa Ana Mountains and rising above Santa Ana Canyon and the Santa Ana River. Weir Canyon Trail offers a gentle introduction to the considerable pleasures of these hills.

Directions to trailhead: From the Riverside Freeway (91) in Anaheim Hills, exit on Weir Canyon Road. Head south 0.7 mile to Serrano Avenue. Turn right (west) and proceed 2 miles to Hidden Canyon Road. Turn left

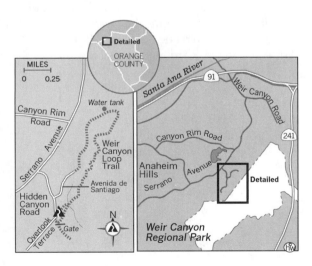

Wildflowers bloom in Weir Canyon.

(south and follow it a half-mile to its end at Overlook Terrace and the signed trailhead. Park along Hidden Canyon Road.

The hike: From the park sign, the trail leads northeast. Ignore a path descending toward the canyon bottom and continue on the main path as it rises and then levels. Enjoy eastward views into Weir Canyon and westward ones of some intriguing sandstone outcroppings.

The path dips into and climbs out of some minor side canyons, skirts some residences at about the 2.5 mile mark, then U-turns and begins heading south. After leading you a mile along the western rim of Weir Canyon, the path drops to the end of Avenida de Santiago. Walk down the steep residential street to Hidden Canyon Road, turn left, and return to the trailhead.

Peters Canyon

Lake View, Lower Canyon, East Ridge Trails
2 to 6 mile loops

In 1899, "green space," in these parts had an entirely different meaning than it does today. Here in a remote canyon, local sportsmen introduced golf to Orange County.

Santa Ana and Orange duffers leased land from the Irvine Company and laid out a nine-hole course. The "greens" were oil-soaked earthen patches and the fairways were little more than brush-cleared canyon bottom. It must have been hard to make par in Golf Canyon, as it became known.

Today Golf Canyon is the site of Peters Canyon Park, located on the edge of more suburbs-in-the-making on the eastern frontier of the communities of Orange and Tustin. The Irvine Company donated the park land in 1992.

Park highlight is a reservoir, gathering place for many migratory and resident waterfowl. Bring binoculars and watch for herons and egrets along the willow-lined shores. Also watch the skies for the red-tailed and Cooper's hawks circling above the eucalyptus groves located in lower Peters Canyon.

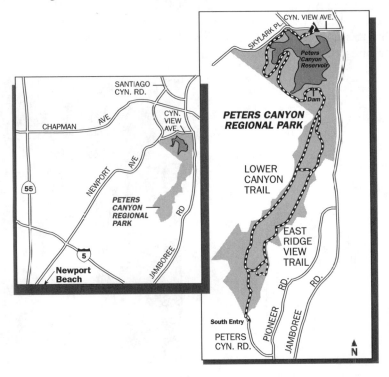

A network of old Irvine Ranch roads and footpaths explore the canyon and its east wall. Most popular is Lake View Trail, a two-mile path that loops around the reservoir. It's a six-mile round trip walk to the eucalyptus groves at the park's south end.

Directions to trailhead: From Highway 55 in Orange, exit on Chapman Avenue and head east 4.5 miles to Jamboree Road. Turn right and proceed a half mile to Canyon View Avenue, then turn right again. The park is a short distance up the road on your left.

The hike: Join signed Lake View Trail as it meanders along the northern edge of Upper Peters Canyon Reservoir, built in 1931 by the Irvine Company to hold water for its agricultural operations. A lower reservoir was built in 1940, but as you'll see when you visit the lower canyon, it's dry these days, and serves as an emergency flood control basin.

The trail joins a dirt road on the west side of the lake, passes a couple of side trails leading down to the lake, then skirts the dam. Loop back along the east side of the reservoir to the parking area or continue along the canyon bottom on Lower Canyon Trail. As you near the south end of the park, you'll pass a World War II "battlefield"; this part of Peters Canyon was used by the U.S. Army during the war to train troops and stage mock battles.

Visit the eucalyptus groves at the park's south end then, if you wish, join East Ridge View Trail for the return back up the canyon. The views promised by this trail's name are of the length of Peters Canyon as well as semi-suburban, semi-pastoral Orange County.

Madame Modjeska

MODJESKA CANYON

Harding Trail
From Tucker Wildlife Sanctuary to Goat Shed Overlook is 3 miles round trip
with 600-foot elevation gain; to Laurel Spring is 10 miles round trip
with 2,300-foot gain

The story of Modjeska Peak and Modjeska Canyon in Orange County began in Warsaw, Poland in the 1870s. Count Karol Bozenta Chlapowski edited a fiercely nationalistic patriotic journal that protested the cultural and political imperialism of Czarist Russia and Germany. He and his wife, acclaimed actress Helena Modrzejewski, and other Polish writers and artists, yearned for the freedom of America and the climate of Southern California.

Helena mastered English, shortened her name to Modjeska, and under the Count's management, began her tremendously popular stage career. Madame Modjeska and the Count bought a ranch in Santiago Canyon and hired professionals to run it. Madame called her ranch Arden after the enchanted forest in Shakespeare's *As You Like It*. Infamous New York architect Stanford White was commissioned to design a dream home, which looked out over a little lake, across which glided swans.

For two decades the Chlapowski/Modjeska household was a center of artistic and literary life in Southern California. Today, a state historical marker on Modjeska Canyon Road commemorates their home.

The natural history of Modjeska Canyon is as intriguing as its human history. In 1939, Dorothy May Tucker, a canyon resident, willed her land to the Audubon Society and the Tucker Bird Sanctuary was created. California State University Fullerton took over its operation in 1969.

The sanctuary is best known for its hummingbirds, which may be viewed from an observation porch. Because the sanctuary includes a mixture of coastal scrub, chaparral and oak woodland environments, it attracts a diversity of bird life. Nearly two hundred species have been spotted in the sanctuary.

Two short nature trails wind through the preserve. One trail interprets chaparral flora, and the other leads along the banks of Santiago Creek.

Tucker Wildlife Sanctuary is the trailhead for Harding Trail, a dirt road that ascends the western slopes of the Santa Ana Mountains. The trail, formerly known as Harding Truck Trail, is used by Cleveland National Forest fire crews and their trucks, but is closed to all other vehicles.

Old Saddleback, comprised of 5,687-foot Santiago Peak and 5,496-foot Modjeska Peak, forms the eastern boundary and highest portion of Orange County. You can reach the peaks via Harding Trail, but this would mean a 20-mile hike. A more reasonable destination, halfway up the mountain, is Laurel Spring, a tranquil rest stop tucked under the boughs of giant bay lau-

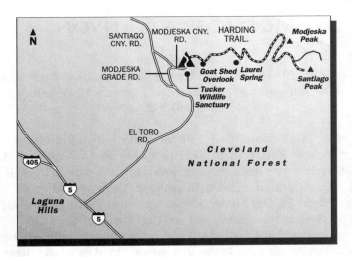

rel. En route to the spring, you'll get great views of Madame Modjeska's peak and canyon, as well as much of rural Orange County.

Directions to trailhead: From the San Diego Freeway (5) in El Toro, exit on El Toro Road (S-18). Drive inland on the road, which after about 7 miles bends north and continues as Santiago Canyon Road. Eight and a half miles from the freeway, veer right onto Modjeska Grade Road, travel a bit more than a mile, then turn right and follow Modjeska Canyon Road a mile to its end at Tucker Wildlife Sanctuary. Park in the gravel lot by a tiny observatory. The trail, signed forest road 5S08, begins at a locked gate on the north side of the road.

The hike: Harding Trail immediately begins a no-nonsense ascent above Modjeska Canyon which, in all but its lower reaches, is officially known as Harding Canyon. To the northwest is Flores Peak, named for outlaw Juan Flores.

As you ascend, notice the lumpy, pudding-like clumps of conglomerate rock revealed by the road cuts. After a mile, the trail descends a short distance (the only elevation loss on the way to Laurel Spring), rounds the head of a canyon, and ascends to the remains of a funny-looking wood structure that locals call the Goat Shed. Enjoy the view of Modjeska Canyon. If you're feeling a bit leg weary, this is a good turnaround point.

Chaparral-lined Harding Trail continues climbing east along a sharp ridgeline. To your left, far below, is deep and precipitous Harding Canyon, and to your right—Santiago Canyon. Four and a half miles from the trailhead, Harding Trail offers clear-day views of the southern end of the Los Angeles Basin, the San Joaquin Hills and the central Orange County coastal plain, the Pacific and Catalina Island. The view serves notice that you're nearing Laurel Spring. A narrow trail descends 50 yards from the right side of the road to the spring. The spring (unsafe drinking water), waters an oasis of toyon, ferns and wonderfully aromatic bay laurel.

WHITING RANCH WILDERNESS PARK

Borrego Canyon, Whiting, Vista Point Trails
From 4 to 6 miles round trip.

Oak-shaded canyons, grassy hills and handsome, rose-colored sandstone cliffs are some of the attractions of Orange County's Whiting Ranch Wilderness Park. The 1,500-acre park, crisscrossed by trails, is a hiker's delight.

First-time visitors are amazed to find a lush oak woodland and rugged hills in such close proximity to suburban developments.

Rancho Canada de los Aliso was the land grant given in 1842 to José Serrano who raised cattle until the great drought of 1864 bankrupted the rancho. Dwight Whiting bought the land in 1885, planting vineyards and olive trees, as well as subdividing it. In 1959 the property was sold to a residential developer and suburbia ensued.

Whiting Ranch Wilderness Park, which opened to the public in 1991, is an oasis of green in a fast-growing area of Orange County. While the park is indeed a wild land as its name suggests (a mountain lion killed a mountain biker and attacked another in the park in 2003), the trailhead is anything but. A shopping center is located across Portola Parkway. Near the trailhead is a sculpture entitled "California song," a windmill-topped tower that depicts native birds and wildlife.

Oak woodland, preserved the way it was at the time of Rancho Trabuco.

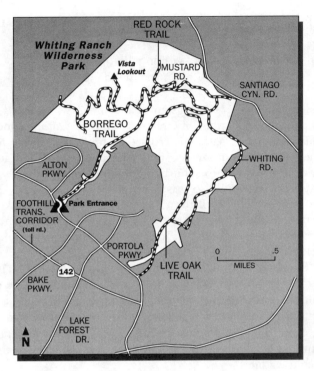

Directions to trailhead: From Interstate 5 in the El Toro area, exit on Lake Forest Drive and proceed east 4.8 miles to Portola Parkway. Turn left and drive 0.5-mile to the entrance and parking lot of Whiting Ranch Wilderness Park.

The hike: Borrego Trail leads a mile through oak-studded Borrego Canyon, a peninsula of parkland surrounded on three sides by residential and commercial development. The path up Borrego Canyon leads to junctions with other trails that lead to more remote sections of the park.

Three popular hikes (mileage calculated from Portola Parkway trailhead) include: Vista Point Trail (4 miles round trip) leads from Borrego Canyon to a high ridge for excellent views of south Orange County.

Red Rock Trail (4 miles round trip) explores what some rock connoisseurs consider to be one of Orange County's finest formations. It's a 1.5-mile hike to reach Red Rock Trail, a 0.5-mile pathway into the strangely eroded sandstone.

The Borrego Trail-Mustard Road-Whiting Road Loop is a grand 6-mile tour of the park. The route climbs through heavily wooded Borrego Canyon, tops out at a junction called Four Corners, then descends Serrano Canyon to Portola Parkway. A mile of walking along the road brings you back to the trailhead.

O'NEILL PARK

O'Neill Park Trail
From Trabuco Canyon to Ocean Vista Point is 3 miles round trip
with 600-foot elevation gain

The soldier marching with Captain Gaspar de Portolá's 1769 expedition who lost his firearm in this hilly region would no doubt be astonished at the number of Orange County placenames inspired by his mistake. Trabuco, which means "blunderbuss" in Spanish, now names a canyon, a creek, a plain, a trail, a road and even a ranger district of the Cleveland National Forest.

If the unknown soldier who lost his blunderbuss trekked this way again he would be amazed at the names on the land, and even more amazed at the land itself, so drastically has it changed. Maybe though, he would recognize Trabuco Canyon, at least that part of it saved from suburbanization by O'Neill Regional Park. Here the modern trekker can explore a small slice of the pastoral Southern California of two centuries ago.

This land of grassy meadows, rolling hills and oak woodland was originally part of Rancho Trabuco, two leagues granted to Santiago Arguello in 1841 by Mexican Governor Alvarado. The rancho had various lessees and owners until it was purchased by James Flood, a wealthy businessman and his partner Richard O'Neill, a packing house owner. O'Neill built up quite a ranching empire here and elsewhere in California. O'Neill's Orange County property passed to various heirs who, in turn, gave 278 acres of Trabuco Canyon to Orange County for a park in 1948. Today, after various gifts and purchases, the park encompasses 1,700 acres of woodland and brushy hills, taking in Trabuco Canyon and neighboring Live Oak Canyon.

A good way to learn about the ecology of Trabuco Canyon is to walk the park's 1.5-mile (round trip) nature trail. Trabuco Creek Trail, with stops keyed to a pamphlet available at the park's entry station, meanders through an oak/sycamore woodland and explores Plano Trabuco, or Trabuco Flat, a level alluvial surface deposited by runoff from the slopes of the Santa Ana Mountains.

Another way to explore a bit of rural Orange County is to hike the park's various fire roads and trails on a route I've dubbed O'Neill Park Trail. The trail ascends to Ocean Vista Point, which offers fine coast and canyon views.

Directions to trailhead: From the San Diego Freeway (5) in El Toro, exit on El Toro Road and drive 7.5 miles to Santiago Canyon Road (S-18). Turn right and proceed 3 miles to O'Neill Regional Park. There is a vehicle entry fee. Park in the day use lot near the entrance.

The hike: From the entry station, walk north on a service road that parallels Live Oak Canyon Road. Soon you'll head left on another paved road that ascends toward some water tanks. After a quarter-mile's travel, leave the pavement and turn right on a dirt road. Two turns bring you to a junction with a dirt road on your right (an optional return route from the top).

Continue your ascent along a ridge. Over your shoulder are two scenes typical of rural Orange County: Red-tailed hawks circling over classic Southland ranching country in one direction, and suburbs-in-the-making in the other.

Continue on a last steep ascent toward what appears to be a Star Trek movie set, but is actually Ocean Vista Point, sometimes known as "Cellular Hill," for the hardware that helps us complete our calls.

From the 1,492-foot summit, enjoy clear-day coastal views from Santa Monica Bay to San Clemente, with Catalina Island floating on the horizon.

For a different return route, head back two hundred yards and make a left at the first fork. Descend to an unused kid's camp, then follow the park's service road back to the trailhead.

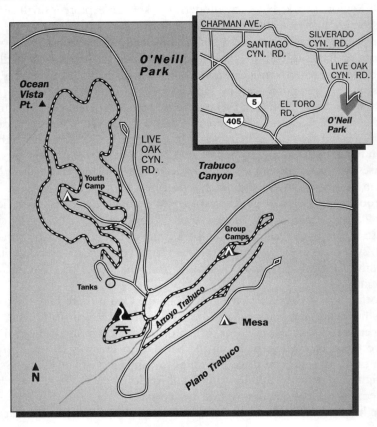

Arroyo Trabuco Wilderness

Arroyo Trabuco Trail
From O'Neill Park to Oso Parkway is 6 miles one way
with 500-foot elevation loss

One way or another the hike through Arroyo Trabuco Wilderness is an engaging experience. In fact, one-way may be the best way to walk this wildland corridor from O'Neill Park to Oso Parkway across southern Orange County. With the help of a car shuttle, the hiker can enjoy a mostly downhill ramble from a nature center to a mini-mall, a journey from the foothills of the Santa Ana Mountains to trail's end near a Taco Bell.

On a recent down-canyon jaunt, I experienced a collage, indeed collision, of images that included a murmuring creek, grand old oaks and sycamores, a doe and fawn browsing a flower-sprinkled meadow, as well as traffic rushing over my head on the Foothill Transportation Corridor (toll road). In places, all traces of the suburbia that sandwiches Arroyo Trabuco recedes to a respectful distance, and the hiker is left only in the company of chirping crickets, croaking frogs and twittering birds.

Part of this leafy retreat was fashioned by humans, not nature. Roadbuilders were required to plant a couple thousand native trees—willow, oak, sycamore and more—in the arroyo in order to offset the environmental effects of the arroyo-crossing parkways

A winter walk can be quite a muddy adventure. A half-dozen knee-high or higher creek crossings can mean a wet and wild journey.

Spring is an excellent time to trek Arroyo Trabuco. Arroyo Trabuco Creek is sprightly, and its banks blossom with monkey flowers, California poppies and lush green grasses.

By summer, the arroyo is all but dry and the temperature too hot for pleasant hiking. In autumn, the arroyo's numerous sycamores don their fall colors. Cool, coastal breezes (and sometimes hot Santa Ana winds) whisk the yellow-brown leaves from the trees and scatter them along the trail.

Directions to trailhead: From the San Diego Freeway (5) in El Toro, exit on El Toro Road and drive 7.5 miles to Live Oak Canyon Road (S-19). Turn right and proceed 3 miles to O'Neill Regional Park. There is a vehicle entry fee.

From the entry station, follow the signs west to the far end of the day-use area and the well-marked trailhead.

If you intend to hike Arroyo Trabuco one-way and would like to arrange a car shuttle, you'll want to leave a vehicle or be met at the commercial center located on the southeast corner of Oso Parkway and San Antonio Parkway. Reach this intersection from the San Diego Freeway (5) in Mission Viejo by exiting on Oso Parkway and traveling west a few miles.

The signed southern end of Arroyo Trabuco Trail is actually located 0.3 mile west of San Antonio Parkway on the north side of Oso Parkway; however, there is no parking whatsoever here, so you need to leave your vehicle at or near the mini-mall on the corner of Oso Parkway and San Antonio Parkway. A variety of eateries offer food and refreshment for the hiker.

The hike: Follow the wide path south under towering oaks and sycamores, then under the even more towering spans of the Foothill Transportation Corridor and Santa Margarita Parkway.

About two miles out, the path angles left up toward a canyon wall, topped by houses. A connector trail leads to Arroyo Vista (a street and trailhead for residential access to the Arroyo). After another mile of travel, the trail descends back toward the creek.

You'll alternate travel between wide meadows and the riparian corridor along the creek. After three creek crossings, you'll spot the Oso Parkway bridge over the arroyo. The path crosses under the bridge, then immediately crosses back to intersect a dirt powerline access road that ascends the west wall of the arroyo to trail's end at Oso Parkway. Walk east 0.3 along the sidewalk to reach the shopping center at the corner of Oso Parkway and San Antonio Parkway.

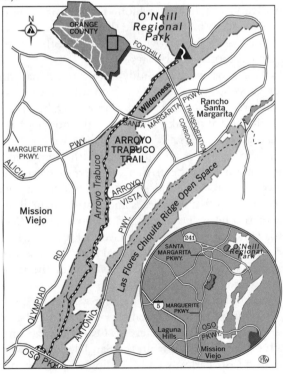

Caspers Wilderness Park

Nature, Oak, Bell Canyon Trails
2- to 4-mile loops

Caspers Wilderness Park has some unusual rules and a permit system for hikers fashioned years ago in response to two highly publicized mountain lion attacks on children. The incidents also resulted in an outpouring of support for the beleaguered mountain lion population, and a questioning of the very meaning of the word "wilderness." It's highly unlikely, however, that you will glimpse a mountain lion in Caspers Wilderness Park.

Visitors to the 7,600-acre park in the Santa Ana Mountains near San Juan Capistrano will, however, have a good chance of sighting other wildlife: Deer, rabbits and coyote, as well as more furtive animals such as foxes and bobcats. Bird-watchers will want to consult the park's bird list and test their skill by identifying the many species found in the park. Crisscrossing Caspers Wilderness Park are thirty miles of trail, which explore grassy valleys, chaparral-cloaked ridges and native groves of coastal live oak and sycamore.

Centerpiece of the park is oak-lined Bell Canyon. Acorns from the oaks were an important food source for the Juaneno Indians who lived in the canyon. As the legend goes, the Indians would strike a large granite boulder with a small rock to make it ring. The sound could be heard for a mile through what is now known as Bell Canyon. "Bell Rock" is now housed in Bowers Museum in Santa Ana.

Bell Canyon, San Juan Canyon, and surrounding ridges were once part of Starr-Viejo Ranch, which was purchased by Orange County in the early 1970s. The park honors Ronald W. Caspers, chairman of the Orange County Board of Supervisors, who was instrumental in preserving the old ranch as a park. Reminders of the park's ranching heritage include a windmill and a wooden corral where the branding and loading of cattle took place. The windmill still pumps a little water, which helps park wildlife make it through the long hot Santa Ana Mountains summers. During summer, the area around the windmill is the park's best bird-watching spot.

To learn more about the region's human and natural history, drop by the park's visitor center. Exhibits interpret Native American life, birds, mammals, geology, and much more.

The mostly level, Nature Trail-Oak Trail-Bell Canyon Trail-loop described below is only one of many possible day hikes you can fashion from the park's extensive trail network.

Directions to trailhead: From Interstate 5 in San Juan Capistrano, take the Highway 74 (Ortega Highway) exit. Drive eight miles inland to the entrance to Caspers Wilderness Park. There is a vehicle entrance fee. Each

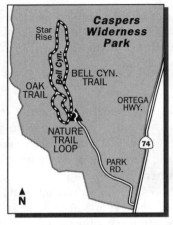

adult in your party must obtain a wilderness permit at the entry kiosk. Remember, no solo hiking, and no kids on the trails.

From the entry kiosk, take the park road 1.5 miles to its end at the corral and windmill. There's plenty of parking near the signed trailhead for Nature Trail.

The hike: Nature Trail loops through a handsome grove of antiquarian oak. You might see woodpeckers checking their store of acorns, which the birds have stuffed in hidey-holes in the nearby sycamores. Beneath the oaks are some huge patches of poison oak, but the trail steers clear of them.

You'll pass a junction with a left-branching trail that leads to Gunsight Pass and West Ridge Trail, and soon arrive at a second junction. (If you want a really short hike, keep right at this junction and you'll loop back to the trailhead via Nature Trail.)

Head north on signed Oak Trail, which meanders beneath the oak and sycamore that shade the west wall of Bell Canyon. The trail never strays far from Bell Creek, its streambed, or sandy washes. During drought years, it's difficult to imagine that in the 19th century, black bears used to catch spawning steelhead trout in Bell Creek. Fragrant sages perfume the trail, which is also lined with lemonade berry and prickly pear cactus.

Oak Trail reaches a junction at Post "12." You may take a short connector trail east to Bell Canyon or head north on another short trail, Star Rise, and join Bell Canyon Trail. A wide dirt road, Bell Canyon Trail travels the canyon floor.

To return to the trailhead, you'll head south on Bell Canyon Trail, which passes through open oak-dotted meadows. Red-tailed hawks roost atop spreading sycamores. The trail returns you to the parking area, within sight of the beginning of Nature Trail, where you began your walk.

CRYSTAL COVE STATE PARK

Moro Canyon Trail
From Park Headquarters to the top of Moro Canyon is 7 miles round trip
with 700-foot elevation gain

Extending three miles along the coast between Laguna Beach and Corona del Mar, and inland over the San Joaquin Hills, 3,000-acre Crystal Cove State Park attracts bird-watchers, beachcombers and hikers.

The backcountry of Crystal Cove State Park is part of the San Joaquin Hills, first used by Mission San Juan Capistrano for grazing land. Cattle raising continued under José Sepúlveda when the area became part of his land grant, Rancho San Joaquín, in 1837. In 1864, Sepúlveda sold the land to James Irvine and his partners and it became part of his Irvine Ranch. Grazing continued until shortly after the state purchased the property as parkland in 1979.

Former Irvine Ranch roads now form a network of hiking trails that loop through the state park. An especially nice trail travels the length of Moro Canyon, the main watershed of the park. An oak woodland, a seasonal stream and sandstone caves are some of the attractions of a walk through this canyon. Bird-watchers may spot the roadrunner, quail, Cooper's hawk, California thrasher, wrentit and many more species.

After exploring inland portions of the state park, allow some time to visit the park's coastline, highlighted by grassy bluffs, sandy beaches, tidepools and coves. The Pelican Point, Crystal Cove, Reef Point and Moro Beach areas of the park allow easy beach access.

Directions to trailhead: Crystal Cove State Park is located off Pacific Coast Highway, about two miles south of the town of Corona Del Mar or one mile north of Laguna Beach. Turn inland on the short park road, signed "El Moro Canyon." Drinking water, restrooms, interpretive displays and plenty of parking is available at the ranger station.

The hike: Below the ranger station, near the park entry kiosk pick up the unsigned Moro Canyon Trail, which crosses the grassy slopes behind a school and trailer park down into Moro Canyon. At the canyon bottom, you meet a fire road and head left, up-canyon.

The hiker may observe such native plants as black sage, prickly pear cactus, monkeyflowers, golden bush, lemonade berry and deer weed. Long before Spanish missionaries and settlers arrived in Southern California, a Native American population flourished in the coastal canyons of Orange County. The abundance of edible plants in the area, combined with the mild climate and easy access to the bounty of the sea, contributed to the success of these people, whom anthropologists believe lived off this land for more than four thousand years.

The canyon narrows, and you ignore fire roads joining Moro Canyon from the right and left. Stay in the canyon bottom and proceed through an oak woodland, which shades a trickling stream. You'll pass a shallow sandstone cave just off the trail to the right.

About 2.5 miles from the trailhead, you'll reach the unsigned junction with a fire road. If you wish to make a loop trip out of this day hike, bear left on this road, which climbs steeply west, then northeast toward the ridgetop that forms a kind of inland wall for Muddy, Moro, Emerald and other coastal canyons.

When you reach the ridgetop, unpack your lunch and enjoy the far reaching views of the San Joaquin Hills and Orange County coast, Catalina and San Clemente Islands. You'll also have a raven's-eye view of Moro Canyon and the route back to the trailhead. After catching your breath, you'll bear right (east) along the ridgetop and quickly descend back into Moro Canyon. A 0.75-mile walk brings you back to the junction where you earlier ascended out of the canyon. This time you continue straight downcanyon, retracing your steps to the trailhead.

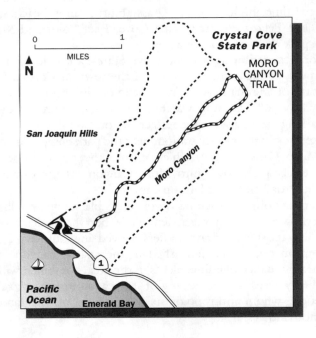

ALISO-WOOD CANYONS REGIONAL PARK

Aliso Creek, Wood Canyon Trails

To Wood Canyon is 3 miles round trip; through Wood Canyon to Sycamore Grove is 6 miles round trip; loop of Wood Canyon is 9 miles round trip

Aliso-Wood Canyons Regional Park, the largest park in the hills above Laguna Beach, preserves 3,400 acres of pastoral Orange County.

Most locals and other hikers refer to the low hills that back the Orange County coast from Corona del Mar to Dana Point as the Laguna Hills or "the mountains behind Laguna Beach." Actually, the northerly hills are the San Joaquin Hills—their cousins to the south are the Sheep Hills.

Here's how nature writer Joseph Smeaton Chase described an outing in the Sheep Hills in his classic 1913 book, *California Coast Trails:* "A few miles along a road that wound and dipped over the cliffs brought us by sundown to Aliso Canyon. The walls of the canyon are high hills sprinkled with lichened rock, sprinkled with brush whose prevailing gray is relieved here and there by bosses of olive sumac. Our camp was so attractive that we remained for several days."

Aliso-Wood Canyons Regional Park is a great place to hike, but it does present a minor access problem: From the parking area to the mouth of Wood Canyon is a less-than-scintillating 1.5 mile walk alongside a road. Some hikers avoid this road walk by bringing their bikes—either mountain bike or standard bicycle will do—and cycling to the "true" trailhead. Cyclists can ride some of the park's trails (the wider dirt roads), then leave their bikes at conveniently placed racks and walk the narrower, hikers-only paths.

Directions to trailhead: From the San Diego Freeway in Laguna Hills/Mission Viejo, exit on La Paz Road. Drive west, then south four miles to Aliso Creek Road. Turn right and proceed a short half-mile to Alicia Parkway. Turn left, then make a right turn on the park service road that crosses Aliso Creek and leads to a parking lot for Aliso-Wood Canyons Regional Park on your left.

The hike: From the parking area and information kiosk, hike along the paved road heading into the hills. The road (sometimes called Aliso Creek Bike Trail) and a parallel dirt path for walkers, heads southeast, meandering just west of Aliso Creek.

After 1.5 miles of walking, you'll arrive at a junction with Wood Canyon Trail on your right. Join this path (a dirt road) as it begins the very gentle ascent of Wood Canyon. Skirting the base of the Sheep Hills, the path visits the remains of an old corral and delivers the trees promised on the park map—Five Oaks Canyon and Sycamore Grove.

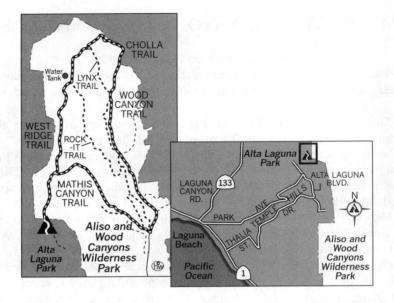

From Sycamore Grove, you can loop back via a trail on the opposite side of Wood Canyon by joining the short connector trail that leads to Coyote Run Trail.

Ambitious hikers will join either Lynx Trail or Cholla Trail (near the end of Wood Canyon Trail), head west over West Ridge Trail, then south to Rock It Trail or Mathis Trail, either of which returns you to Wood Canyon and the way back to the trailhead.

LAGUNA COAST WILDERNESS PARK

Laurel Canyon, Willow Canyon Trails
Laurel-Willow canyons loop is 3.5 miles with 600-foot elevation gain;
to Bommer Ridge Overlook is 7 miles round trip

Laguna Coast Wilderness Park is the Orange County of the 19th century, a lovely diversity of landscapes highlighted by woodlands, grasslands and scenic ridgelines with handsome sandstone outcroppings. The new 5,000-acre park also contains Orange County's only natural lakes, which provide habitat for fish as well as for such waterfowl as geese, grebes, coots, cormorants and kingfishers.

James Irvine and his partners purchased the one-time Rancho San Joaquin in 1865 and the company grazed cattle on it for more than a century. Now, with the Irvine Company's cooperation, substantial acreage in and around Laguna Canyon is becoming parkland under the stewardship of the Orange County Parks Department.

That these hills and canyons don't resemble the developed Orange County of the 21st century is a tribute to three decades of exemplary work by local conservationists, as well as state and local park agencies and municipalities. Preservationists, with the support of then-California Senator Alan Cranston attempted to create Orange Coast National Park in the late 1970s. In 1989, 8,000 people marched along Laguna Canyon Road to show their commitment to preserving the Laguna Hills. A year later the citizens of Laguna Beach voted overwhelmingly to tax themselves $20 million in order to purchase land alongside Laguna Canyon Road and far up into the hills. Lengthy negotiations among public entities and private parties, as well as increased preservation efforts spearheaded by the Laguna Canyon Foundation took place during the 1990s.

For more than a decade, access has been restricted to an extent that only the most connected local hikers have been able to figure out when, where and how to hike this park-in-the-making. Currently the park is open for hiking only on weekends.

Directions to trailhead: From the San Diego Freeway (405) in Irvine, a few miles north of this freeway's junction with the Santa Ana Freeway (5), exit on Laguna Canyon Road (133) and head south toward the coast and Laguna Beach. Look for the main (Laurel Canyon) entrance to the park on the right (west) side of the road.

The hike: Join the path leading north parallel to Laguna Canyon Road and soon pass a sandstone boulder sculpted by wind and water into a very small cave. Keep an eye out for more such caves and rock formations crowning the park's ridges.

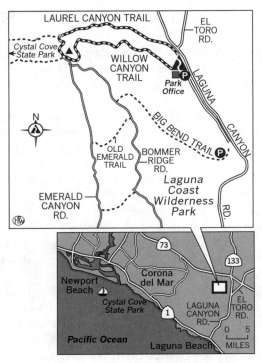

The trail traverses an open slope that, with an end to cattle grazing, is making the environmental transition from annual grassland to coastal sage scrub. Buckwheat and sage line the path which turns away from Laguna Canyon Road and enters the quiet of Laurel Canyon.

Begin a westward ascent among live oaks and sycamores. The oaks appear to have recovered far better than the sycamores from the terrible 1993 Laguna Fire that blackened Laurel Canyon and thousands of acres around it. Certainly the vegetation in the canyon bottom regenerated quickly: what is now a brush-crowded narrow footpath up Laurel Canyon was actually a fairly wide ranch road before the fire.

The path leads by a seasonal creek (look for an ephemeral waterfall during the rainy season) and ascends to meet a dirt road. Turn left on this road and begin an ascent to a saddle on Willow Ridge and another junction. Go left again and descend Willow Canyon Road.

Most of the view on your descent east is of parkland, with the major exception of the San Joaquin Hills Toll Road which, alas, bisects Laguna Coast Wilderness Park. Your journey ends at the park office, a short walk from the trailhead and parking area.

JAMES DILLEY PRESERVE

Canyon, Edison, To the Lake Trails
From Laguna Canyon Road to Barbara's Lake is 3.5-mile loop with 300-foot elevation gain

Lakes are few and far between in Orange County and for the most part are decorative contrivances created for city parks, golf courses and suburban neighborhoods.

Orange County's only natural lakes are the Laguna Lakes in Laguna Canyon. The largest of the three lakes is delightful to visit, particularly for the hiker, because it's accessible only by a trail through the engaging James Dilley Preserve.

Early maps referred to the lakes as laguna, Spanish for pond, while modern maps generally opt for the rather redundant Laguna Lakes. The lakes are replenished by rainfall and possibly some water from underground springs.

Barbara's Lake, largest of the lakes, honors conservation activist Barbara Stuart. Fringed by bulrush, cattail and willows, the lake offers habitat for coots, grebes and mallards.

From the preserve's high points, hikers get good views of Bubbles Lake, named for the hippopotamus Bubbles who escaped from Lion Country Safari in the mid-1970s and took up residence in the little lake located on the west side of Laguna Canyon Road. For a time, the wayward hippo eluded capture, staying underwater by day and emerging only at night. Alas for Bubbles, she was shot with tranquilizers and died while attempting to elude her captors.

In the 1960s, James Dilley, a Laguna Beach bookseller, began promoting his vision: the creation of a band of parks and preserves surrounding Laguna Beach. Dilley's notion of a greenbelt ringing the coastal town was enthusiastically supported by local conservationists, and a broad cross-section of the community.

Thanks to "The Father of the Greenbelt," plus four decades of cooperative efforts among conservation groups, park agencies and the area's major landowner, the Irvine Company, Laguna Beach is green on three sides and Pacific blue on the fourth. All Southland communities should be so fortunate!

The preserve, owned by the city and managed by the county's parks department was established in 1978 and is the oldest portion of Laguna Coast Wilderness Park. Spearheaded by the nonprofit Laguna Canyon Foundation, conservation efforts continue in order to expand the park, preserve other hills and canyons, and open up the greenbelt to increased public use.

The preserve is something of an island on the land. It's bordered by Laguna Canyon Road on the west, El Toro Road and Leisure World on the east and the San Joaquin Hills Transportation Corridor (toll road) on the south. The Laguna Lakes form the preserve's north boundary. James Dilley

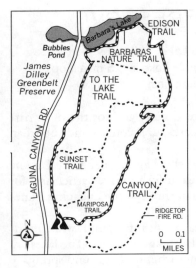

Preserve's "islandness" is apparent from looking at the map and even more obvious when contemplating the landscape from atop the preserve's ridges.

Access to the preserve is strictly regulated. James Dilley Preserve is open for hiking on Saturdays only, from 8 A.M. to 2 P.M.

Canyon Trail, part of my suggested loop around the preserve, is the first leg of a nature trail with numbered wooden markers keyed to an interpretive pamphlet (sometimes available at the trailhead). The pamphlet is by no means necessary to enjoy the hike.

Directions to trailhead: From the San Diego Freeway (405) in Irvine, exit onto the Laguna Freeway (133), which soon becomes Laguna Canyon Road. Drive south miles to the signed entrance for James Dilley Preserve on the left (east) side of the road and park in the dirt lot. The preserve entrance is just north of San Joaquin Hills Transportation Corridor (toll road).

The hike: From the parking area, take the dirt road east and soon join Canyon Trail. The path swings north up the canyon, which is lined with coastal live oak and sycamore, white sage, black sage and buckwheat.

Leaving the moist canyon bottom, the path climbs higher slopes with a change in elevation to prickly pear cactus, lemonadeberry and monkeyflower. Near a ridgeline the path forks. The left branch, sometimes called the Eagle Scout Trail, descends south toward the trailhead.

Continue up the remains of a dirt road to the top of the hill and you'll see a gravel road leading downhill west toward Laguna Canyon Road and a steep Edison fire road Edison Trail) heading north. I prefer taking the Edison Trail for the views, which can include the San Gabriel Mountains on a clear winter day.

The more immediate view from the trail is of Orange County's largest natural lake, with a surface area of about 12 acres. Cattle grazed the slopes back of the lake for more than 150 years.

Barbara's Nature Trail, another interpretive trail, leads along the lakeshore to an old pump house, and an intersection with To The Lake Trail, which heads south, parallel to Laguna Canyon Road back to the trailhead.

Alta Laguna Park

West Ridge, Mathis, Wood Canyon, Cholla Trails

Loop From Alta Laguna Park to Aliso and Wood Canyons Regional Park is 8 miles round trip with 600-foot elevation gain

Most park-goers use the Alicia Parkway entrance to Aliso and Wood Canyons Wilderness Park to begin their self-propelled adventures from the canyon bottoms. Another, less crowded way to go is by way of a second trailhead at Alta Laguna Park, perched atop a ridge on the big park's west boundary. This handsome little park offers every hiker amenity including water, restrooms, picnic area, play area for the kids and plenty of parking.

Hikers should be forewarned that Aliso and Wood Canyons Wilderness Park is extremely popular with mountain bicyclists. Beginning riders cruise the nearly flat canyon bottoms in the main part of the park while advanced riders careen down the steep ridgelines and along the rocky single tracks.

Vistas from Alta Laguna Park are superb. Hike the short trail to Carolynn Wood View Knoll and admire the coastal panorama to the southwest: Laguna Beach and the shoreline to the south, northward to the prominent Palos Verdes Peninsula, then across the great blue Pacific to San Clemente Island and Santa Catalina Island.

Gaze east to the San Joaquin Hills and the modern communities of Aliso Viejo, Lake Forest and more. Behind the hills and suburbs rise the Santa Ana Mountains and its two most distinctive peaks—Modjeska and Santiago—which team together to form Old Saddleback. On a clear day, the observant hiker can pick out several San Gabriel Mountains high points including Mt. Wilson and Mt. Baldy.

This top-down approach to Aliso-Woods park that I've suggested can be shortened or lengthened to your time and inclination. Four trails extend from the park's West Ridge and offer the hiker several loop trip opportunities of varying lengths.

Directions to trailhead: From Pacific Coast Highway (1) in Laguna Beach, turn inland on Park Avenue and ascend two miles to Alta Laguna Boulevard. Turn left and after a block turn right into Alta Laguna Park.

The hike: The most eager among us can get right to the walk by stepping out onto the wide West Ridge Trail, but I recommend following the more roundabout trail to Carolynn Wood View Knoll and taking in the panoramic vistas. Thanks to some slope restoration efforts these hilltops are healing from the effects of off-road vehicle use that occurred prior to the creation of the park. While enjoying the view, realize that the knoll's "purpose" is actually more utilitarian than aesthetic: below ground is a reservoir containing some 3 million gallons of water.

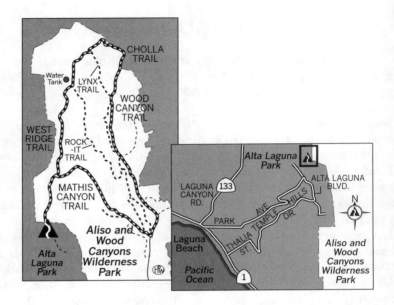

From atop the knoll, a footpath corkscrews down to a spur road that, in turn, connects to West Ridge Trail. A half-mile northward descent leads to a park bulletin board, bench and signed intersection with Mathis Trail. If you're not up for a long hike, contemplate the park below, then retrace your steps back to the trailhead.

Mathis Trail drops southwest very quickly. It's a hairy mountain bike ride and even a steep route for hikers. The trail finally levels out and a better graded dirt road leads to the grassy, oak-dotted bottom of Mathis Canyon.

Turn north on Wood Canyon Trail through the heart of the park. Follow the mellow path along the seasonal creek on a gentle 2.5 mile ascent to the north end of the park and a junction with Cholla Trail. Bear left and head up Cholla Trail to the ridge line. A final 2.5 miles along West Ridge Trail returns you to the trailhead.

7. Chino Hills

C HINO HILLS STATE PARK, located in Orange, San Bernardino, and Riverside counties, preserves some much needed "breathing room" in this fast-growing area. Nearly three million people live within sight of the Chino Hills and more than nine million people live within a 40-mile radius of the park!

The park is the state's most expensive ever, with in excess of $50 million spent by the time it opened for full time use in 1986. The park has remained undeveloped, the province of horseback riders, mountain bikers and hikers.

While some 3 million people live within sight of the Chino Hills and some 9 million within a 40-mile radius of the state park, the park trails offer surprisingly tranquil and away-from-it-all hiking.

On some days, it seems like almost no one uses the park's excellent trail network. On a recent spring Saturday I counted only six vehicles, including the park ranger's pickup, in the heart of the state park. Perfect walking

weather, not a cloud in the sky, sunny but not hot, air quality as good as it gets out here, and...where was everybody?

Well, the parking lots of the nearby malls were full. Everyone was shopping? How else to explain why I counted more rabbits than people in the 13,000-acre park?

Summer is the one season to steer clear of the park. High temperatures, often combined with heavy smog, suggest that a summer visit can be something of an ordeal. The Chino Hills are much more pleasurable in the cooler months and especially delightful in spring.

The 13,000-acre park is located near the northern end of what geologists call the Peninsular Ranges Geomorphic Province. The Chino Hills are part of the group of hills that include the Puente Hills to the northwest. These hills form a roughly triangular area of approximately 35 square miles of valleys, canyons, hills and steep slopes.

Considering the proximity of so much 21st century civilization, the hills harbor an admirable biodiversity. Most obvious are some lovely oak woodlands as well as stands of native California walnut, which thrive in the park's larger canyons.

Extensive grasslands blanket the slopes. The hills are covered with wild oats, rye, black mustard and wild radish. On south-facing slopes is the soft-leaved shrub community, dominated by several varieties of sage.

Rising to about the same height as another, far more famous, metropolitan-crossing range—the Hollywood Hills—the Chino Hills top out at about 1,800 feet. But summits short in stature can deliver very long views, particularly on a clear winter day. Stand on the summits of park high points such as Gilman Peak and San Juan Hill and you can see parts of four counties and a glorious amount of room to roam in this special state park.

Telegraph Canyon

Hills-for-Everyone Trail
Along Ranch Road to McDermont Spring is 4 miles round trip
with 400-foot gain; to Carbon Canyon Regional Park is
7.5 miles one way with 800-foot loss

Hills-for-Everyone Trail was named for the conservation group that was instrumental in establishing Chino Hills State Park. The trail follows a creek to the head of Telegraph Canyon. The creek is lined with oak, sycamore and the somewhat rare California walnut.

Directions to trailhead: Chino Hills State Park can be a bit tricky to find. The park is located west of Highway 71 between the Riverside Freeway (91) and the Pomona Freeway (60).

From Highway 71, exit on Soquel Canyon Parkway and travel one mile to a signed left turn at Elinvar Road, which bends sharply left. Look immediately right for a signed dirt road—Bane Canyon Road. Enter the park on this road (which returns to pavement in two miles) and follow signs to the park office and ranger station.

The road forks just before the ranger station. To the right is the ranger station and visitor center. Bear left one-half mile on the dirt road to a vehicle barrier and trailhead parking. The signed trailhead is located a short distance past the vehicle barrier on the right of the road.

The hike: Hills-for-Everyone Trail descends to a small creek and follows the creek up canyon. Shading the trail—and shielding the hiker from a view of the many electrical transmission lines that cross the park—are oaks, sycamores and walnuts. Of particular interest is the walnut; often the 15- to 30-foot tall tree has several dark brown trunks, which gives it a brushy appearance.

The trail, which can be quite slippery and muddy after a rain, passes a small (seasonal) waterfall. The slopes above the creekbed are carpeted with lush grasses and miners lettuce.

Along the trail is found evidence of the park's ranching heritage, including lengths of barbed wire fence and old cattle troughs. For more than a century this land was used exclusively for cattle ranching.

Near its end, the trail ascends out of the creekbed to the head of Telegraph Canyon and intersects a dirt road. McDermont Spring is just down the road. Some of the livestock ponds, constructed during the area's ranching days, still exist, and hold water year-round. McDermont Spring—along with Windmill and Panorama ponds—provides water for wildlife.

To Carbon Canyon Regional Park: Telegraph Canyon Trail (a dirt road closed to public vehicular traffic) stays close to the canyon bottom and its

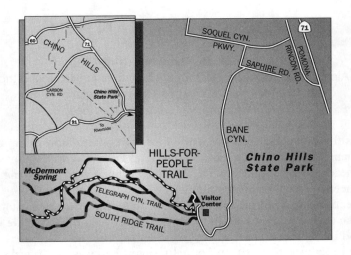

creek. It's a gentle descent under the shade of oak and walnut trees. The walnuts are particularly numerous along the first mile of travel and the hiker not inclined to hike the length of Telegraph Canyon might consider exploring this stretch before returning to the trailhead.

The route passes an old windmill. Farther down the canyon, the walnuts thin out. A lemon grove, owned by the state park but leased to a farmer, is at a point where the dirt road intersects Carbon Canyon Road. Walk along the broad shoulder of the latter road 0.5 mile to Carbon Canyon Regional Park.

WATER CANYON

Water Canyon, South Ridge, Aliso Trails
5 miles round trip with 400-foot elevation gain

Water Canyon may just be the single most compelling locale in the Chino Hills. Grand old oaks and sycamores, along with willows and walnut trees shade this quiet enclave, one of the great natural treasures and pleasures of the Inland Empire.

The steep walls of the canyon add to the hiker's sense of isolation and adventure. Water Canyon is located nearly astride the boundary line between Orange and San Bernardino counties, but seems a hundred miles away from those fast-growing areas.

The canyon is particularly attractive to hikers because it's accessible only by foot. This foot-traffic only designation is something of a rarity in Chino Hills State Park, which has a system of dirt roads that is often heavily used by mountain bikers and horseback riders.

Directions to trailhead: Chino Hills State Park can be a bit tricky to find. The park is located west of Highway 71 between the Riverside Freeway (91) and the Pomona Freeway (60).

From Highway 71, exit on Soquel Canyon Parkway and travel one mile to a signed left turn at Elinvar Road, which bends sharply left. Look immediately right for a signed dirt road—Bane Canyon Road. Enter the park on this road (which returns to pavement in two miles) and follow signs to the park office and ranger station.

About 0.5 mile before the park office, turn left into the park campground and follow the camp road to its end at a vehicle gate, parking area and signed trailhead.

The hike: Aliso Canyon Trail (a dirt road) heads south across a wide, fairly flat grassland. About 0.5 mile along, the road dips to cross the creek at the bottom of Aliso Canyon. Just before the crossing, note unsigned (upper) Aliso Canyon Trail (your return route on this loop hike) on the right.

Just ahead is a junction with another road. A left on the road leads south to lower Aliso Canyon. Go right about 100 yards. At a hairpin turn, the road bends back south and heads toward Skull Ridge, but you join signed Water Canyon Trail.

The footpath trends west through the lovely, wooded canyon. After a mile, and after passing a towering clump of prickly pear cactus and a sign indicating the end of the trail, the path reaches an open area.

(To continue your exploration of Water Canyon, follow the trail-less canyon bottom west. After 0.25 mile or so, when you encounter more stinging nettle and poison oak than you can avoid, you might decide discretion is the better part of valor and retreat.)

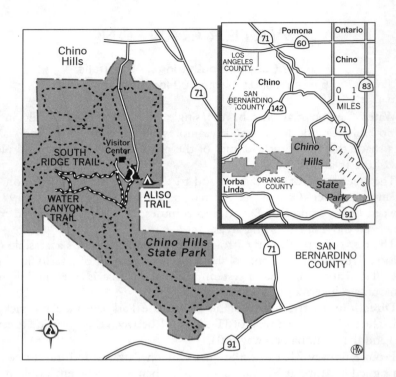

A more pleasant option might be to follow the path, faint, but passable, which veers northwest away from Water Canyon and climbs rather steeply about 0.4 mile to meet South Ridge Trail, a dirt road. Turn right (east) on the road and enjoy good views to the south and east of the park's rolling hills.

A mile's descent brings you within sight of park headquarters and leads to a junction with the main park road. The signed beginning of Aliso Canyon Trail is also located at this junction. Join this footpath for a 0.75 mile saunter with great views of a windmill (a reminder of this land's pre-park ranching heritage) and some handsome alisos (sycamores). The trail meets (Lower) Aliso Canyon Trail, a dirt road. Turn left and retrace your steps back to the trailhead.

GILMAN PEAK

North Ridge and Gilman Peak Trails
From Carbon Canyon Regional Park to Gilman Peak is 7 miles round trip
with 1,200-foot elevation gain

Gilman Peak, a 1,685-foot Chino Hills promontory, is far from the top
of the world but offers the hiker magnificent vistas—particularly on a clear
winter's day. The San Gabriel Mountains, wearing a mantle of snow, rise to
the north above the San Gabriel Valley. The Santa Ana Mountains border
the southeastern vista while to the southwest the Orange County
suburbanopolis spreads to the sea.

To the approaching hiker, Gilman Peak itself does not inspire great
expectations. It appears as little more than just another bump on the
ridgetop, a bald crown scarcely higher than neighboring peaklets. Ah, but
the inspirational views from the summit more than make up for the dull
appearance of the peak.

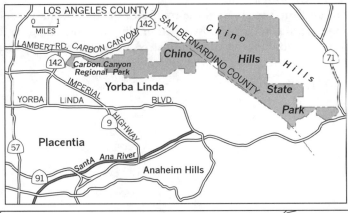

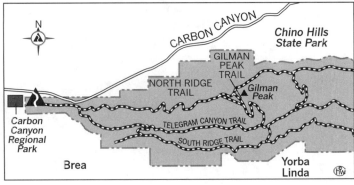

The three reasons for Gilman Peak's success at delivering views are location, location, and location. The peak is located at the far frontier of three counties: Los Angeles, Orange and San Bernardino. Parts of a fourth county—Riverside—can be viewed from the peak also.

Surrounded by all manner of residential, commercial and industrial developments, as well as four freeways, the wilder parts of the Chino Hills are indeed an island on the land. The range's "island" nature is apparent to the hiker on the trail to Gilman Peak.

Directions to trailhead: From the Orange Freeway (57) in Brea, exit on Lambert Road. Drive 4 miles east on Lambert (which changes to Carbon Canyon Road east of Valencia Avenue) to the entrance of Carbon Canyon Regional Park. There's a vehicle entry fee. Limited legal parking (free) also exists on the south shoulder of Carbon Canyon Road. From wherever you park, join the dirt road angling southeast just below the road.

The hike: Walk up the dirt road past a citrus orchard to a state park bulletin board and a signed junction. Telegraph Canyon Trail (a dirt road) heads south, but you join North Ridge Trail (also a dirt road) on a climb past scattered California walnut.

A bit more than 2 miles from the trailhead, the path gains a sparsely vegetated ridgeline and travels across it. After dipping and rising to a couple "false" summits, you'll reach Gilman Peak. A wide summit trail takes you to the top.

SAN JUAN HILL

South Ridge Trail
To the top of San Juan Hill is 6 miles round trip with 1,200-foot elevation gain

When the land for Chino Hills State Park was purchased in the mid 1980s, there was a lot of grumbling about the high cost—from the public, from politicians, and even from some conservationists who figured purchasing a redwood grove or two was a better use of hard-to-come-by funds.

Nowadays the large park seems like a bargain. And nowhere is this more apparent than on the trail to the park's high point, San Juan Hill.

The first glimpse of the park's great value is obvious when hiking the half mile of South Ridge Trail and looking at what you're leaving behind: all manner of brand-new suburbia pushing right up to the park's southern boundary. Without a park, every build-able slope would likely be smothered in subdivisions.

Farther up the trail, most traces of civilization vanish, and the hiker enters a wonderfully pastoral landscape of rolling grassland and drifts of oak. It would be difficult to place a dollar value on this wonderful experience.

Deer gambol through the high grasses, hawks circle overhead and a refreshing breeze (often) keeps the temperature down. Atop San Juan's slopes, hikers are often joined by kite-flyers, who take advantage of the robust gusts.

While that famed San Juan Hill in Cuba was a difficult charge for Theodore Roosevelt and his Rough Riders to make in an 1898 battle of the Spanish-American War, you should have a rather mellow time conquering the San Juan Hill perched on the border of Orange and San Bernardino counties. The trail to 1,781-foot San Juan Hill is a well-graded fire road.

Directions to trailhead: From the Orange Freeway (57) in Brea, exit on Imperial Highway (90) and head southeast 4.5 miles to Yorba Linda Boulevard. Turn left (east) and drive 1.3 miles to Fairmont Boulevard. Turn left (east) and drive 1.5 miles to Rim Crest Drive. Turn left and proceed 0.3 mile to the signed trailhead on the right. Park alongside Rim Crest Drive.

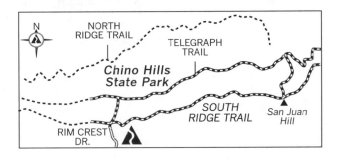

Charge up San Juan Hill for views of four counties.

Heed the curbside parking signs because public parking is permitted only on some lengths of Rim Crest Drive; some parking is for residents (by permit) only.

The hike: Walk 40 yards up the fire lane to the park information bulletin board and the signed beginning of South Ridge Trail. Begin your journey east with an ascent that soon removes you from all sights and sounds of civilization.

The moderate climb leads over hills covered with wild oats, rye, mustard and wild radish. Trees are few and far between atop these hills, which means both little shade and unobstructed views of the surrounding countryside. Only the high-voltage powerlines bisecting the hills detract from the near-pastoral landscape.

Nearly three miles out, you'll reach a junction with the signed path to San Juan Hill. Walk 50 yards up a fire road toward a powerline tower, then join the narrow, unsigned footpath on the right leading 0.1 mile to the summit of San Juan Hill.

Crowning the hilltop is a concrete, hexagon-shaped column that reads: San Juan 1896. Puzzle over this number as you enjoy the billowing grass and the usually breezy summit, as well as commanding vistas of the Chino Hills.

8. SANTA ANA MOUNTAINS

T HE SANTA ANA MOUNTAINS may be the most overlooked and underutilized recreation area in Southern California. Extending the entire length of Orange County's eastern perimeter, the Santa Anas roughly parallel the coast. This coastal range is only about twenty miles inland and the western slopes are often blanketed with fog. The coast has a cooling influence on what is often a very hot range of mountains. Except for the dog days of summer, most days offer pleasant hiking.

The Santa Anas offer no dramatic escarpment to compare with that of the San Jacintos, nor do they have the rugged tumbled look of the San Gabriels; these mountains are round, brushy, inviting. At first glance, they seem to be inundated by a monotonous sea of chaparral. But the chaparral teems with wildlife, and even the most casual hiker will be amazed at the number of rabbit and quail who hop and flutter from the dense undergrowth. The range is covered with great masses of buckthorn, greasewood, sumac and scrub oak. Alternating with the chaparral are oak woodlands, wide potreros, and boulder-strewn creeks with superb swimming holes.

The range is a granite block, which has been uplifted and depressed below sea level several times. On top of the mountains, marine sediments occur in successive formations. The Santa Anas increase in altitude from north to south, culminating in the twin peaks of Old Saddleback—Mt. Modjeska (5,440 feet) and Mt. Santiago (5,860 feet). The crest of the range has been filed down and eroded by wind and weather exposing the hard granite at the surface.

The mountains came under federal protection in 1893 when the Trabuco Canyon Forest Reserve was formed. The name was changed to the Trabuco National Forest in 1906; the forest later was enlarged and eventually assigned to the Cleveland National Forest in 1908. Today, 136,500 acres of the Santa Ana Mountains are included in the national forest's Trabuco District.

The Ortega Highway, which crossed the Santa Anas from San Juan Station to Lake Elsinore, opened up the mountains to camping and hiking, but not to the same extent the Rim of the World Highway opened up the San Bernardinos or the Angeles Crest Highway opened up the San Gabriels. Portions of the Santa Anas are infrequently visited because trailheads require travel on rough dirt roads.

Highlight of the range is the San Mateo Canyon Wilderness, set aside by Congress in 1984. The 40,000-acre preserve protects San Mateo Canyon, a relatively untouched land of 200-year-old oaks, potreros and quiet pools.

Silverado Canyon

Silverado Trail
From Silverado Canyon Road to Bedford Peak is 7 miles round trip
with 2,100-foot elevation gain

When experienced hikers refer to a trek as "a conditioning hike" you know you're in for a workout. The path to Bedford Peak most definitely fits into the getting-fit category.

From the west (most populated) side of the Santa Ana mountains, Silverado Trail is the shortest and quickest way to Main Divide, the ridge-crest of the range. Of course, short and quick add up to steep as well, which is why this trail offers an aerobic workout.

Reward for the ascent to 3,800-foot high Bedford Peak is a great clear-day panorama of the Santa Ana, San Gabriel and San Bernardino ranges, along with the O.C. suburbanopolis and the Pacific Ocean.

The name Silverado comes from the high hopes of prospectors who swarmed into the canyon during the late 1870s. A few years later, the silver ore played out, and the boom went bust. These days the canyon is a surprisingly rural enclave of homes, general store and fire station.

On old maps, and on most new ones as well, Silverado Trail is labeled as Silverado Motorway. Originally constructed for fire patrol and control purposes, the fire road deteriorated over the years and de-evolved (evolved in the opinion of we hikers) into a footpath. Hikers might find it difficult to believe this now-vanished motorway was ever passable by vehicles.

Directions to trailhead: From the Newport Freeway (55) in Orange, exit on Chapman Avenue and drive east. About 6 miles out, Chapman becomes Santiago Canyon Road and, some 11 miles from the freeway, you'll intersect Silverado Canyon Road. Bear left and continue 5.5 miles to the parking area.

The hike: Walk up the wide, shaded Maple Springs Road (a continuation of Santiago Canyon Road) for 0.1 mile. Just after crossing a seasonal creek, look and turn left (west) on unsigned Silverado Trail. At first it appears the path intends to return you to the trailhead, but it soon turns north and begins a steep, zigzagging ascent of the north wall of the canyon.

The trail is flanked by sage and exposed outcroppings of stratified sedimentary rock known as the Bedford Canyon Formation. Higher and higher you climb on switchbacks that offer ever-grander vistas of Silverado Canyon, until the entire canyon comes into view.

A bit more than 2 miles out, you'll reach a flat spot on the ridge between Silverado and Ladd canyons and a so-so view of the Santa Anas. If you feel sufficiently "conditioned", this is a good turnaround point.

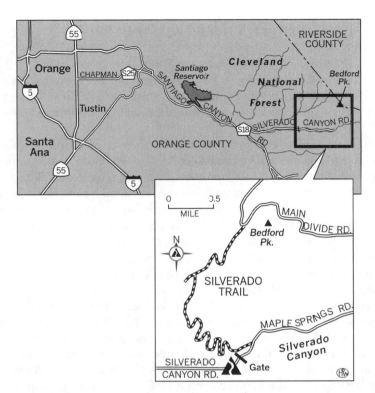

Otherwise, continue along the ridgeline on a steep, but quite inspiring mile of trail to meet Main Divide Road. Turn right and walk 0.3 mile up the road to Bedford Peak.

Bedford is really more of a big bump in the road than a proper peak, but it does provide a modest platform from which to survey peaks near and far, as well as the advancing metropolis on both sides of the range.

HOLY JIM CANYON

Holy Jim Trail
From Holy Jim Creek to Falls is 2.5 miles round trip with 200-foot elevation gain; to Bear Springs is 10 miles round trip with 2,200-foot gain; to Santiago Peak is 16 miles round trip with 4,000-foot gain

Holy Jim Trail, creek and canyon take their names from Cussin' Jim Smith, an early Santa Ana Mountain settler who, when displeased, unleashed a string of unholy epithets. Mapmakers back then were unwilling to geographically honor such a blasphemer, so they changed his name to "Holy."

The trail is one of the most popular in the Santa Anas, though many hikers go only as far as the falls. Holy Jim Trail is often in fair-to-mediocre shape and is sometimes overgrown with brush. The trail is something of a Santa Ana Mountains sampler, giving the hiker a creek, a lush canyon, a waterfall, oak woodland and chaparral-covered slopes. All this and a view, too!

Directions to trailhead: Take Interstate Highway 5 to the El Toro Road exit (S-18); go east through Mission Viejo. Turn right on Live Oak Canyon Road (S-9). One mile after passing O'Neill Park, the road crosses Trabuco Wash. Turn left into the wash and head up rocky Trabuco Road. Don't be intimidated; the road gets better, not worse, as it heads up the wash, and it is suitable for most passenger cars. In 5 miles, you'll pass a volunteer fire department station and reach Holy Jim turnoff on your left. Park in the dirt area near the turnoff.

The hike: Walk up Holy Jim Road, passing a number of summer homes. Beyond the last home, you'll reach a gate. Holy Jim Trail (6W03) begins on the other side of the gate and heads up vine- and oak-filled lower Holy Jim Canyon. The trail stays near Holy Jim Creek for the first mile, crossing and recrossing the bubbling waters near some stone fish dams. A mile from the gate, the trail crosses the creek one last time. At this creek crossing, an unsigned, but well-used side trail heads upstream to Holy Jim Waterfall. It's 0.25 mile to the falls and well-worth a visit. Push your way through the wild grape, and boulder-hop up the creekbed to the cool grotto. The falls will seem even more spectacular if you engage in a little delayed gratification and save them for your return from Bear Springs.

To Bear Springs: At the creek crossing, the Holy Jim Tail turns downstream for a few hundred yards. You're treated to a good view of the northern Santa Ana Mountains. The trail soon takes you on a stiff climb up the west side of the canyon. If the trail is severely overgrown, it's time to put on your long pants and forge on. After some hearty switchbacking through thick brush, the trail begins a long contour along the canyon wall. As the trail nears Bear Springs, it gets less brushy, and there is some flora you can

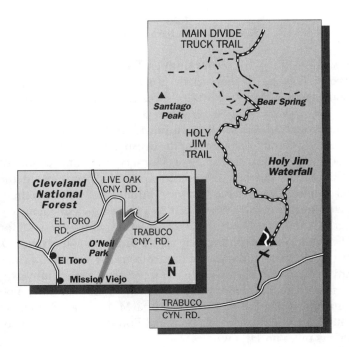

look up to: shady oaks, with an occasional Douglas fir or Coulter pine. Santiago Peak comes into view. The northern Santa Anas were once known as Sierra de Santiago for this dominant peak. You can't miss Santiago Peak; it's the only mountain road around with a forest of antennae atop it.

Bear Springs is located at the intersection of the Holy Jim Trail and the Main Divide Truck Trail. An enclosed concrete water tank is at the intersection, but the tank does not dispense water to thirsty hikers. You can get plenty of water from the creek, but it should be purified. The shady area around the springs is cool and pleasant, an ideal lunch stop.

To Santiago Peak: Return the same way or, if you're feeling rambunctious, continue another three miles (gaining 1,800 feet) on the Main Divide Truck Trail to Santiago Peak, the highest summit in the Santa Anas. On a clear day, you can see a hundred miles from the 5,687-foot peak.

Bear Canyon

Bear Canyon Trail
From Ortega Highway to Pigeon Springs is 5.5 miles round trip with 700-foot elevation gain; to Sitton Peak is 10.5 miles round trip with 1,300-foot gain

Bear Canyon Trail offers a pleasant introduction to the Santa Ana Mountains. The trail climbs through gentle brush and meadow country, visits Pigeon Springs, and arrives at Four Corners, the intersection of several major hiking trails through the southern Santa Anas. One of these trails takes you to Sitton Peak for a fine view. Along the trail, refreshing Pigeon Springs welcomes hot and dusty hikers to a handsome oak glen.

Directions to trailhead: Take the Ortega Highway (California 74) turnoff from the San Diego Freeway (5) at San Juan Capistrano. Drive east 20 miles to the paved parking area across from the Country Cottage store. Bear Canyon Trail starts just west of the store on Ortega Highway.

Departing from the parking lot is the two-mile San Juan Loop Trail, another nice introduction to the Santa Ana Mountains. Obtain trail information and purchase a Cleveland National Forest map at El Cariso Station, located a few miles up Highway 74.

The hike: From the signed trailhead, the broad, well-graded trail climbs slowly up brushy hillsides. The trail crosses a seasonal creek, which flows through a tiny oak woodland.

Few have discovered the wide variety of trails found in the Santa Ana Mountains.

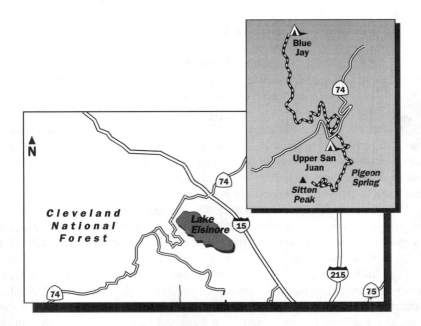

A half mile from the trailhead, you'll enter the San Mateo Canyon Wilderness. After a mile, a deceptive fork (the west end of Morgan Trail) appears on the left. Ignore it. The trail climbs on, skirts the periphery of a meadow and crests a chaparral-covered slope. Just before the trail joins the Verdugo Trail, there's a nice view down into San Juan Canyon. Turn right (south) on Verdugo Trail and proceed 0.75 mile to Pigeon Springs.

Pigeon Springs includes a storage tank and horse trough. Forest rangers recommend that you purify the water before drinking. The springs are located among oaks on the left of the trail.

To continue on to Sitton Peak, hike down the Verdugo Trail another half mile and you'll arrive at Four Corners, a convergence of trails (fire roads). The Verdugo Trail pushes straight ahead to an intersection with the Blue Water Trail. To the left is Blue Water Fire Road leading down to Fisherman's Camp in San Mateo Canyon. To proceed to Sitton Peak, bear right on the Sitton Peak Trail.

Follow the trail as it begins to climb and contour around the peak. There are a few trees up on the ridge but little shade en route. In a mile you'll be at the high point of Sitton Peak Trail, a saddle perched over San Juan Canyon. Follow the trail another mile until you reach the southeast face of the peak. Leave the trail here and wend your way up past the rocky outcroppings to Sitton Peak. On a clear day, there are superb views of the twin peaks of Old Saddleback (Mt. Modjeska and Mt. Santiago), Mt. San Gorgonio and Mt. San Jacinto, Catalina and the wide Pacific.

LION CANYON

Chiquito Basin Trail
From Ortega Highway to Lion Canyon is 11.5 miles round trip
with 1,100-foot elevation gain

"Chiquito," which names a basin, a spring and the trail, is not named after a major brand of banana, as you might guess, but rather, was the name bestowed upon these features by a forest ranger in 1927 to honor his horse. The trail leads past a sparkling little waterfall, over brushy hillsides and oak-studded slopes to shady Lion Canyon Creek.

Directions to trailhead: Take the Ortega Highway 74 turnoff from the San Diego Freeway (5) in San Juan Capistrano, and drive east 19.5 miles to the paved parking area across from Country Cottage store. The trailhead is at the east end of the parking area and is signed as the San Juan Loop Trail.

The hike: From the signed trailhead, you'll embark on the San Juan Loop Trail in a counterclockwise direction. Bear right at the first fork. The loop trail circles the base of a small peak, following a creek much of the way. Soon the trail arrives above San Juan Falls, a pleasant place for the return visit after you've completed this hot hike. The trail then drops down into a narrow, oak-lined canyon.

A mile from the trailhead, near the junction of Bear Creek and San Juan Creek, there's a flat area and the signed intersection with the Chiquito Basin Trail. You cross San Juan Creek, then follow an unnamed creek. All too soon, the trail leaves this peaceful creek and begins switchbacking up the west side of the canyon. Up, up, up the dry slopes you climb on this trail lined with toyon, buckwheat and chamise. The slopes are alive with lizards and horned toads. In spring and early summer, wildflowers abound along the trail. Views are excellent when you emerge in open areas and atop ridges. Just as you despair of ever finding any shade, an oak magically appears.

Five miles from the trailhead, the trail rounds a ridge and bears north toward Lion Canyon. Three-quarters of a mile after rounding the ridge, you'll arrive at a meadow watered by Lion Canyon Creek. There are a number of large oak groves in Lion Canyon. Any one of them makes a splendid picnic spot.

Return the same way. When you arrive at the junction with the San Juan Loop Trail, you may want to bear right and follow this trail through a campground back to your car. Or take the left fork and retrace your steps back to inviting San Juan Falls.

LOS PINOS PEAK

North Main Divide, Los Pinos Trails
From Main Divide Road to Los Pinos Peak is 4.5 miles round trip
with 900-foot elevation gain.

Trail Trivia Question: Name the four highest peaks in Orange County.
1. Santiago Peak (5,687 feet
2. Modjeska Peak (5,496 feet)
3. Trabuco Peak (4,604 feet)
4. Los Pinos Peak (4,510 feet)
Experienced hikers—and others with more than a passing interest in the county's geography—may have guessed numbers one and two—the peaks comprising the landmark Old Saddleback. Orange County's number 3 and number 4 peaks are much more obscure.

Los Pinos Peak, located about three miles as the hawk flies from the southeast corner of Orange County where it meets both San Diego and Riverside counties, offers terrific clear-day vistas and is well worth the moderate hike. From the summit, the hiker looks down to Lake Elsinore and up at snowcapped Mt. Baldy and the high peaks of the San Gabriel Mountains, as well as over to the San Bernardino Mountains and San Jacinto Mountains. Gaze west over miles of hills and valleys to the great blue Pacific.

The wary trekker might suspect that such a view would come at enormous cost but in the case of Los Pinos Peak, only a modest effort is required in order to earn this rewarding panorama.

Another selling point of this hike is that one gets to the trailhead by paved roads. (Veteran travelers of the range's rough dirt roads can tell you what a pain in the axle some of them can be!) The trail itself presents a moderate (but not mountain goat-like) climb.

A great time to scale Los Pinos is in the springtime when lupine, bush poppy and ceanothus splash color on the slopes of the mountain. Crisp, clear autumn days are good ones to head for the peak, too. Winter sometimes dust the crest of Los Pinos with a bit of snow. Stay away from this summit and others in the Santa Anas in summer. It's way too hot for hiking.

Directions to trailhead: From Interstate 5 in San Juan Capistrano, exit on Highway 74 and follow it 22 miles northeast to Long Canyon Road. Turn left (northwest) and follow this paved road 2.5 miles to Blue Jay Campground, then another mile to a pullout on your left. The gated road is signed "North Main." Park in the pullout.

Another way to go: From Interstate 15 in Lake Elsinore, exit on Highway 74 and drive 11 miles southwest to Long Canyon Road, then follow the above directions.

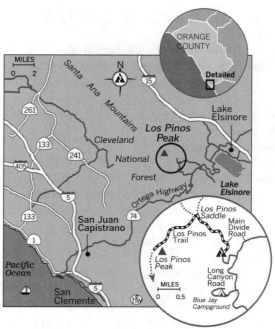

From Highway 74 you can also turn west on Main Divide Road (signed "To Blue Jay Campground") and follow this paved road 4 miles to the trailhead.

Located on Highway 74 between the turnoffs to the trailhead, the hamlet of El Cariso hosts the Country Store, which features an exceptionally well-stocked candy counter guaranteed to please the hiker with a sweet tooth.

The hike: From the gate, follow the wide dirt road, which soon gains elevation and good views. A mile out, look for a particularly good vista of Lake Elsinore and out to high mountain peaks to the north and east.

About 1.25 mile from the start, the road brings you to Los Pinos Saddle, where you'll spot guardrails and a convergence of trails. Leave Main Divide Road, which goes right, and step onto signed Trabuco Trail. Almost immediately look left and fork left onto signed Los Pinos Trail. The path soon gains the top of the ridge and you quickly learn why Los Pinos Trail is often called Los Pinos Ridge Trail.

The steep path gains a high point that is only 20 feet lower in elevation than your goal, then dips, climbs again, dips some more, and finally climbs steeply to the top of Los Pinos Peak. Savor the great views and retrace your steps back to the trailhead.

TENAJA FALLS

Tenaja Falls Trail
1.5 miles round trip with 300-foot elevation gain.

When the Southland is blessed with a rainy, rainy season, Tenaja Falls spills over granite ramparts with great vigor. With five tiers and a drop of some 150 feet, it's a large waterfall, particularly in comparison to other falls in the Santa Ana Mountains.

Tenaja's size is all the more a delightful surprise considering its locale: a rather dry section of the Cleveland National Forest near the boundary of Orange and Riverside counties. Some hikers claim Tenaja Falls is the most intriguing natural highlight of the national forest, and even in that crown jewel of the mountains—the San Mateo Canyon Wilderness.

For Tenaja Falls-bound hikers, there's good news and bad news. Good news: the trail is a wide dirt road, easy enough for the whole family. Bad news: the drive to the trailhead is circuitous to say the least.

For nature photographers, there's one more minor bit of bad news: No viewpoint allows an angle of the whole of Tenaja Falls, that is to say, all five cascades at once.

Two tiers at a time is the usual view from the trail.

For those looking for a longer hike in the area, an adventure awaits: an exploration of the San Mateo Canyon Wilderness. I recommend a 5-mile loop that begins just 1.5 miles down the road from the Tenaja Falls trailhead.

Walk down an old fire road, now a footpath, often lined with wildflowers in spring. About 1.5 miles of travel brings you to Fisherman's Camp, once a drive-in campground and now an oak-and sycamore-shaded trail camp.

From the camp, the path angles north toward San Mateo Canyon and a junction with San Mateo Canyon Trail on the west side of the creek.

To make a loop, hike right, northeast up San Mateo Canyon. You'll cross the creek a couple of times, traveling along brushy banks dotted with oaks. After two miles you'll meet Tenaja Falls Trail just below Tenaja Road. Walk 1.5 miles south on the dirt road back to the trailhead.

Directions to trailhead: Take either Highway 74 or Interstate 15 to Lake Elsinore, and from there drive about 12 miles southeast on I-15 to Wildomar and exit on Clinton Keith Road. Proceed 5 miles southwest, then another 1.8 miles west on Tenaja Road to a signed junction. Fork right on Tenaja Road and continue west for 4 miles. Turn right on paved Rancho California Road and drive a mile to Tenaja Station and a junction with dirt Tenaja Road. Continue another 4.5 miles north to a hairpin turn and a parking area.

The hike: Meander over to the fence that bars motorized entry to the San Mateo Canyon Wilderness. Cross the creek on the concrete vehicle

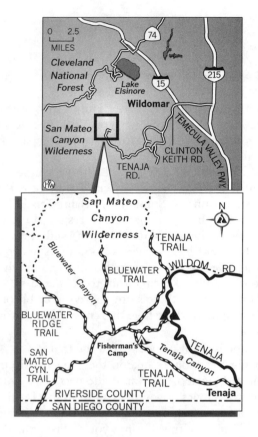

ford. If the creek is high, you'll have to wade across, though skilled rock-hoppers can sometimes cross without getting their boots wet. Another creek-crossing option is to walk along the creek until you find a narrower place to cross.

The trail/road ascends northward over brush-clad slopes and before long serves up distant vistas of Tenaja Falls. Just keep walking toward the falls.

The trail leads right to Tenaja's top tier. Exploration of the lower cascades is tricky, and for experienced rock-climbers only. Those granite boulders are darn slippery.

If you're bound and determined to reach the lower falls, a somewhat safer and saner way to go is retrace your steps back down the trail, then bushwhack through the brush to the banks of the creek.

San Mateo Canyon Wilderness

Fisherman's Camp, San Mateo Canyon Trails
From Tenaja Road to Fisherman's Camp is 3 miles round trip with 300-foot loss; loop via Tenaja Road is 5 miles round trip with 400-foot elevation gain; to Lunch Rock is 8 miles round trip with 400-foot loss

Two-hundred-year-old oaks, tangles of ferns, nettles and wild grape, and the quiet pools of San Mateo Creek make the bottom of San Mateo Canyon a wild and delightful place. This section of the Santa Ana Mountains is steep canyon country, sculpted by seasonal, but vigorous streams. San Mateo Creek, a cascading waterway in winter, slows to a gurgle in summer and flows above ground only sporadically in the fall.

San Mateo Canyon Wilderness, set aside by Congress in 1984, protects 40,000 acres of the Cleveland National Forest, including the headwaters and watershed of San Mateo Creek. During the 1930s, anglers were attracted by superb fishing for steelhead and trout. San Mateo Canyon Trail was a favorite route to the fishing holes. Steelhead ran these waters then; current environmental efforts are being made to coax them back.

San Mateo Canyon takes its name from one of the padres' favorite evangelists and holy men. It's the crown jewel of the Santa Ana Mountains, a relatively untouched wilderness of oaks, potreros and cattail-lined ponds. It's a haven for turtles and rabbits. Spring brings prolific wildflower displays. The canyon drops from 3,500 feet to the coastal plain at Camp Pendleton.

This day hike plunges through the southern part of San Mateo Canyon, easily the wildest place in the Santa Ana Mountains. The San Mateo Canyon Trail and other riding and hiking trails in the wilderness have been in use for more than a century. Volunteers work on the trail, but it's often in rough shape. Creek crossings are sometimes difficult to spot.

You can travel almost as far down the canyon as you like in one day. It's nine miles from Fisherman's Camp to the Marine base, with a hundred ideal picnic spots along the way.

Directions to trailhead: Take either Highway 74 or Interstate 15 to Lake Elsinore, and from there drive southeast on I-15 to Wildomar and exit on Clinton Keith Road. Proceed 5 miles southwest, then another 1.8 miles west on Tenaja Road to a signed junction. Fork right on Tenaja Road and continue west for 4 miles. Turn right on paved Rancho California Road and drive a mile to Tenaja Station and a junction with dirt Tenaja Road. Continue another 3 miles north to small parking area.

The hike: Walk down an old fire road, now a footpath, often lined with wildflowers in spring. About 1.5 miles of travel brings you to Fisherman's Camp, once a drive-in campground and now an oak-and sycamore-shaded trail camp.

From the camp, the path angles north toward San Mateo Canyon and a junction with San Mateo Canyon Trail on the west side of the creek.

To make a loop, hike right, northeast up San Mateo Canyon. You'll cross the creek a couple of times, traveling along brushy banks dotted with oaks. After two miles you'll meet Tenaja Falls Trail just below Tenaja Road. Walk 1.5 miles south on the dirt road back to the trailhead.

Those hikers heading down San Mateo Canyon will follow the trail that climbs among ceanothus to a ridge that offer a view of the canyon. After 0.5 mile, the path switchbacks down to San Mateo Creek and follows it along the heavily vegetated canyon bottom.

Along the creek, the trail may be indistinct; simply continue down-creek. About a mile after reaching the creek, you'll come to a small potrero dotted with oaks and sycamore. Here Bluewater Creek flows into San Mateo Creek and the Bluewater Trail leads off three miles to the Clark Trail and Oak Flat. You can picnic under the oaks near the trail junction and return, or continue down the canyon.

Continue down the creek on the San Mateo Canyon Trail, which follows the right side of the canyon, now and then dropping to wide sandy beaches along bends in the creek. The boulders get bigger, the swimming holes and sunning spots nicer. One flat rock, popular with hikers, has been nicknamed "Lunch Rock." A cluster of massive boulders form pools and cascades in the creek. It's a nice place to linger.

9. RIVERSIDE COUNTY

CROSSING RIVERSIDE COUNTY is a little like crossing the continent: You journey from suburbia to desert spas, from rich agricultural land to pine forests, from snow-capped mountains to sand dunes. This ecological diversity is reflected in the many hiking adventures the county offers from alpine meadows high in the San Jacinto Mountains to the palm oases near Palm Springs.

In addition to the huge recreation areas found wholly or partly within county boundaries—Joshua Tree National Park, Santa Rosa National Scenic Area, San Bernardino National Forest—Riverside also entices the hiker with parks and preserves close to population centers. The Bernasconi Hills near Lake Perris and the Box Springs Mountains behind Riverside are not well-known destinations, but they offer a pleasant time for the sojourner afoot.

Formed in 1893 from parts of San Bernardino and San Diego Counties, Riverside County's rich soil and benign climate made it an ideal location for growing navel oranges. By 1900, residents of the "Orange Empire" around Riverside enjoyed one of the largest per capita incomes in the world.

In recent decades, the county has witnessed phenomenal Inland Empire-style growth; that is to say the construction of many highways and suburbs. The short hike to the top of 1,337-foot Mt. Rubidoux, located on the west side of Riverside, offers a superb 360-degree panorama of the county—one very different from the view of a century ago.

With such rapid development, the county's parks have a critical "breathing room" role to play. Riverside has an enthusiastic county parks department, which has ambitious plans to improve its trail system.

MT. RUBIDOUX

Mt. Rubidoux Trail
3 mile loop with 500-foot elevation gain

The isolated, 1,337-foot high granite hill towering above the Riverside's western edge has long been a landmark to travelers and residents alike, ever since the 1880s when Riverside emerged as the quintessential Southern California citrus town. The mountain was named for one of its 19th-century owners, wealthy ranchero Louis Robidoux.

Frank Miller, owner of the lavish, pride-of-Riverside Mission Inn, purchased the mountain in 1906 with the intention of using the mountain as an attraction to sell residential lots at its base. Mt. Rubidoux was landscaped and a road constructed to the summit, where a cross was planted. Some historians believe America's first Easter sunrise service took place atop Rubidoux in 1909 and inspired similar observances around the continent.

Credit the developers for going all out on the road; they hired the engineer who designed Yellowstone National Park's road system. While the developers originally viewed Rubidoux strictly as a way to boost lot sales, their vision (particularly Miller's) soon expanded dramatically.

The road to Rubidoux was designed to be more than a mere recreational walk or drive; it was a pilgrimage to a cross and to monuments of famous men of the time. This "trail of shrines" ascended to a long white cross honoring missionary Father Junipero Serra credited, by early developers anyway, for "the beginning of civilization in California." Thus today's pilgrim views an assortment of plaques, monuments and memorials on Rubidoux that is eclectic and eccentric.

Rubidoux's most significant sights-to-see are the Peace Tower and Friendship Bridge. Frank Miller was a lifelong advocate for world peace and his friends constructed the distinct tower to honor him in 1925.

For many, many years, Mt. Rubidoux was a drive, not a hike. Arrows painted on rocks indicated an "up" route and "down" route for autos. The mountain has been closed to vehicles since 1992.

Autumn sunsets, when nearby mountains glow red, purple and blue, are particularly memorable. Winter brings vistas of snow-capped summits.

Locals access the mountain from several trailheads, but the best route for first-time Rubidoux ramblers is by way of the Ninth Street gate, an inspired beginning for what can be an inspiring jaunt.

Directions to trailhead: From the Pomona Freeway (60) in Riverside, exit on Market Street and proceed east into downtown. Turn west (right) on Mission Inn Avenue and drive 7 blocks to Redwood Drive. Turn left and head 2 blocks to 9th Street, turn right and continue 2 more blocks to the distinct trailhead (gated Mt. Rubidoux Drive) on the left. Park safely and courteously on adjacent residential streets.

From the Riverside Freeway (91) in Riverside, exit on University Avenue and head west through downtown to Redwood Drive. Turn left, travel one block, then turn right on 9th Street. Proceed two more blocks to this hike's start on the left.

The hike: Pass through the entry gate and walk along and landscaped lane past pepper trees, eucalyptus and huge beaver tail cactus. After 0.3 mile of southbound travel, the road makes a very tight hairpin turn north and nearly—but not quite—intersects the downward leg of Mt. Rubidoux Road, which makes a similar hairpin turn from north to south. Note this junction because on your return journey you'll need to cross from one leg of the road to the other to close the loop.

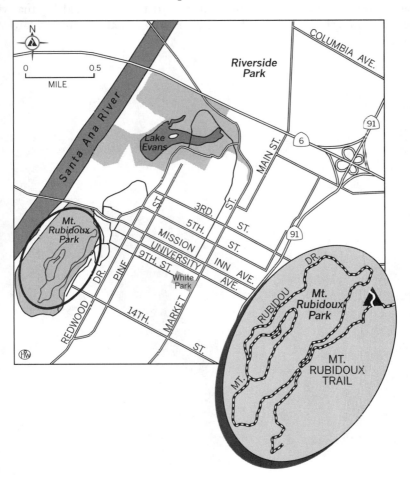

The road ascends rather bare slopes, dotted with brittle bush, mustard and century plant. Lupine and California poppies brighten the way in spring.

After passing a memorial to Henry E. Huntington, "man of affairs, large in his bounty, yet wise," the road bends west, then south. City views are exchanged for more rural ones, including the Santa Ana River that gave Riverside its name.

The main Mt. Rubidoux road junctions a circular summit road, which you'll join to see the sights—the Peace Tower, Friendship Bridge and plenty of plaques. From the Father Junipero Serra Cross at the summit or from one of the peak's other fine vista points, partake of the 360-degree panorama of great mountains and metro-Riverside.

Return to the main Mt. Rubidoux Road for a short (0.75 mile) descent that loops south, east, then back north. Just as this downward leg bends sharply south, leave the road and step over to the other road leg that you used to ascend the mountain. Retrace your steps a final 0.3 mile back to 9th Street.

Box Springs Mountain

Skyline Trail
4- to 6-mile loop with 500-foot elevation gain

Far too steep for suburban housing developments, the Box Springs Mountains in Riverside County remain a place to get away from it all. "It" in this instance is the hustle and bustle of the Inland Empire which surrounds this little-known mountain range.

Little-known the mountains may be, but remote they are not. Four freeways—the San Bernardino, Riverside, Pomona and Escondido—surround the Box Springs Mountains. Their location might remind football fans of a quarterback barking signals: "10-91-60-215-Hike!"

The peaks of the range rise sharply from the floor of the Moreno Valley to 3,000 feet and offer commanding clear-day views of the city of Riverside, the San Bernardino and San Jacinto Mountains, as well as a great portion of the Inland Empire.

The mountain's namesake peak, as well as 2,389 acres of native Southern California coastal sage terrain is preserved in Box Springs Mountain Park under the jurisdiction of Riverside County. The park is a natural island amidst one of the fastest growing urban and suburban areas in California.

Vegetation includes members of the coastal sage scrub community: chamise, lemonade berry, brittlebush, white sage, black sage and buckwheat. More than 30 types of wildflowers brighten the park's slopes in the spring.

Wildlife—coyotes, jackrabbits, skunks and kangaroo rats—is attracted by the tiny springs that trickle from the mountain. Wildlife biologists call Box Springs Mountain a "habitat island" because it provides a home for animals while being surrounded by development.

The mountains, along with "The Badlands" to the east of the range, were shaped in part by the San Jacinto Fault, a major branch of the San Andreas system. Some geologists believe that the granites of Box Springs were once attached to the granites of the San Jacinto Mountains but were moved to their present location, some 20 miles, by lateral displacement along the fault.

Perhaps the most eccentric resident of Box Springs Mountain was Helene Troy Arlington, who moved to the mountain in 1945. The self-styled hermit secluded herself in a mountain retreat she called Noli Me Tangere, a Latin phrase meaning "Do Not Touch Me."

Arlington was devoted to dogs, particularly Dalmatians, and kept many of them in her home. She wrote canine poems and magazine articles under the pen name "Dear Dog Lady." On a plot of land next to her home she established "Arlington Cemetery," a final resting place for her four-legged friends.

Dogs, in fact, were her only friends. She sold her land to the Riverside

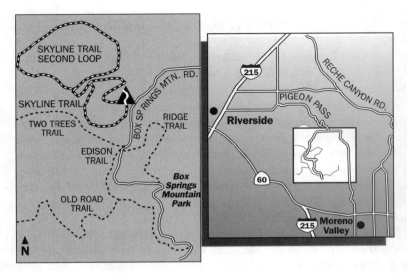

County Parks Department in 1974 and moved to Arlington, Virginia to be near the grave of her long-dead husband Masefield. She wrote the parks department: "There was no reason to remain there any longer, as I still do not have one friend in California."

Park trails include 3-mile long Pigeon Pass Trail, which offers great views, and 1.5 mile long Ridge Trail which travels over Box Spring Mountain. (Avoid Two Trees Trail, which climbs from Two Trees Road in Riverside to meet Box Springs Mountain Road inside the park. Trailhead access is poor, as is the trail itself.)

The park's premier path is Skyline Trail, which loops around Box Springs Mountain. If Riverside can be said to have a skyline, this is it; not tall office buildings but skyscraping granite and a top-of-the-world view.

Directions to trailhead: From the Pomona Freeway (60) in Moreno Valley, exit on Pigeon Pass Road. Proceed some 4.5 miles north, then a short distance west. Pigeon Pass Road turns north again, but you continue west, joining a dirt road and following the signs into Box Springs Mountain Park. Signed Skyline Trail is on your right.

The hike: From Box Springs Mountain Road, Skyline Trail heads west, soon serving up views of the city of Riverside. Next the trail contours north, passing rock outcroppings that are geologically and aesthetically similar to those found atop Mt. Rubidoux, Riverside landmark and site of a long-popular Easter service.

The path comes to an unsigned junction. Skyline Trail angles east and begins contouring around a hill back to the trailhead. Hardier hikers will join an extension of the trail known as "Second Loop" and make an even larger circle back to the trailhead.

LAKE PERRIS

Terri Peak Trail

From Campfire Center to Terri Peak is 3.5 miles round trip with 800-foot elevation gain; to Indian Museum, return via lakeshore, is 6 miles round trip

Perris in the Spring. No need to battle the hordes of tourists flocking to that other similar-sounding place of romance across the Atlantic. No need to travel 6,000 miles and spend lots of money to have a good time.

For just a few francs you can visit a manmade wonder, Lac de Paris, otherwise known as Lake Perris State Recreation Area. So pack *du pain et du vin* and head for the most romantic Pomona Freeway offramp in all of Southern California.

Few nature lovers—or lovers of any kind—have discovered the romance of Perris. True, a million and a half visitors come to the lake each year, but the only nature most are interested in is that found wriggling on the end of a hook.

While the parc is oriented to *les autos et les bateaux,* there is a network of trails for those visitors who wish to explore Perris à pied. Perris pace-setters will enjoy the trek to Terri Peak, easily the most romantic spot in all of the Bernasconi Hills.

Springtime colors the hills with a host of wild fleurs, including goldfields, California poppy, fiddleneck, baby blue eyes and blue dicks. The view from Terri Peak on smog-free days is *très fantastique.*

Directions to trailhead: From the Pomona Freeway (60), a few miles east of its intersection with I-215, exit on Moreno Beach Drive and proceed 4 miles to the park. Immediately after paying your state park day use fee at the entry kiosk, turn right on Lake Perris Drive. Look sharply right for the strange-looking international symbol indicating a campfire and an amphitheater. Park in the campfire/interpretive center lot. The unsigned trail begins to the left of the campfire area.

The hike: The trail ascends gradually west and occasionally intersects a horse trail. The unsigned path is tentative at first but an occasional wooden post helps keep you on the trail, which climbs boulder-strewn slopes.

The coastal scrub community—sage, buckwheat, chamise and toyon predominates. Also much in evidence are weedy-looking non-native species, as well as mustard, prickly pear cactus, morning glory and Russian thistle.

The trail climbs to a small flat meadow then turns southwest and climbs more earnestly to the peak. From atop Terri Peak, enjoy clear-day views of the San Bernardino Mountains to the northeast and the Santa Ana Mountains to the southwest. Below is fast-growing Moreno Valley, checkerboarded alternately with green fields and subdivisions. You can see all of Lake Perris, Alessandro Island, and hundreds of boaters, anglers and swimmers.

The trail from Terri Peak down to the Indian Museum is sometimes in poor condition. You may lose the trail a couple of times; however you won't get lost because it's easy to stay oriented with the lakeshore on your left and the Indian Museum ahead.

After a steep descent, the trail bends sharply east and deposits you at the Indian Museum's parking lot. The museum includes exhibits interpreting the Cahuilla, Chemehuevi, Serrano and other desert tribes and how they adapted to life in the Mojave Desert region.

From the museum, you follow the asphalt road down to Lake Perris Drive, cross this main park road and continue down to Perris Beach. Here, and at Moreno Beach one mile to the west, you may cool off with a swim.

Improvise a route along the lakeshore using the sidewalk and bicycle trail until you spot the main campground entrance on your left. Enter the campground, pass the kiosk, then pick up the intermittent footpath that winds through the campground. This path and some improvisation will bring you to Lake Perris Drive and back to the trailhead.

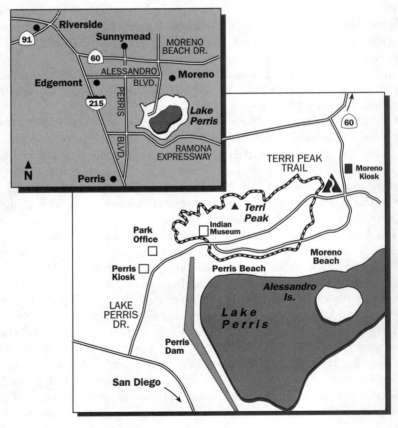

Santa Rosa Plateau Preserve

Trans Preserve Trail
4-mile loop

Hard-riding Spanish vaqueros called the deep holes in creekbeds tenajas. The holes held water year-around and provided crucial summer water sources for both cows and cowboys. Today the tenajas (Spanish for "tanks") offer habitat for such amphibians as the western pond turtle and red-legged frog.

Tenajas, ancient Engelmann oaks, and more than 3,000 acres of rolling grassland are preserved in Santa Rosa Plateau Preserve, located at the southern end of the Santa Ana Mountains in Riverside County. The plateau is pastoral Southern California at its finest, that is to say the least changed since the days of the caballeros and gracious haciendas. Atop the plateau, time seems to have stopped at 1840.

Off the plateau, it's very much the 21st century; that is to say, huge housing developments have pushed up Clinton Keith Road and left the plateau something of an island on the land. The island was saved from Inland Empire-style development when, in 1991, a major plateau land owner agreed to sell 3,800 acres to the Nature Conservancy, greatly increasing the size of the preserve.

The preserve is more than a park or some much-needed breathing room in this fast-developing part of the Southland; it's an ecological treasure. Santa Rosa Plateau has been recognized by UNESCO as a biosphere reserve, one of only three such special places in all of California.

Now protected is one of the last healthy stands of Engelmann oaks; these trees were once widespread throughout the western U.S., but now range only between San Diego and Santa Barbara. For reasons researchers can't quite figure, most stands of Engelmann oaks contain just a few venerable specimens that are incapable of regeneration. The Engelmann oaks on Santa Rosa Plateau, however, are quite healthy.

Engelmann oaks are gnarled fellows, with a kind of checkered trunk and grayish leaves. When you visit the preserve you'll observe that Engelmanns are noticeably different from their more common cousins, the coast live oaks. Coast live oaks are fuller, with smoother bark and leaves that are shiny green. Usually, the coast live oaks grow in lower, wetter locales, while the Engelmanns take higher and drier ground.

Directions to trailhead: From Interstate 15 in Riverside County, southeast of Lake Elsinore and northwest of Murrietta and the junction with Interstate 215, exit on Clinton Keith Road. Follow the road about 5 miles south. Just as the road makes a sharp bend west and becomes Tenaja Road, you'll spot a turnout and the main gate of Santa Rosa Plateau Preserve. Park in a safe manner off the road.

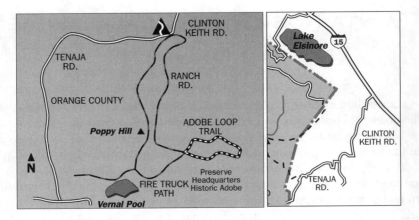

The hike: At the main gate, scan the bulletin boards, pick up a preserve map, then join the Trans Preserve Trail.

The trail heads south across grassy slopes, dips into an oak-filled draw, then contours around Poppy Hill. To the west you'll see Ranch Road, your return route to the trailhead, and to the east, on private land, some cows grazing.

If you use your imagination, you can step back a century and a half in time, when Santa Rosa Plateau was part of 47,000-acre Rancho Santa Rosa given to cattle rancher Juan Moreno by Governor Pio Pico. The land was held by various ranching companies until 1984 when the Nature Conservancy acquired the land from the Kaiser Corporation and established the preserve.

Follow Trans Preserve Trail and signs to Mesa de Colorado and Vernal Pools. Atop the mesa, you'll find (at least after winter rains) a couple vernal pools, some of the last in Southern California. The mesa is capped with basalt, which means its an ideal rainwater collector. Depressions in the rock collect water into seasonal ponds called vernal pools. When winter and spring rains fill the ponds, the pools are visited by ducks, geese and other waterfowl. Wildflowers—particularly goldfields—are much in evidence when the water recedes.

After visiting the pools, decend to the main dirt road called Ranch Road and head east toward a windmill. You'll soon come upon an old adobe and some ranch buildings, now used as preserve headquarters.

If you want to tour a little more of the preserve, continue east past preserve headquarters on Ranch Road, which becomes a footpath. On a clear day, you might be able to get a glimpse of Oceanside and the wide blue Pacific, about twenty miles away. Pick up signed Adobe Trail which meanders among old oaks, passes an olive grove, and loops back to headquarters.

Follow Ranch Road back to the trailhead.

10. SAN BERNARDINO MOUNTAINS

When that restless breed of American—the trapper, the trader, the Army mapmaker—pushed westward, they had to reckon with the arid country beyond the lower Colorado River. The Mojave Desert gave sustenance to few, and mercy to none. And if crossing the desert's uncharted sands wasn't enough of a problem, another formidable obstacle barred the way west—the San Bernardino Mountains. Sheer granite cliffs, thorny chaparral, snowbound passes.

The San Bernardino range is a vast fault block about sixty miles long and thirty miles wide, extending in a southwesterly direction across Southern California. The western portion is plateau-like with some rather broad uplands—unusual for Southern California mountains. At its western end, the mountains terminate abruptly at Cajon Pass, which separates the range from the San Gabriel Mountains. Geologists speculate that the two ranges may originally have been one. Rocks on both sides of the pass suggest the earth's convulsions wrenched the mountains fifteen to twenty-five miles apart. The earth is still shuddering in this area; the San Andreas Fault runs through the pass. It's an excellent place to observe fault features and view this Maker and Shaker of Continents.

Although the two ranges look something alike at first glance, they aren't the same age. The San Gabriels are more sheer, more faulted. The San Bernardinos are younger, less fractured by earthquakes.

The southern slopes of the San Bernardinos consist of high ridges cut by many deep stream gorges. At the western end of the highest ridge is San Bernardino Peak. The ridge culminates toward the east in Mt. San Gorgonio (Old Grayback, 11,502 feet), the highest peak in Southern California. To the south, San Gorgonio Pass separates the San Bernardinos from the San Jacinto Range. The discovery of the pass in 1853 enabled Los Angeles to be tied to the rest of the United States by railroad line.

By the mid-nineteenth century, industrious Mormons and other settlers invaded the San Bernardinos. They drove the Serrano and Cahuilla Indians into the desert. Newcomers clear-cut miles of forest, dammed and channeled the wild rivers into irrigation ditches, and dynamited the mountains in search of gold.

But not all visitors blasted, mined and milled. Some came to relax in the alpine air and enjoy the good life. Summer tents and homes clustered around high-country lakes. To many people, the San Bernardinos no longer seemed so remote, so formidable.

A large portion of the San Bernardino Mountains was protected by the establishment of the San Bernardino Forest Reserve, created by President Benjamin Harrison in 1893. Subsequently, the name "Reserve" was changed to "National Forest." In 1908, the San Bernardino National Forest and Angeles National Forest were brought together and administered under the latter's name, but in 1925, President Coolidge divided them.

The San Bernardino National Forest is a huge parcel of land, bigger than the state of Rhode Island, the second-largest national forest in California (first is Los Padres). It's also one of the most heavily used national forests in the nation.

Rim of the World Highway, leading from San Bernardino to Lake Arrowhead and Big Bear Lake, opened up the mountains to recreation on a large scale. Chiseled into rock walls, the road takes many a switchback and hairpin turn, following the crest of the range and ascending to more than 7,000 feet. Even the highway's primitive forerunners—with their forty-one percent grades—didn't stop thousands of guns and fishing rods from assaulting the wilderness. Big Bear and Arrowhead Lakes became one of Southern California's most popular resort areas. The rustic hotels, spas and lodges delighted Southern Californians in the same manner the Catskills and Berkshires served the needs of New Yorkers and New Englanders.

Many quiet places in the 700,000-acre San Bernardino National Forest beckon the hiker to behold waterfalls, stunning fields of flowers, and golden eagles soaring above lofty crags. The San Gorgonio Wilderness contains all the delights of these mountains, and none of its "civilization." The San Gorgonio Wild Area was created by a law in 1931 as a place free of restaurants and roads, camps and resorts. In 1965, Congress declared it a Wilderness.

Seventy-one miles of hiking trails wind through this high-country wilderness, a 56,000-acre refuge from the glass and chrome world far below. On the high spine of the range, Mt. San Gorgonio and other 10,000-plus foot peaks—Dobbs, Jepson, Charlton and San Bernardino—stand shoulder to shoulder. When you reach the summit on one of these peaks, you'll be only 90 miles from downtown Los Angeles and two miles high, but the city will seem more remote than the map indicates, and you'll feel much higher.

DEEP CREEK

Pacific Crest Trail
From Highway 173 to Deep Creek Hot Springs is 12 miles round trip
with 800-foot elevation gain; from Mojave River Forks Dam to
Deep Creek Hot Springs is 8 miles round trip with 800-foot gain

Kick off your boots and slip into the relaxing waters of Deep Creek, site of the only hot spring in the San Bernardino Mountains. Float awhile and gaze up at the sky. Feel your urban anxieties vaporize in one of nature's hot tubs.

Deep Creek is a study in contrasts. Upstream it contains pools of great size, flanked by sheer masses of stone. The water has scoured great basins and the creek bounds down the water-worn rocks from one pool to the other. The pools are home to rainbow trout, which attract anglers. Downstream Deep Creek is but a shadow of its former self. It ends ingloriously in the desert sands; only water-polished stones indicate its path.

This fine hike travels a well-built stretch of Pacific Crest Trail. The trailhead, formerly at Mojave River Forks Dam, has been relocated to Highway 173. The Army Corps of Engineers has closed the dam to the public. However, many day hikers still begin this trail at the dam. Call the San Bernardino National Forest, Arrowhead Ranger District, in Rimforest for the latest trail information.

The trash situation sometimes gets out of hand in the vicinity of the hot springs. Make sure you pack out what you packed in. Due to frequent injuries caused by broken glass, the Forest Service now prohibits the possession of glass containers in the Deep Creek area.

The hot springs can be crowded on weekends. Bronzed children frolic at water's edge, adults emit gurgles of delight as they settle into the soothing

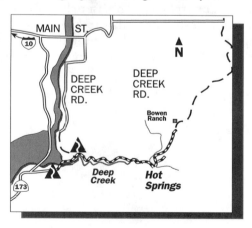

heat, and hikers of all ages enjoy a reward for a hike well-done. Weekdays, the springs are deserted you'll probably "take the cure" by yourself.

Directions to trailhead: From Interstate Highway 15, a few miles north of Cajon Pass, take the Hesperia turnoff. Go east through Hesperia on Main Street, following it as it curves south at the outskirts of town. Turn left (east) on Rock Springs Road. If the bed of the Mojave River is dry, you're in luck. Cross it and turn right (south) on Deep Creek Road. Follow this road to pavement's end. Bear left on a dirt road and drive straight up the spillway of the Mojave River Forks Flood Control Dam. Don't worry, you won't drive into a reservoir; the dam holds no water. The trail begins at the east (left) end of the parking lot.

Directions to Highway 173 trailhead: Exit Interstate 15 on Highway 138. Go right (east) 9 miles and veer left on Highway 173, following the latter highway 8 miles to pavement's end. At the point where the dirt road begins, you'll find parking and a signed trailhead for the Pacific Crest Trail.

The hike: (From Highway 173) The trail heads on a straight line for Deep Creek Canyon. It follows the roadbed of an asphalt road (broken-up, but not removed) through sagebrush down into the lower reaches of Deep Creek near its meeting with the Mojave River. Uncontrolled motorcycle and all terrain vehicle use has seriously eroded the creekbed.

The trail proceeds on the right bank of the creek. Cross the creek and pick up the trail on the other side. You can scramble around to the top of the dam and make your way over to the spillway, where good trail resumes.

Past the spillway, you'll find another signed trailhead for Pacific Crest Trail. Ascend five easy switchbacks to the north canyon wall. You stay high on the almost-barren wall for 2 miles until the trail descends to Deep Creek, then crosses it on an arched bridge. Now you follow the south slope for another mile and reach oak-shaded McKinley Creek. This is a good area for picnicking, cooling-off, or exploring. The last mile of trail contours along the south slope, then drops down close to the creek just before the hot springs.

The hot springs, enclosed by rocks bordering the creek, range from warm to hot. Pick your spot. After you've mellowed out, return the same way.

Lake Arrowhead

North Shore Trail
From North Shore Campground to Little Bear Creek is 5 miles round trip
with 600-foot elevation gain; Season: April-November

The Lake Arrowhead country is the prettiest alpine area in the San
Bernardino Mountains. A nice place to stroll when you're visiting Arrowhead is the tranquil canyon cut by Little Bear Creek, a woodsy retreat shaded by sugar pines and Jeffrey pines, oaks, sycamores and incense cedars

This is an easy hike, suitable for the whole family, but keep in mind that
it's an upside-down walk; the elevation gain occurs on the way back.

Directions to trailhead: From Interstate 10 in San Bernardino, take the
Waterman Avenue/Highway 18 exit and wind 20 miles north into the San
Bernardino Mountains. When Highway 18 junctions with 173, take the lat-
ter highway and proceed 3.5 miles to Hospital Road and turn right.

Late in the year, when the snow sticks, the Forest Service closes North-
shore Campground until spring. However, day hikers may park in the upper
lot at Mountains Community Hospital and walk the short distance into the
campground. The trailhead is just off the campground road between campsites 10 and 11.

The hike: Head down-slope, continue straight at an unsigned four-way
junction and drop to a dirt road. On the other side of the road you'll join
signed Trail 3W12, pass by a seasonal creek and descend into the handsome
canyon of Little Bear Creek.

Bracken ferns line the trickling creek. Keep an eye out for the wild
turkeys that patrol the canyon. Enjoy the sounds of the wind blowing
through the pines, the murmuring creek. Norman-style Arrowhead Village
and a shopping mall are just over the next ridge, but the resort might as well
be a hundred miles away.

The trail leaves the creek, humps over a knoll, then rejoins it after 0.25-
mile. Hang out along one of the bends in the creek before returning the way
you came. If you want to walk
every foot of North Shore Trail,
continue to a creek crossing,
boulder-hop over Little Bear
Creek, and soon come to the
trail's inglorious end at Hook
Creek Road and an area popular
with off-highway vehicles.

Heap's Peak

Heap's Peak Trail
0.75-mile loop through Arboretum. Season: April-November

San Bernardino National Forest is not only huge, it's botanically diverse; the forest hosts ecological communities ranging from sage brush to sub-alpine, from Joshua tree to limber pine. One of the best places to learn about national forest flora is at Heap's Peak Arboretum, located near the tiny San Bernardino Mountains community of Running Springs. Most of the arboreteum is filled with mixed stands of pine and fir—the typical forest community of these parts. In addition, the arboretum grows trees and shrubs that are representative of other parts of the forest.

A walk through the arboretum is a relaxing—and quite educational—experience. Numbered stops along the trail are keyed to a pamphlet which can be picked up at the trailhead. The entertaining pamphlet, published by the Rim-of-the-World Interpretive Association, is a mini-botany course.

Nature lovers of all hiking abilities will learn something from the interpretive displays along Heap's Peak Trail. Did you know that the willow contains salicylic acid, the active ingredient in asprin? Did you know that the Coulter pine's 8-pound pine cones are the world's largest?

It's hard not to like a nature trail that begins with the forest philosophy of Buddha and ends with the natural history of the gooseberry.

Directions to trailhead: From Interstate 10 in Redlands, exit on Highway 30 and doggedly follow the highway signs through minor detours and suburbs-in-the-making. As Highway 30 begins to climb into the San Bernardino Mountains, it becomes Highway 330. Eighteen miles from Redlands, you'll reach a highway junction on the outskirts of Running Springs. You'll bear northwest on Highway 18 (following signs toward Lake Arrowhead). Four miles of driving along this winding mountain road brings you to Heap's Peak Arboretum. There's plenty of parking just off the road.

Siberia Creek

Siberia Creek Trail
From Forest Road 2N11 to Champion Lodgepole Pine is 1 mile round trip
with 100-foot loss; to The Gunsight is 3 miles round trip with 600-foot loss;
to Siberia Creek Trail Camp is 8 miles round trip with 2,500-foot loss;
Season: April-November

California nurtures some superlative trees. The tallest tree on Earth is a coast redwood, the oldest tree a bristlecone pine. And in the San Bernardino Mountains gows the world champion lodgepole pine.

It's a pleasant stroll, suitable for the whole family, to the world champion. More ambitious hikers will enjoy tramping down Siberia Creek Trail to the appropriately named rock formation "The Gunsight," and on to Siberia Creek Trail Camp for a picnic.

Siberia Creek, born atop the high mountains near Big Bear Lake, is a delightful watercourse. It flows southwest through a deep coniferous forest and lush meadowlands, then cascades down a steep rocky gorge and adds it waters to Bear Creek.

From Forest Road 2N11, Siberia Creek Trail passes the Champion Lodgepole, the largest known lodgepole pine in the world. It then travels alongside Siberia Creek through a wet tableland, detours around a ridge while Siberia Creek crashes down a precipitous gorge, then rejoins the creek at Siberia Creek Trail Camp.

This is an "upside-down" hike; the tough part is the trek uphill back to the trailhead. Pace yourself accordingly.

Directions to trailhead: From Highway 18 at the west end of Big Bear Lake Village, turn south on Tulip Lane. You'll pass Coldbrook Campground on the right, and 0.5-mile from the highway, turn right on Forest Road 2N11. Follow the "Champion Lodgepole" signs five miles to the signed trailhead. Parking is alongside the road.

The hike: The trail follows a fern-lined little brook. You'll notice some tall cornstalk-like plants—corn lilies—and a generous number of red flowers—Indian paintbrush.

A half-mile's travel brings you to a signed junction. Go right 75 yards to the Champion Lodgepole, which towers above the east end of an emerald green meadow. You can't miss it. It's the only 110-foot tree around.

Lodgepole—also called tamarack—pines are usually found at higher elevations, but here at 7,500 feet, nurtured by the rich, well-watered soil, they not only thrive, but achieve mammoth proportions. The World Champion is 75 inches in diameter (the species usually measures 12 to 24 inches), and is estimated to be more than 400 years old. Lodgepoles are easily identified by their yellow-green paired needles.

While hiking in Southern California, these pines are probably the only ones you'll come across that have two needles per bundle. By way of comparison, you might notice that the pinyon pine has one needle, the ponderosa three, and the limber pine five.

To The Gunsight: Return to the main trail and continue through open forest, skirting the meadowland. You cross and recross Siberia Creek. After the second crossing, the meadowland ends and the creek crashes down the gorge. The trail avoids the gorge and swings down and around the steep slopes of Lookout Mountain. About one mile from the Champion Lodgepole, an interesting rock formation called the Gunsight appears. Squint through the Gunsight at the metropolis trapped in the haze below.

From The Gunsight, the trail descends the slopes of Lookout Mountain. A series of switchbacks brings you to a trail junction. Bear right (north) on the Seven Pines Trail and proceed 0.75-mile to Siberia Creek Trail Camp. For the day hiker, this oak- and alder-shaded camp makes a nice picnic spot or rest stop.

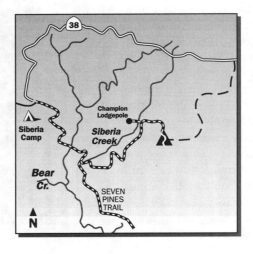

FAWNSKIN

Grout Bay, Grays Peak Trails
From Grout Bay Picnic Area to Grays Peak is 6 miles round trip
with 1,000-foot elevation gain

Even today, Grout Bay doesn't sound like a place to play. The name suggests mortar, not lakeshore, and offers no clue to the considerable attractions offered by the bay and the woodsy hiking trail that offers vistas of Big
Bear Lake.

Back in 1919, Los Angeles businessmen William Cline and Clinton
Miller ran into serious consumer resistance when they tried to lure vacationers to the upscale summer resort they were developing on the north shore
of Big Bear Lake. Marketing a community called Grout was difficult to say
the least; Grout had to go.

The developers changed the name to Fawnskin, appropriating the name
from a nearby meadow. While the name evokes images of Bambi, Fawnskin's
origin is one guaranteed to upset an animal rights activist. Back in 1891,
hunters shot many deer fawns, stretched their hides on trees, and promptly
disappeared. As the story goes, subsequent travelers observed the fawn skins
and began referring to the meadow and surrounding area as Fawnskin.

During the 1920s, Fawnskin expanded to include the Swiss chalet-style
Fawn Lodge, complete with tea room, a general store, post office, more
than 100 fairly pricey homes along the lakeshore and in the surrounding
woods, as well as the Theatre of the Stars, a stage for musicals and dramas.

A bit west of Fawnskin proper stood Gray's Lodge, a pier, store and
rental cabins owned by Alex Gray. Gray's name now graces a boat landing
and a 7,880-foot peak.

As for the name Grout, it didn't entirely slip between the cracks: Grout
Bay and Grout Bay Trail remain on the map, perhaps a reminder that a
name isn't everything.

Grout Bay Trail begins in the piney woods above the lake and climbs to
the summit of Grays Peak. The trail begins at the outskirts of the drowsy
hamlet of Fawnskin, where a couple of eateries offer the hiker pre-hike sustenance or post-hike refreshment.

Directions to trailhead: From the far west end of Big Bear Lake at the
junction of Highway 18 (Big Bear Boulevard) and Highway 38 (North
Shore Drive), take the latter highway northeast 2.5 miles to the outer fringe
of Fawnskin. Turn west into the trail parking lot of the Grout Bay Picnic
Area.

The hike: The well-graded, signed path begins a moderate ascent over
wooded slopes and soon offers views of Fawnskin, Grout Bay and Windy

Point. Vistas soon close up as the trail traverses more heavily timbered terrain.

A bit less than a mile out, Grout Bay Trail meets and joins dirt Forest Service Road 2N68E. Assisted by a couple of "Trail" signs, follow the road west about 0.4 mile. (Grout Bay Trail resumes as a footpath and heads north toward Fawnskin Valley.)

This hike leaves the road and follows the signed trail west toward Grays Peak. Long, finely engineered switchbacks aid the ascent past conifers, jumbo boulders and impressive specimens of manzanita.

The trail ends just short of the peak at a rock outcropping, which provides a superb overlook of the lake, valley and surrounding San Bernardino Mountains, as well as fine picnic spot.

Big Bear Lake

Pine Knot Trail
From Aspen Glen Picnic Area to Grand View Point is 6.5 miles round trip
with 1,200-foot elevation gain; Season: April-November

Rim of the World Highway offers the traveler a fine view of Big Bear Lake. A better view, a hiker's view, is available from Pine Knot Trail, which climbs the handsome, pine-studded slopes above the lake and offers far-reaching panoramas of the San Bernardino Mountains.

Big Bear Lake is a great place to escape the crowded metropolis, and Pine Knot Trail is a great way to escape sometimes-crowded Big Bear Lake.

The idea for Big Bear Lake came from Redlands citrus growers, who wanted to impound a dependable water source for their crops. Farmers and city founders formed Bear Valley Land and Water Co. and in 1884, at a cost of $75,000, built a stone-and-cement dam, thus forming Big Bear Lake. In 1910 a second, larger dam was built near the first one. This second dam is the one you see today.

Pine Knot Trail takes its name from the little community of cabins, stores and saloons that sprang up when Rim of the World Highway was completed. After World War II the town of Pine Knot changed its name to Big Bear Lake Village.

While Pine Knot Trail offers grand views of the lake, this hike's destination—Grand View Point—does not overlook the lake. The grand view is a breathtaking panorama of the San Gorgonio Wilderness and the deep canyon cut by the Santa Ana River.

Grand views of Big Bear Lake from Pine Knot Trail

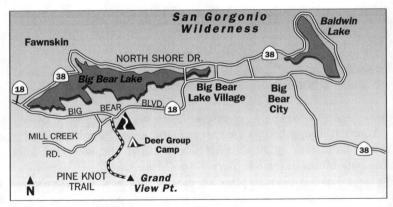

Directions to trailhead: From California 18 in Big Bear Lake Village, turn southwest on Mill Creek Road and proceed about a half-mile to Aspen Glen Picnic Area on your left. The signed trail departs from the east end of the picnic area by Mill Creek Road.

The hike: From Aspen Glen Picnic Area, Pine Knot Trail climbs a low, lupine-sprinkled ridge. The path follows a fence line for a short distance, then dips into and out of a willow-lined creek bed. You will get great over-the-shoulder views of the south shore of Big Bear Lake.

Ascending through Jeffrey pine and ponderosa pine forests, the trail meets and joins a fire road; after a short distance, it again becomes a footpath. Now your over-the-shoulder view is of the north shore of Big Bear Lake.

Pine Knot Trail passes near one of the runs of the Snow Forest Ski Area, then meanders through an enchanted area of castellated rocks. About 2 miles from the trailhead the trail intersects dirt Forest Service Road 2N17. Before you is a meadow, a rather amusing-looking landscape decorated with boulders, ponderosa pine, Indian paintbrush and skunk cabbage. Bear left on the dirt road for just 50 feet or so, then pick up the signed footpath again.

Passing black oak and willow, Pine Knot Trail skirts the moist meadow and soon arrives at Deer Group Camp. Benches and tables suggest a picnic or rest stop.

From the camp, continue on Pine Knot Trail, which crosses and then parallels another dirt Forest Service road. Ahead of you are tantalizing views of San Gorgonio Wilderness peaks—just a hint of things to come when you reach trail's end.

About a mile from Deer Group Camp, the trail intersects dirt Forest Service Road 2N11. Cross the road and follow the signed trail on a 0.25-mile ascent to the top of a ridgeline.

From Grand View Point, enjoy views of the San Gorgonio Wilderness, a panorama of Southern California's highest peaks.

COUGAR CREST

Cougar Crest Trail
From Highway 38 to Bertha Peak is 6 miles round trip with 1,100-foot elevation gain; Season: April-November

Cougar Crest, the forested ridge between Big Bear Lake and Holcomb Valley is a treat for hikers. From the ridge, as well as from the ridge's two prominent peaks—Bertha and Delamar—enjoy great views of the lake, towering Mt. San Gorgonio and tranquil Holcomb Valley.

Holcomb Valley wasn't always so tranquil. In 1860, Billy Holcomb was out bear hunting and wandered over the ridge of hills that separates Bear Valley from the smaller, parallel valley to the north. He found gold. Prospectors swarmed into the valley from all over the West.

This day hike climbs the forested slopes above Big Bear Lake to a junction with the Pacific Crest Trail. From the PCT, you can ascend to Bertha Peak or to more distant Delamar Mountain for grand views of the middle of the San Bernadino Mountains.

Directions to trailhead: From Highway 18 in the town of Big Bear Lake, turn north on Stanfield cut off, crossing to the north shore of the lake and a junction with Highway 38. Turn left, drive a mile to the Big Bear Ranger Station, then a short distance beyond to the signed Cougar Crest trailhead and parking area off the north side of the highway.

The hike: From the signed trailhead, join wide Cougar Crest Trail, a retiring dirt road. You climb through a pine and juniper woodland and pass a couple of old mining roads. After a mile, the trail narrows and begins ascending forested Cougar Crest via a series of well-constructed switchbacks. Soon you'll begin enjoying over-the-shoulder views of Big Bear Lake and its dramatic backdrop—the high peaks of the San Gorgonio Wilderness.

A bit more than two miles from the trailhead, Cougar Crest Trail reaches a signed junction with the Pacific Crest Trail. To reach Bertha Peak you'll bear right (east) and continue along the ridge crest for 0.5 mile to an intersection with an old dirt road. PCT continues straight at this junction, but you bear right on the dirt road and ascend 0.5-mile through pinyon pine and juniper woodland to the small relay station atop Bertha Peak. Best views are a bit below the peak.

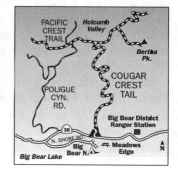

MILL CREEK, ALGER CREEK

Momyer Trail

From Forest Falls to Alger Camp is 7.5 miles round trip with 1,600-foot elevation gain; to Dobbs Camp is 11 miles round trip with 1,700-foot gain; to Saxton Camp is 14.5 miles round trip with 2,900-foot gain; to Dollar Lake Saddle is 20 miles round trip with 4,500-foot gain; Season: May-November

Thanks to the urging of retired San Bernardino postal superintendent Joe Momyer and Harry James, co-founders of the conservation group Defenders of the San Gorgonio Wilderness, Congress set aside the San Gorgonio Wilderness in 1965. Momyer Trail is a pleasant day hike in itself, or you can extend your trip deep into the wilderness by joining other paths. Hikers will enjoy the forested hollows en route, as well as the superb wilderness views.

Directions to trailhead: From Interstate 10 in Redlands, exit on Orange Avenue/State 38. Follow State 38 some eight miles east to Mill Creek Ranger Station. Pick up the required wilderness permit. Continue east on the state highway to the Forest Home turnoff and drive to the signed Momyer trailhead and parking area on the left side of the road.

The hike: Momyer Trail drops into Mill Creek Canyon. Cross Mill Creek. The signed trail resumes on the other side of the creek. The well-constructed trail switchbacks up the brushy divide between Momyer Creek to the west and Alger Creek to the east. Several pockets of oak and Jeffrey pine offer shade and a chance to catch your breath.

After an ascent of nearly three miles, a sign welcomes you to the San Gorgonio Wilderness, and shortly thereafter you'll arrive at a signed junction. (Continuing north is a rather rough and tough path climbing four steep miles toward San Bernardino Peak.) You angle east a short mile to Alger Creek Camp. Relax a while in the shade of pine, alder and incense cedar.

The trail ascends again, then contours around pine- and fir-dotted slopes before reaching a junction. To reach Dobbs Cabin Camp, head right and drop down a steep quarter-mile to Falls Creek and the shady camp.

Most day hikers will call it a day at Dobbs. However, the intrepid will return to the above-mentioned junction and tackle Falls Creek Trail for the stiff climb over forested slopes to Saxton Camp, on the fringe of damp Plummer Meadows.

Truly heroic day hikers will continue up manzanita-covered slopes to Dollar Lake Saddle and an intersection with three more wilderness trails. Dollar Lake Trail drops to Dollar Lake and lush South Fork Meadows. The western stretch of San Bernardino Peak Divide Trail climbs to San Bernardino Peak; the eastern length travels toward San Gorgonio Mountain.

SAN BERNARDINO PEAK

San Bernardino Peak Trail

From Camp Angelus to Columbine Spring Camp is 9 miles round trip with 2,000-foot elevation gain; to Limber Pine Bench Camp is 12 miles round trip with 3,200-foot gain; to San Bernardino Peak is 16 miles round trip with 4.700-foot gain; Season: May-November

Mt. San Bernardino, together with its twin peak, Mt. San Gorgonio, just five miles away and 900 feet higher, anchors the eastern end of the San Bernardino Mountains. At 11,499 feet, Mt. San Gorgonio is the peak by which all other Southern California peaks are measured. Mt. San Bernardino, too, is quite a landmark.

In 1852, Colonel Henry Washington and his Army survey party were directed to erect a monument atop Mt. San Bernardino. The monument was to be an east-west reference point from which all future surveys of Southern California would be taken.

The colonel's crew took many readings, but heat waves from the San Bernardino Valley below befuddled their triangulations. The surveying party ingeniously solved this dilemma by lighting bonfires atop the peak in order to make their calculations at night.

This trail takes you from deep pine forest to exposed manzanita slopes and visits the old survey monument. The higher slopes of Mt. San Bernardino are beautiful and rugged subalpine terrain. A number of trail camps along the way offer spring water and rest.

High elevation, coupled with a steep ascent, means this trail is best left to experienced hikers in top form. Beyond Columbine Spring the trail becomes very steep.

Camp Angelus trailhead is less visited than others at the edge of the San Gorgonio Wilderness, but it receives a lot of use, especially during summer weekends.

Directions to trailhead: Drive east on Interstate Highway 10 to Redlands, leaving the freeway at the highway exit (Orange Street). Follow Highway 38 twenty miles east to Camp Angelus. Turn right near the ranger station at a sign that reads "San Bernardino Peak Trail." Follow the dirt road 0.25-mile to the large parking area. The signed trailhead is at the north end of the lot.

The hike: The trail begins ascending through a mixed forest of pine, fir and oak, switchbacking up the beautifully wooded slope. You mount a ridge, walk along its crest for a brief distance, then continue climbing. You're welcomed into the glories of the San Gorgonio Wilderness by a wooden sign, two miles from the trailhead. A little beyond the wilderness

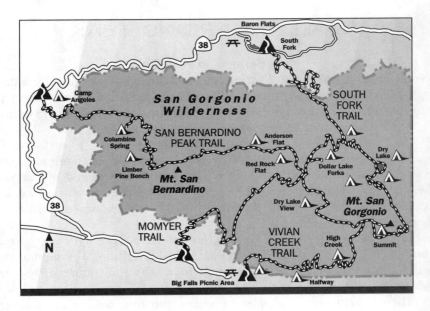

boundary, the grade grows less severe. As you climb above 8,000 feet, the Jeffrey pine become widely spaced. Shortly, the trail penetrates a manzanita-covered slope. You pass a side trail leading down to Manzanita Springs. Don't drink the water. The side trail continues on 0.25 mile to Columbine Springs Trail Camp, which usually has water later in the season than Manzanita.

To San Bernardino Peak: A short distance beyond Manzanita Springs Trail Junction, the trail begins climbing more earnestly. The trail ascends in fits and starts over slopes covered with manzanita and homely chinquapin; in 1.5 more miles, it reaches Limber Pine Springs Camp. (Actually, all the shade in the area is provided by lodgepole pines.) Another 0.25-mile up the trail is Limber Pine Springs, usually a dependable source of water.

The trail begins a long traverse south, switchbacking up to Camp Washington, a trail camp with plenty of view, but nothing to drink. One hundred yards from the trail is Colonel Washington's baseline monument, which looks like little more than a pile of stone rubble. The trail climbs another 0.5-mile, where it intersects a brief side trail that takes you to the summit of Mt. San Bernardino (10,624 feet).

Sign the summit register, enjoy the view, and return the way you came.

Mt. San Gorgonio

South Fork Trail
From South Fork to South Fork Meadows is 8 miles round trip with 1,500-foot elevation gain; to Dollar Lake is 12 miles round trip with 2,500-foot gain; to Mt. San Gorgonio Summit is 21 miles round trip with 4,600-foot gain; Season: June-November

Most of us in the Southland have looked east and marveled at Mt. San Gorgonio, the highest peak in Southern California. The 11,499-foot mountain is most striking in winter when its snow-covered peak can be seen reaching far above the metropolis. In summer, the view from the basin is not so spectacular; the dull gray granite summit is hard to find among the hydrocarbons.

But summer and early autumn are the best seasons in the alpine high country, allowing you to look down at what you left behind. From the top, there's a 360-degree panoramic view from the Mexican border to the southern Sierra, from the Pacific Ocean to the far reaches of the Mojave Desert.

Native American legend has it that San Gorgonio and San Jacinto peaks were brothers and among the first born of Earth Mother, who made all things. It would be hard to improve on Earth Mother's handiwork here. Mt. San Gorgonio's alpine vegetation includes carpets of buttercups, and that venerable survivor of inclement weather, the limber pine. Mountain lions, mule deer and bighorn sheep roam the high slopes, and golden eagles soar over the summit.

The mountain got its name from an obscure fourth-century Christian martyr but irreverent Americans began calling the mountain "Grayback." Its bare, gravelly summit stretches laterally for some distance above the timberline, giving the appearance of a long, gray back.

Below the peak is some fine hiking on good trails that tour the heart of the San Gorgonio Wilderness. You'll pass through lovely meadows and visit two small lakes, Dry and Dollar. Ambitious hikers in top form will want to make the 21-mile round trip trek all the way to the top of Old Grayback for the best view of Southern California available to a hiker.

Directions to trailhead: From Interstate 10 in Redlands, exit on California 38. As you head up the highway into the San Bernardino National Forest, remember to stop at the Mill Creek Ranger Station just beyond the hamlet of Mentone and pick up your wilderness permit.

Follow the highway 19 miles past the ranger station to Jenks Lake Road. Turn right and proceed 3 miles to the South Fork trailhead.

The hike: From the parking area, you cross Jenks Lake Road and pick up the unsigned trail. The path ascends moderately through a mixed pine forest. Enjoy the occasional views of Sugarloaf Peak behind you and San Gorgonio ahead. About 1.5 miles from the trailhead, you'll intersect Poopout Hill Road, now closed to vehicle traffic. Continue straight ahead. Another 0.75 mile of travel brings you to an intersection with the old Poopout Hill Trail. Bear right here.

Continue ascending through the woods. In a mile, South Fork Creek appears on your left, and you parallel it toward South Fork Meadows, also known as Slushy Meadows.

Dozens of tiny streams, which form the headwaters of the Santa Ana River, roam through the ferns and wispy waist-high grasses. Lower South Fork Meadows Trail Camp and Middle South Fork Meadows Trail Camp offer places to picnic.

Locate an idyllic picnic spot beneath the ponderosa pine and white fir. If you're not feeling especially energetic, you could spend a day in South Fork Meadows and be quite happy.

The more energetic will continue on the trail as it skirts the west edge of the meadow and reaches a junction. The left fork, Whitewater Trail, heads toward Dry Lake (another fine day hike destination) and the summit of Mt. San Gorgonio. You take the right fork, South Fork Trail, and begin switch-backing up wooded slopes.

After a mile of climbing, first through ponderosa pine and then through lodgepole pine, you'll begin a long contour around the wall of the basin that holds Dollar Lake. The trail passes a manzanita-covered slope and reaches a junction 1.75 miles from South Fork Meadows. Go left.

In a few hundred yards you reach another junction and turn left again. Follow the easy 0.25-mile trail down the basin wall to the lake.

Dollar Lake, so named because it gleams like a silver dollar, is one of the most popular backcountry spots in the San Gorgonio Wilderness and is another ideal place to picnic or laze away a day. Return to the main trail the way you came.

If you're headed for the summit, resume climbing for another mile to Dollar Lake Saddle (approx. 10,000 feet) and a three-way junction. One half mile beyond the junction, you pass another junction with the rocky side-trail that ascends Charlton Peak. In another 0.5 mile you pass Dry Lake View Camp, a waterless trail camp amidst great boulders. From here, you can look down into Dry Lake Basin, where you'll pass if you return from the peak via Sky High Trail. Soon you'll pass junctions with the Vivian Creek Trail and the Sky High Trail. Keep to your left at both junctions. Cross a last rise and climb to the summit of San Gorgonio.

No other Southern California mountain commands such an uninterrupted panoramic view. To the north are the deep green meadowlands of the upper valley of the Santa Ana River. To the west is the murky megalopolis.

Inviting lakeside campsites beckon weary Mt. San Gorgonio hikers.

To the east is the Mojave. South is San Gorgonio Pass and just across from it, nearly level with your feet, is Mt. San Jacinto.

After enjoying this 360-degree view from the top of the world, return the way you came or via the Sky High Trail, which descends the east slope of San Gorgonio to Mine Shaft Saddle and Dry Lake and deposits you in South Fork Meadows where you intersect the trail back to South Fork.

From the summit, retrace your steps on the main trail to its intersection with the Sky High Trail. Begin your descent from the clouds on the latter trail, circling first east, then north around the mountain's great shoulders. As you descend there are good views of the Whitewater drainage, gorges bearing snowmelt from San Gorgonio and carrying waters to the desert sands below. The awesome Whitewater country was in 1984 added to the San Gorgonio Wilderness.

As you round the east ridge, you'll pass the wreckage of a DC-3 squashed against the mountain. Three and a half miles from the summit you reach Mine Shaft Saddle on the divide between Dry Lake Basin and the Whitewater River.

Continue your descent, and in two more miles you'll reach Dry Lake at 9,200 feet. In dry years it is dry by midsummer, but some years the lake is filled to the brim, its water lapping against the trail that surrounds the lake.

From the Dry Lake basin, you switchback down through pine and fir 1.75 miles to South Fork Meadows, where you intersect the trail back to South Fork trailhead.

Vivian Creek

Vivian Creek Trail

From Mill Creek Canyon to Vivian Creek Trail Camp is 2.5 miles round trip with 1,200-foot elevation gain; to Halfway Trail Camp is 5 miles round trip with 1,800-foot gain; to High Creek Trail Camp is 8 miles round trip with 3,400-foot gain; to Mt. San Gorgonio Peak is 14 miles round trip with 5,300-foot gain; Season: May-November

"The mountains"—he continued, with his eyes upon the distant heights—"are not seen by those who would visit them with a rattle and clatter and rush and roar—as one would visit the cities of men. They are to be seen only by those who have the grace to go quietly; who have the understanding to go thoughtfully; the heart to go lovingly; and the spirit to go worshipfully."
—HAROLD BELL WRIGHT, *The Eyes of the World, 1914*

A half-dozen major trails lead through the San Gorgonio Wilderness to the top of Mt. San Gorgonio, Southern California's highest peak. Oldest, and often regarded as the best, is Vivian Creek Trail.

Not long after the formation of San Bernardino Forest Preserve in 1893, pioneer foresters built Government Trail to the top of San Gorgonio. This path was later renamed Vivian Creek Trail because it winds along for a few miles with its namesake watercourse before climbing the steep upper slopes of San Gorgonio.

Vivian Creek Trail begins in Mill Creek Canyon. The lower stretches of the canyon, traveled by Highway 38, displays many boulders, evidence of great floods in years past.

Upper Mill Creek Canyon is where Big Falls falls. Tumbling from the shoulder of San Bernardino Peak, snowmelt-swollen Falls Creek rushes headlong over a cliff near Mill Creek Road. (Unfortunately, too many foolish people were killed or injured by trying to climb Big Falls and the Forest Service has closed the 0.5-mile path leading to Big Falls Overlook.)

Mill Creek Canyon was the retreat for pastor-turned-novelist Harold Bell Wright (1872-1944). His wholesome, tremendously popular novels featured rugged individualists, as well as Southwest and Southland settings. One novel, *Eyes of the World,* uses the San Bernardino Mountains as a setting and explores the question of an artist's responsibility to society and to himself.

Leaving the head of Mill Creek Canyon, Vivian Creek Trail climbs into the valley cut by Vivian Creek, visits three inviting trail camps—Vivian Creek, Halfway and High Creek—and ascends rocky, lodgepole pine-dotted slopes to the top of Old Grayback.

Directions to trailhead: From Interstate 10 in Redlands, exit on Highway 38 and proceed 14 miles east to a junction with Forest Home Road. (Halfway to this junction, on Highway 38, is Mill Creek Ranger Station, where you must stop and obtain a wilderness permit.) Follow Forest Home Road 4.5 miles to its end.

The hike: The trail, an old dirt road, travels 0.75 mile through (closed) Falls Campground to another (the former) Vivian Creek trailhead. The trail, a dirt path from this point, crosses boulder-strewn Mill Creek wash, then begins a steep ascent over an exposed, oak-dotted slope. Soon you'll reach Vivian

Big Falls

Creek Trail Camp, where pine- and fir-shaded sites dot the creek banks.

Past the camp, Vivian Creek Trail follows its namesake, crossing from one side to the other and passing little lush meadows and stands of pine and cedar.

Halfway, a relatively new trail camp, about halfway between Vivian Creek and High Creek Camps, is another welcome retreat. Another 1.5 miles of steep climbing up forested slopes brings you to High Creek Camp.

Above High Creek, located at 9,000-foot elevation, you leave behind the Ponderosa pine and cedar and encounter that hearty, high altitude survivor, the lodgepole pine. Two miles high, you start getting some great views; at 11,000 feet, the trail ascends above the timberline.

When you reach a junction with the trail coming up from Dollar Lake you'll turn right. Soon you'll pass a junction with the Sky High Trail, cross a last rise and climb to the summit of San Gorgonio.

Sugarloaf Mountain

Sugarloaf National Recreation Trail
From Green Canyon to Wildhorse Creek Trail Camp is 5 miles round trip
with 700-foot elevation gain; to Sugarloaf Mountain is 10 miles round trip
with 2,000-foot gain; Season: May-November

Sugarloaf Mountain, highest peak in the San Bernardino Mountains outside the San Gorgonio Wilderness, is a particularly fine destination on a hot
summer's day. The ridgeline leading to the summit is forested with pine, fir
and cedar. A breeze cools the massive round shoulders of the mountain.

The first part of the trail—as far as Wildhorse Trail Camp—offers a family trip of moderate difficulty. Well-conditioned hikers will enjoy the challenge of the second part of the trail—a vigorous ascent to the summit of
9,952-foot Sugarloaf Mountain.

Directions to trailhead: From Big Bear City, head east on State Route
38. The highway turns south, and about 3 miles from town, turn right on
Forest Road 2N84. Take note here that the Forest Service has posted "passenger car not recommended" signs; those with low-slung cars should proceed with caution—or be prepared to walk part of the 1.5 mile-distance to
the trailhead if the road is poor. When 2N84 veers left, proceed straight
ahead on Forest Road 2N93, which climbs a mile to Green Creek crossing.
On the other side of the creek, turn right (south) onto an unsigned dirt
road and follow it a few hundred yards to a parking area at a locked gate.

The hike: Ascend on the steep dirt jeep road which stays close to Green
Creek. Two miles of hiking brings you to a saddle on the ridgeline and a
trail junction. (Straight ahead, the trail continues a short distance to
Wildhorse Meadows Trail Camp—a fine picnic and rest stop.)

Turn right (west) and ascend on the Sugarloaf Trail. Above 9,000 feet,
the trail passes through thick stands of lodgepole pine. The trail contours

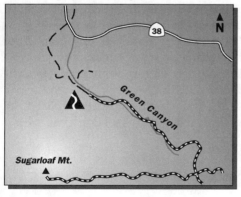

around Peak 9775 and dips into a
saddle. Gnarled and picturesque
junipers hug the ridgeline. The
trail then ascends to the forested
summit of Sugarloaf Peak.
Eastern San Bernardino
Mountains peaks and the San
Gorgonio Wilderness are part of
the fine view.

SANTA ANA RIVER

Santa Ana River Trail
From South Fork Campground to Heart Bar Campground is 9 miles round trip with 800-foot elevation gain; Season: March-November

For most of its length, Southern California's largest river is not a thing of beauty. Concrete-lined and channelized, the Santa Ana River that crosses Orange County is a thoroughly domesticated watercourse. Its riverbed has been covered with subdivisions, its natural course altered for human convenience. Glimpsing the river as it passes Costa Mesa backyards, Anaheim Stadium or the I-10/I-15 interchange does not inspire further exploration.

Fortunately for hikers and nature lovers, there's another Santa Ana River, unfettered and unchanneled. At its headwaters high in the San Bernardino Mountains, the river waters a beautiful meadow and cuts through a deep canyon that separates the high peaks of the San Gorgonio Wilderness from the mountains of the Big Bear Lake area. The river, born of natural springs and snowmelt, is an important wildlife habitat in its upper reaches.

The most intriguing segment of the Santa Ana River Trail begins at Heart Bar, first settled by Mormon pioneers in the 1850s. During the latter part of the 19th century and the first half of the 20th, cattle ranchers sent their herds to graze the lush Santa Ana River meadows. It was one rancher's brand—a heart with a bar beneath it—that gave the land its name.

Santa Ana River Trail parallels the river as it winds from South Fork Campground to Heart Bar Campground. The path stays in piney woods for most of its length. A few side trails allow passage to the river.

Directions to trailhead: From Interstate 10 in Redlands, take the Highway 38 exit and proceed north 32 miles to South Fork Campground. Almost opposite the entrance to the camp, on the north side of the highway, you'll find the Santa Ana River trailhead parking lot and the signed trail.

Santa Ana River Trail ends at Forest Road 1N021, near Heart Bar Campground. If you want to make a one-way hike, you can arrange to have transportation waiting at the Forest Road 1N021 trailhead. To reach this trailhead from the South Fork Campground trailhead, you would continue east on Highway 38 to the signed Heart Bar Campground turnoff, then drive a mile past the campground on the dirt Forest Road 1N021 to the second signed Santa Ana River trailhead.

The hike: From the parking area opposite South Fork Campground, Santa Ana River Trail meanders by its namesake, then veers under the Santa Ana River Bridge. Notice the rugged construction of the bridge and the wide bed of the river, two indications of the Santa Ana's size and strength after a storm.

The trail makes a short circle, reaches a second signed trailhead at the entrance to South Fork Campground and heads west.

Switchbacking up a slope, the trail soon turns east—your direction for the rest of this hike.

During the first mile you will intersect a number of dirt roads, but strategically placed signs keep you on the path. Most of the climb occurs in the first mile. The trail travels through a mixed forest of ponderosa and Jeffrey pine, white fir and black oak. Ground squirrels are abundant, and deer are seen occasionally.

Above you to the southwest is the San Gorgonio Wilderness, dominated by its 11,499-foot signature peak, highest point in Southern California. To the north, above the forested canyon of the Santa Ana River, is Sugarloaf Mountain (9,952 feet), highest peak in the San Bernardinos outside the wilderness.

About the trail's midpoint you'll spot Heart Bar Station, headquarters for a Forest Service fire crew. Continuing east, the trail offers great views of well-named Big Meadow. Watering the meadow are Heart Bar Creek, Coon Creek, Cienega Seca Creek and the headwaters of the Santa Ana. Big Meadow is especially pretty when a breeze sways the willows and tall grasses. During late spring and summer the meadow is splashed with colorful wildflowers. The meadows where cattle once grazed are now a valuable habitat for rabbits, foxes, skunks and raccoons. California golden beaver were brought into the area, and several pairs of them maintain dams on the Santa Ana River.

About a mile from trail's end you will intersect an unsigned side trail leading left down to Big Meadow and over to Heart Bar Campground. Continue straight at this junction to the end of this segment of Santa Ana River Trail at Forest Road 1N021.

Aspen Grove

Aspen Grove Trail
From Forest Road 1N05 to Fish Creek Meadows is 5 miles round trip with 600-foot elevation gain; Season: May-November

One of the prettiest sights of autumn is the fluttering of the aspen's golden-yellow leaves. From a distance, the trees stand apart from the surrounding dark forest. In the right light, the aspens seem to burn, like fire in the wind.

Botanists say the aspen is the most widely distributed tree on the North American continent. Even rough American fur trappers and mountain men of the last century were impressed by the tree's range and beauty.

The water-loving aspen is a rarity in Southern California, but there is a handsome little grove in the San Bernardino Mountains. Aspen Grove, reached by a trail with the same name, is an ideal autumn excursion.

The hike to Aspen Grove is particularly inviting after Jack Frost has touched the trees. After the first cold snap, the aspens display their fall finery, a display of color unrivaled in Southern California.

It's only a short 0.25-mile saunter to the aspens that line Fish Creek, but the trail continues beyond the grove, traveling through a pine and fir forest and a lovely meadow.

Directions to trailhead: From Interstate 10 in Redlands, exit on Highway 38 and proceed 32 miles east to the signed turnoff for Heart Bar Campground. (As you head up 38 into the San Bernardino National Forest, remember to stop at Mill Creek Ranger Station just beyond the hamlet of Mentone and pick up a wilderness permit.) Turn south (right) on dirt Forest Road 1N02, and drive 1.25 miles to a fork in the road. Stay right at the fork and follow it on a 1.5-mile climb to a small parking area and signed Aspen Grove Trail on your right.

The hike: The trail, for its first 0.25-mile an abandoned dirt road, descends toward Fish Creek. The very beginning of Aspen Grove Trail offers the best view of San Gorgonio Wilderness peaks—the highest in Southern California. To the west stands mighty Grinnell Mountain, named for turn-of-the-century University of California zoologist Joseph Grinnell, who studied the animals of the San Bernardino Mountains. To the south is Ten Thousand Foot Ridge, headwaters for Fish Creek, which you soon see and hear meandering below.

At Fish Creek, a sign marks the boundary of the San Gorgonio Wilderness. Cross the creek and enjoy the aspen grove that lines Fish Creek. It's a small grove, but a pretty one. No one will blame you if you picnic among the whitewashed trunks and quaking leaves and hike no farther.

The aspens have been suffering of late at the hands of—or more accurately, the jaws of—a creature that loves the trees even more than humans. The aspen-chomping California golden beaver is not a native of the San Bernardino Mountains, but since its introduction it has found the area—and the aspens to its liking. Forest Service wildlife experts are working on a plan to manage the native aspens and the beaver.

After admiring the aspens, continue on Aspen Grove Trail, which heads up-creek. The path soon wanders a bit away from Fish Creek and travels through a forest of ponderosa pine, Jeffrey pine and Douglas fir.

About a mile from Aspen Grove, the trail passes little Monkey Flower Flat. During late spring and early summer, columbine and lupine join the monkeyflowers in bedecking the flat.

Beyond Monkey Flower is a much larger flat—Fish Creek Meadow. Aspen Grove Trail skirts this meadow and ends at a signed junction with Fish Creek Trail. The left fork of Fish Creek Trails leads a bit more than 0.5 mile to Forest Road 1N05. Take the right fork of the trail, which angles toward Upper Fish Creek. The path ascends above the creek, passes through a pine and fir forest and, a bit more than a mile from the junction with Aspen Grove Trail, reaches Fish Creek Camp. This fir-shaded camp is an ideal place to relax.

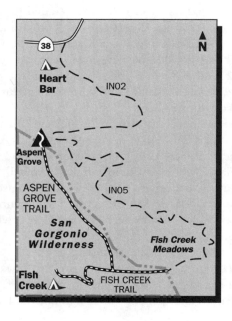

11. San Jacinto Mountains

ANY HIKERS IN THE SAN JACINTO MOUNTAINS can't resist comparing this range with the High Sierra. While comparisons often leave low chaparral-covered mountains on the short end, the alpine San Jacintos fare well because the range shares many geologic similarities with the Sierra Nevada. Both ranges are bold uplifted masses of granite. Both are westward tilted blocks located near powerful earthquake faults. Both veer abruptly out of the desert without the geologic fanfare of foothills preceding them.

Author Carey McWilliams called Southern California an "island on the land." The San Jacintos could well be described the same way. The 10,000-foot peaks of the San Jacintos and their shorter, but no less majestic, stony neighbors are completely separated from the rest of Southern California by low passes and desert valleys. The range is bounded by San Gorgonio Pass on the north, the San Jacinto Valley on the west, the Colorado Desert and the great Coachella Valley on the east, and Anza-Borrego Desert State Park to the south.

The San Jacintos seem an island in the sky because of their incredibly rapid rise from the desert floor. No other place in California do alpine and desert vegetation thrive in such close proximity. Six distinct life zones, from cactus-dotted desert and palm canyons to arctic alpine summits, can be encountered within five horizontal miles of travel. On the base is Lower Sonoran vegetation of creosote and ironwood. Above this is the Upper Sonoran or manzanita and scrub oak, soon giving way with rise in elevation to dense mountain forests of pine and cedar. In narrow belts around the high summits are those hearty survivors—the lodgepole pine and limber pine. Finally some stunted species, including alpine sorrel, grow on the peaks and are classified in the Arctic-Alpine Zone. Each life zone has a unique set of inhabitants. Shy and reclusive bighorn sheep patrol the desert-facing high country, mule deer browse the verdant meadows, golden eagles soar over the high peaks.

During the great logging boom of 1880-1910, timber barons sent their choppers farther and farther up the slopes of the San Jacintos. Ranchers grazed thousands of sheep and cattle in the alpine meadows. Even the most shortsighted could see the destruction of the mountain watershed, and with local settlers urging protection for the range, President Grover Cleveland established the San Jacinto Timberland Reserve in 1897. It was a huge chunk of land, extending from the San Gorgonio Pass to the Mexican border. The San Jacinto Reserve was later combined with a portion of the Santa Ana Mountains to create the Cleveland National Forest. After several devastating fires in 1924, federal foresters decided the huge tract of land was too unwieldy for fire suppression purposes, and the San Jacintos were taken from the Cleveland National Forest and attached to the nearby San Bernardino National Forest, where they remain today.

In the mid-1930s, Civilian Conservation Corps workers camped in Round and Tahquitz Valleys, and built an extensive, well-engineered trail system through the San Jacintos.

The wild areas in the San Jacinto Mountains are now administered by both state park and national forest rangers. The middle of the region, including San Jacinto Peak, is included within Mt. San Jacinto Wilderness State Park. On both sides of the peak, north and south, the wilderness is administered by the San Jacinto District of the San Bernardino National Forest.

Access to the San Jacintos was difficult until Highway 243, "The Banning to Idyllwild Panoramic Highway" was built. As late as World War II, it was a muffler-massacring, steep, narrow, unpaved route that forded streams. A new paved "high gear" road opened in 1948, with actress Jane Powell performing the ribbon-cutting duties as the Banning High School Band played.

Palm Springs Aerial Tramway makes it easy for hikers to enter Mt. San Jacinto State Wilderness. Starting in Chino Canyon near Palm Springs, a tram takes passengers from 2,643-foot Lower Tramway Terminal (Valley Station) to 8,516-foot Upper Tramway Terminal (Mountain Station) at the edge of the Wilderness.

The Swiss-made gondola rapidly leaves terra firma behind. Too rapidly, you think. It carries you over one of the most abrupt mountain faces in the world, over cliffs only a bighorn sheep can scale, over several life zones, from palms to pines. The view is fantastic.

Construction of the Tramway was opposed by conservationists who pointed out that Mt. San Jacinto slopes were totally unsuited to its stated purpose—skiing. First proposed in the 1930s, the project was finally completed in 1963 after approval and funding from by the State of California.

Now, most nature-lovers enjoy witnessing flora and fauna changes equivalent to those viewed on a motor trip from the Mojave Desert to the Arctic Circle in just minutes. In pre-tramway days, John Muir found the view "the most sublime spectacle to be found anywhere on this earth!"

The range is one of those magical places that lures hikers back year after year. The seasons are more distinct here than anywhere else in Southern California. Hikers also enjoy the contrasts this range offers—the feeling of hiking in Switzerland while gazing down on the Sahara.

Saunders Meadow

Ernie Maxwell Scenic Trail
Humber Park to Saunders Meadow 5 miles round trip with 300-foot
elevation gain; Season: May-November

The founder of the *Idyllwild Town Crier* and longtime Idlyllwild conservationist, is honored by the Ernie Maxwell Scenic Trail, a woodsy, 2.5-mile path through the San Jacinto Mountains. Maxwell, longtime Idyllwild conservationist, has hiked his namesake trail many times.

Maxwell explained that his trail came into being as a result of his horse's inability to get along with automobiles. After riding through the San Jacinto Wilderness, Maxwell and his fellow equestrians were forced to follow paved roads back through town to the stables.

Maxwell's barn-sour pack horses, so slow and sullen on the trail, would become suddenly frisky and unmanageable as they neared home. Equine-auto conflicts were frequent. Maxwell thought: Why not build a trail from Humber Park, at the edge of the San Jacinto Wilderness, through the forest to the stables, thus avoiding the horse-spooking congestion of downtown Idyllwild?

Maxwell got cooperation from the U.S. Forest Service and from Riverside County inmates, who provided the labor. Ernie Maxwell Trail was completed in 1959.

And a lovely trail it is. The path meanders through a mixed forest of pine and fir and offers fine views of the granite face of Marion Ridge.

Since founding the newspaper in 1946, Maxwell has often written about what he wryly calls "the urban-wildlands interface issue. That's the one that deals with more and more people moving into the hills."

People began moving into the hills with their axes and sheep more than a hundred years ago. Fortunately, the San Jacinto Mountains have had many conservation-minded friends, including Ernie Maxwell, who for many years served as president of the local chapter of the Izaak Walton League. Maxwell has seen the emphasis of the surrounding national forest change

Ernie Maxwell and his Scenic Trail.

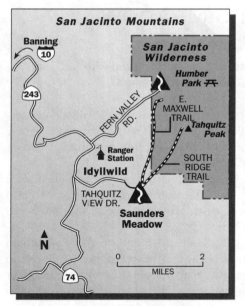

from commodity production to recreation; seen isolated Idyllwild become a (sometimes too) popular weekend getaway. Conservationists are aware that the future of the mountains depend to a large extent on the attitude of the millions of Southern Californians living 7,000 feet below and a 1.5-hour drive away from Idyllwild.

Directions to trailhead: From Interstate 10 in Banning, exit on California 243 (Banning-Idyllwild Highway) and proceed about 25 miles to Idyllwild County Park Visitor Center. A small museum interprets the history and natural history of the area.

From downtown Idyllwild, head up Fern Valley Road. Following the signs to Humber Park, drive two miles to the large parking area. Signed Ernie Maxwell Trail departs from the lower end of the parking lot.

The hike: The trail begins at Humber Park, the main jumping-off point to the San Jacinto Wilderness for hikers and rock climbers. You'll get frequent over-the-shoulder views of the dramatic pinnacles popular with Southern California climbers.

The mostly level trail (the inmates did a great job!) contours gently around wooded slopes. Ponderosa, Jeffrey and Coulter pines, fir and incense cedar grace the mountainside and carpet the path with needles.

This hike's destination, Saunders Meadow, is named for Amasa Saunders, who in 1881 operated a huge sawmill not too far down slope in Strawberry Valley. Take a moment to be thankful that not all the pine and fir became grist for Saunders' mill, then scout the tree tops for the abundant bird life. Look for Steller's jays, the white-headed woodpecker, and the colorful orange-headed, yellow-breasted western tanager.

Ernie Maxwell Scenic Trail ends somewhat abruptly and ingloriously at dirt Tahquitz View Drive. Maxwell had envisioned that his trail would continue another few miles around Idyllwild and connect to the path leading to Suicide Rock, but this trail plan ended in a bureaucratic thicket.

Contemplating the notion that half a terrific trail is better than none, return the same way.

Idyllwild County Park

Yellow Pine Forest, Hillside & Loop Trails
Nature trail is 0.5 mile loop; a longer loop is 2.5 miles round trip

With its towering pines and incense cedar, great boulders and lively creeks, Idyllwild County Park offers a family-friendly introduction to the pleasures of the San Jacinto Mountains. Such pleasures are visited by a couple of miles of trail that tour the forest and climb to viewpoints for far-reaching vistas of the stony ramparts of the range.

The adventure begins at the Idyllwild Nature Center, located just a mile north of the town of Idyllwild. Exhibits present the natural and cultural history of the mountains. Many of Idyllwild's slopes, including this parkland, were logged in the 19th century; thus, a majority of the forest is second-growth.

Still, there are some impressive trees in these parts, as you'll soon observe when you set out on Yellow Pine Forest Nature Trail, which departs

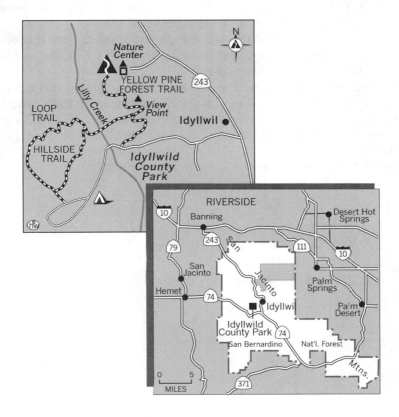

from the nature center (where you can pick up an interpretive pamphlet for the path). The trail passes some impressive specimens of manzanita, and meanders past black oak and boulders. With its soft reddish bark and stately stature, the incense cedars en route seem to personify tranquility.

About halfway along, the nature trail travels near Lily Creek and arrives at an impressive bit of bedrock where the native Cahuilla ground seeds and acorns. The resultant grinding holes (morteros) are evidence of exactly where the Cahuilla went to work—a scenic spot indeed for such labor!

The longer loop trail begins behind the visitor center and after a short, modest, ascent southward, reaches a turnoff for a Viewpoint. Enjoy grand mountain views, particularly of Lily Rock—or Tahquitz Peak if you prefer.

Continue south on the main trail on a switchbacking descent to a junction. The left fork heads down to the park campground, but you'll take the right and meander over a slope punctuated by some impressive boulders as well as a mixed forest of oak, pine and cedar.

Cross Lily Creek on a log bridge to a junction with the left-forking Hillside Trail and the straight-ahead bearing Loop Trail. (The two trails form a loop) I like starting out with the more aggressive Loop Trail, which switchbacks steeply upward while offering great views.

After looping back toward the park campground, you'll close the loop, then retrace your steps. Re-cross the log bridge over Lily Creek and take the connector trail back to the nature center.

Directions to trailhead: From the town of Idyllwild, drive a mile north on Highway 243 to the signed turnoff for Idyllwild County Park. Proceed to the last parking lot and walk up the path to the Idyllwild Nature Center, where Yellow Pine Forest Trail begins. The longer trail loop begins behind the nature center.

There is a park entrance fee for both adults and children.

Tahquitz Peak

South Ridge Trail
From South Ridge Road to Tahquitz Peak is 6 miles round trip with 2,000-foot elevation gain; Season: May-October

Tahquitz Peak dominates the southern San Jacinto Mountains, lording over Strawberry Valley and Idyllwild on one side, and Tahquitz Valley on the other. A fire lookout tower is perched on the summit. The view from the peak is inspiring: clear-day vistas of the San Jacintos, the desert and the distant Santa Rosas.

You may notice what appear to be insect-like creatures high on the rock walls of the mountain. Southland rock climbers often come to practice their craft on the superb rock walls of Tahquitz.

Lily Rock, named for a surveyor's daughter, is the official name of the great rock, though most climbers prefer the more rugged-sounding Tahquitz. After taking one of the hundred routes (some quite hazardous) up the several faces of the rock, you can't blame the climbers for preferring something more dramatic than Lily.

South Ridge Trail, true to its name, ascends the steep south ridge of Tahquitz Peak. The trail climbs through stands of fine and fir and offers great views of Strawberry Valley and the storybook hamlet of Idyllwild.

If you want a longer hike than the six-mile round trip to Tahquitz Peak, there are a number of ways to extend your trek. By arranging a car shuttle, you could descend Tahquitz Peak to Humber Park at the outskirts of Idyllwild. For a very long loop hike, you could even follow the Ernie Maxwell Trail from Humber Park down to the foot of South Ridge Road, then up the road to the South Ridge trailhead.

Directions to trailhead: From Interstate 10 in Banning, exit on Highway 243 (Banning-Idyllwild Highway) and proceed about 25 miles to Idyllwild. After you've obtained your wilderness permit from the Forest Service Station in Idyllwild, you'll double back a wee bit to the south edge of town and make a left turn on Saunders Meadow Road. Turn left on Pine Avenue, right on Tahquitz Drive, then right on South Ridge Road. (If the gate across this road is closed (it's usually open during good weather), you'll have to park at the base of South Ridge Road. Otherwise, passenger cars with good ground clearance may continue 1.5 miles up part dirt–part paved, potholed South Ridge Road to its terminus at signed South Ridge trailhead.

The hike: From the trailhead at the top of South Ridge Road, the well-constructed path zigzags through a forest of Jeffrey Pine and white fir. You'll get fine south views of Garner Valley and Lake Hemet, Thomas

Mountain and Table Mountain. Far off to the west, on a clear day, you'll be able to pick out the Santa Ana and San Gabriel Mountains.

South Ridge Trail climbs to a boulder-strewn saddle, which marks the trail's halfway point. Here you'll find a rock window-on-the-world, a great place to rest or to frame a picture of your hiking mate.

From the saddle, the trail climbs in earnest past thickets of spiny chinquapin, and past scattered lodgepole pine. You'll sight the fire lookout tower atop Tahquitz Peak and many a switchback above you, but the last mile of trail goes by faster than you might expect with a slow, steady pace.

Enjoy the summit views, then either return the same way or follow your heart and forest service map through the San Jacinto Wilderness down to Humber Park and Idyllwild.

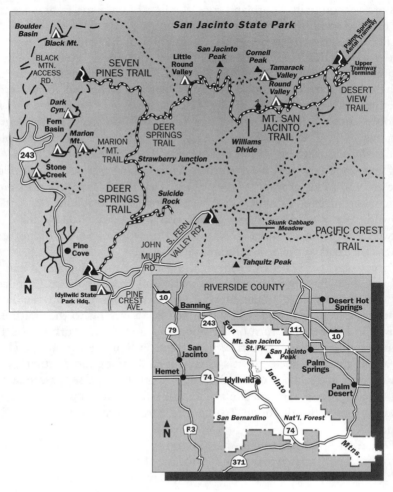

SUICIDE ROCK

Deer Springs Trail

From Idyllwild to Suicide Rock is 7 miles round trip with 2,000-feet elevation gain; Season: May-November

Suicide Rock is a sheer granite outcropping that provides the romantic with a tale of star-crossed lovers, and rewards the hiker with splendid views of Strawberry Valley and a forest wonderland of pine and fir. Legend has it that the rock got its tragic name from an Indian princess and her lover who leaped to their deaths over the precipice rather than be separated, as their chief had commanded.

Suicide Rock is a splendid place to observe the ever-changing four seasons (though you'll have a hard time climbing the rock in winter). The seasons fade in and out with clarity and distinction in the San Jacintos. Fall colors tint the black oak and azalea, winter brings a white blanket, spring is heralded by a profusion of wildflowers, and the long, hot summers are tempered with thunder and lightning displays. Views like this bring hikers back again and again to sample the beauty of the San Jacinto Mountains.

Directions to trailhead: Deer Springs Trail begins across the highway from the Idyllwild County Park Visitor Center parking area, one mile west of town on the Banning-Idyllwild Highway 243. If you'd like to learn something about the history of the area, the nature museum at the county park is helpful.

The Forest Service's Idyllwild Ranger Station is on California 243 at Pine Crest Avenue; the Mt. San Jacinto State Park Ranger Station in Idyllwild is at 25905 California 243.

The hike: Signed Deer Springs Trail picks its way through an elfin manzanita forest, then ascends past spreading oaks and tall pines. You switchback up a ridge to Suicide Junction, 2.3 miles from the trailhead. Here you leave the Deer Springs Trail and bear east, contouring across Marion Ridge. You cross Marion Creek, whose performance is seasonal, and on wet years, inspiring. A long mile from Suicide Junction you reach the back side of Suicide Rock.

From the white granite rock you'll be able to look down and see tiny Idyllwild and Strawberry Valley. On the far horizon are Tahquitz Peak and Lily Rock.

LITTLE ROUND VALLEY

Seven Pines Trail

From Dark Canyon to Deer Springs is 7.5 miles round trip with 2,600-foot elevation gain; to Little Round Valley Camp is 10.5 miles round trip with 3,600-foot elevation gain; to San Jacinto Peak is 13.5 miles round trip with 4,400-foot gain; Season: May-November

Seven Pines Trail ascends the cascading North Fork of San Jacinto River to its headwaters at Deep Springs. Energetic hikers will join the Deer Springs Trail for an ascent of Mt. San Jacinto.

Remember to obtain a wilderness permit and map from park headquarters, off California 243 just before you get to the town of Idyllwild.

Directions to trailhead: Take Highway 243 (Banning-Idyllwild Road) about 20 miles from Banning or 6 miles from Idyllwild. Just south of Alandale Forest Service Station, take the turnoff (4S02) toward Dark Canyon Campground. After a mile's travel on the dirt road, veer left at a junction. Pass through the camp and bear left at Azalea Trail junction to the trailhead.

The hike: Seven Pines Trail ascends the ridge between Dark Canyon and the canyon cut by the North Fork. You hike out of the San Bernardino National Forest into Mt. San Jacinto State Park. After a mile, the trails tops the ridge and descends eastward to the North Fork. In spring, when the river is swollen with snowmelt, the North Fork has quite a heady flow.

The trail climbs along a pine- and fir-covered slope, recrosses the river, and reaches a junction with Deer Springs Trail. (A right turn on the trail leads to Strawberry Junction, past Suicide Rock). Another possibility is to bear south on the Marion Mountain Trail which descends steeply a little more than two miles to Marion Mountain Camp. A three-mile car shuttle or three-mile walk leads back to Dark Canyon Campground and the trailhead.)

Follow Deer Springs Trail left (east) 0.25 mile to the former site of Deer Springs Trail Camp. The camp, overused in past years, has been abandoned by Mt. San Jacinto State Park. However, its all-year water supply and pleasant locale makes it an ideal lunch or rest stop.

To Little Round Valley Camp: A short walk up Deer Springs Trail from the former camp brings you to another junction. The leftward fork is Fuller Ridge Trail, which leads northwest 5 miles to Black Mountain Camp. Bear right at this junction. The trail passes through some meadowland on the way to Little Round Valley Trail Camp.

To Mt. San Jacinto: From Little Round Valley, the trail climbs through stands of lodgepole pine, and in a little more than a mile arrives at a junction with San Jacinto Peak Trail. A left turn on this trail takes you 0.25 mile past a stone shelter cabin to the top of the 10,084-foot peak.

MT. SAN JACINTO

Mt. Jacinto Trail
From Mountain Station to Round Valley is 4 miles round trip with 600-foot elevation gain; to San Jacinto Peak is 11 miles round trip with 2,300-foot gain; Season: May-November

Palm Springs Aerial Tramway makes it easy for hikers to enter Mt. San Jacinto State Wilderness. Starting in Chino Canyon near Palm Springs, a tram takes passengers from 2,643-foot Lower Tramway Terminal (Valley Station) to 8,516-foot Upper Tramway Terminal (Mountain Station) at the edge of the wilderness.

The day hiker accustomed to remote trailheads may find it a bit bizarre to enter Valley Station and find excited tourists sipping drinks and shopping for souvenirs. But the gondola rapidly leaves the station and carries you over one of the most abrupt mountain faces in the world. When you disembark at Mountain Station, your ears will pop and you'll have quite a head start up Mt. San Jacinto.

There's a strong geologic similarity between the High Sierra and the San Jacintos. While standing upon the summit of Mt. San Jacinto, the perceptive mountaineer may notice a subtle atmospheric similarity—both the San Jacintos and Sierra Nevada can be called a "range of light." powerful sunlight illuminates the San Jacintos, creating sharp contrasts between light and shadow, the kind of contrast found in an Ansel Adams photograph. There may be a six f-stop difference between the bright light shimmering on the rocky summit and the dark forest primeval below. The sun burns upon the lower slopes

Mt. San Jacinto

of Mt. San Jacinto like a fire in the wind, but the upper elevations receive a more gentle incandescent light and a fraction of the heat dispersed below. Our civilization measures time by the sun, yet as you watch sunlight and shadow play tag across the slopes, you are left with a feeling of timelessness.

Directions to trailhead: From Interstate 10, exit on California 111 (the road to Palm Springs). Proceed nine miles to Tramway Road, turn right, and follow the road four miles to its end at Mountain Station. Contact the Tramway office for information about prices and schedules.

The hike: From Mountain Station, walk down the cement walkway through the Long Valley Picnic Area. Soon you will arrive at the state park ranger station. Obtain a wilderness permit here.

Continue west on the trail, following the signs to Round Valley. The trail parallels Long Valley Creek through a mixed forest of pine and white fir, then climbs into lodgepole pine country. Lupine, monkeyflower, scarlet bugler and Indian paintbrush are some of the wildflowers that add seasonal splashes of color.

After passing a junction with a trail leading toward Willow Creek, another 0.3 of a mile of hiking brings you to Round Valley. A trail camp and a backcountry ranger station are located in the valley, as well as splendid places to picnic in the meadow or among the lodgepole pines.

An alternative to returning the same way is to retrace your steps 0.3 of a mile back to the junction with the Willow Creek Trail, take this trail a mile through the pines to another signed trail north back to Long Valley Ranger Station. This alternative route adds only about a 0.25 mile to your day hike, and allows you to make a loop.

To Mt. San Jacinto Peak: From Round Valley, a sign indicates you may reach the peak by either Tamarack Valley or Wellman Divide Junction. Take the trail toward Wellman Divide Junction. From the Divide, a trail leads down to Humber Park. At the divide, you'll be treated to spectacular views of Tahquitz Peak and Red Tahquitz, as well as the more distant Toro Peak and Santa Rosa Mountain. You continue toward the peak on some vigorous switchbacks. The lodgepole pines grow sparse among the crumbly granite. At another junction, a half-mile from the top, the trail continues to Little Round Valley but you take the summit trail to the peak. Soon you arrive at a stone shelter—an example of Civilian Conservation Corps handiwork during the 1930s. From the stone hut, you boulder-hop to the top of the peak.

The view from the summit—San Gorgonio Pass, the shimmering Pacific, the Colorado Desert, distant Mexico—has struck some visitors speechless, while other have been unable to controle their superlatives. Helen Hunt Jackson's heroine Ramona found "a remoteness from earth which comes only on mountain heights," and John Muir found the view "the most sublime spectacle to be found anywhere on this earth!"

MARION MOUNTAIN

Marion Mountain, Pacific Crest Trails
From Fern Basin to San Jacinto Peak is 11 miles round trip
with 4,400-foot elevation gain

It's the shortest, the steepest and, in the opinion of some hikers, the most scenic ascent of San Jacinto Peak. Marion Mountain Trail gains 2,400 feet in just 2.5 miles. The rest of the climb to the peak via Pacific Crest and Deer Springs trails is nearly as steep.

While reaching the summit of the great mountain is ample reward for most hikers, Marion Mountain Trail scatters additional rewards along the way. This is a hike for tree-lovers, a climb to remember through Conifer-Land.

Marion Mountain's lower elevations support stands of Jeffrey pine and even some oaks. Higher up the mountain grow ranks of sugar pine and white fir and higher still, some lofty lodgepole pine.

Marion Mountain Trail is a great conditioning hike for anyone planning a High Sierra adventure. The altitude and altitude gain of this hike approximates some Sierra sojourns.

Get an early start and allow plenty of time for this hike—six to nine hours, depending on your pace and how long you linger on the summit. Even if you're a well-conditioned hiker, don't be discouraged if it takes you four hours or more to make San Jacinto Peak. And don't rush the descent: the steep and rocky trail has a high ankle-turning and knee-wrenching potential.

The majority of Marion Mountain Trail traverses the Mt. San Jacinto State Park Wilderness; this means the hiker must obtain a wilderness permit, available from the state park headquarters at 29505 Highway 243 in Idyllwild.

Directions to trailhead: From Interstate 10 in Banning, exit on Highway 243 and ascend south some 19 winding miles. Just about opposite the Forest Service's Alandale Station, turn left (east) on the road leading to Stone Creek Campground. You'll soon fork left and follow the signs for Marion Mountain Campground 1.5 miles to the start of Marion Mountain Trail on the right side of the road and trailhead parking on the left.

The hike: Signed Marion Mountain Trail begins what is briefly (0.2 mile) a mellow ascent through the piney woods. You'll soon pass a spur trail leading north down to Marion Mountain Campground and begin the vigorous ascent of the northwest flank of Marion Mountain.

A bit more than 1.25 miles up the trail, a sign informs hikers they've entered the Mt. San Jacinto State Park Wilderness. Like a window on the world you left behind, the trailside view briefly opens up to reveal Highway 243 snaking through the mountains far below and the murky flatlands of the Inland Empire to the north.

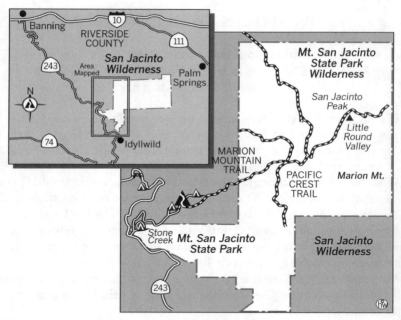

Almost immediately, it's back to the trees, interspersed with ferns and big boulders. That hammering you hear could be from a high altitude headache but is more likely the rat-a-tat-tat of a woodpecker working away high atop one of the many snags near the trail.

After what may seem like one of the longest 2.7-mile stretches of trail in the Southland, you'll come to a junction. It's not quite the perfect four-way intersection pictured on trail maps, but it's well signed. You'll first encounter Pacific Crest Trail (Deer Springs Trail) coming in from the right (south). Turn left and walk 50 feet to a second junction. Seven Pines Trail descends to the north, but you continue your climb east on the signed PCT.

After a 0.3-mile ascent on the very well engineered and maintained PCT, you'll pass gurgling Deer Springs. The modest springs-spawned creek forms part of the headwaters of the North Fork of the San Jacinto River.

The ascent continues another 0.25 mile up the other side of the creek canyon and junctions Fuller Ridge Trail. Keep right, and keep switchbacking for another mile to Little Round Valley, where a small trail camp is located.

The trail curves east, still climbing, still switchbacking for another 1.3 miles and 800-foot elevation gain to San Jacinto Peak's summit ridge. A final 0.3-mile ascent via the summit trail leads past a stone mountaineers hut to the peak.

Fuller Ridge

Pacific Crest Trail
From Fuller Ridge to San Jacinto Peak is 15 miles round trip
with 3,200-foot elevation gain

True, you get a 7,700-foot head-start, but that doesn't make the ascent from Fuller Ridge the easiest route to the top of Mt. San Jacinto.

Do the math and the hike seems a moderate enough exercise: a climb that averages under 500 feet per mile.

Do the hike and the math seems fuzzy—and downright irrelevant. Fuller Ridge presents the hiker with a much more difficult ascent than its numbers suggest.

Other paths to the peak lead through cool forest and, while by no means a walk in the park, seem to offer a kind of woodsy solace to the ascending hiker. The trail following Fuller Ridge is a challenging (the word "tortuous" comes to mind as well) series of tight switchbacks zigzagging amongst stone ramparts and wind-thrashed fir.

The attraction of ascending the mighty mountain by way of Fuller Ridge is more obvious to veteran hikers than novices. What you get is a trek on a grand, seldom-used stretch of Pacific Crest Trail, fabulous views of mountain ranges, the desert and the San Andreas Rift Zone, as well as the satisfaction of seeing the quizzical looks of the hikers who join you on the final mile of trail when you tell them you came by way of Fuller Ridge: "You came from where?" is the usual response from those taking shorter and easier ways to the top of San Jacinto.

Not to discourage you further, but Fuller Ridge is also the hardest of San Jacinto's trailheads to reach and requires a lengthy drive on dirt Black Mountain Road (closed from about late autumn to mid-spring depending on snow conditions).This is a good conditioning hike for, say, that trek to Nepal. If you're not in the mood for an all-day adventure, make the 4-mile round trip hike to the Fuller ridgeline and enjoy the far-reaching views.

Get an early start and allow plenty of time for this hike—seven to ten hours, depending on your pace and how long you linger on the summit. Even if you're a well-conditioned hiker, don't be discouraged if it takes you longer than you think to make San Jacinto Peak by this route. And don't rush the descent: the steep and rocky trail has a high ankle-turning and knee-wrenching potential.

Directions to trailhead: From Interstate 10 in Banning, exit on Highway 243 and ascend southeast some 15 winding miles to Black Mountain Road. (From the town of Idyllwild, drive about 8.5 miles north to Black Mountain Road.) Proceed 6.5 miles north Black Mountain

Campground then another 1.5 miles to a brief, right-forking spur that leads to parking and Fuller Ridge Trailhead.

The hike: The path ascends a mile (in a mellow manner at first) through open forest to a saddle. Another mile of ascent, passing the aptly named Castle Rocks, brings you to the ridge.

The path twists atop the ridgeline, dodging great boulders and contorted white fir. Savor eye-popping vistas of Mt. San Gorgonio, the Southland's 11,499-foot high point, as well as other tall peaks of the San Bernardino Mountains. Far, far below is San Gorgonio Pass, which separates the San Bernardino and San Jacinto ranges. You'll also get impressive views of the Coachella Valley.

After a bit more than a mile of squirming atop the ridgeline, PCT abandons it for the southern slopes of Mt. San Jacinto. PCT switchbacks and contours across the broad shoulders of the mountain past the headwaters of the north fork of the San Jacinto River and reaches a junction 5 miles from the start.

PCT continues south to soon meet up with Seven Pines and Marion Mountain trails, but you turn northeast and keep switchbacking for another mile to Little Round Valley, where a small trail camp is located.

The trail curves east, still climbing, still switchbacking for another 1.3 miles with a 800-foot elevation gain to San Jacinto Peak's summit ridge. A final 0.3-mile ascent via the summit trail leads past a stone mountaineers hut to the peak.

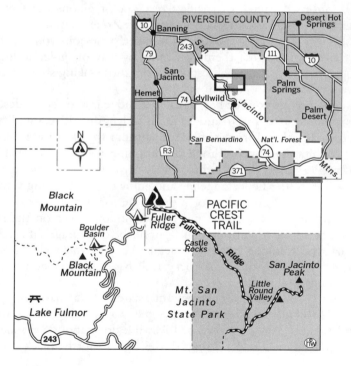

DESERT DIVIDE

Spitler Peak, Pacific Crest Trails

From Apple Canyon to Desert Divide is 10 miles roundtrip with 2,000-foot gain; to Apache Peak is 12 miles round trip with 2,600-foot gain; to Antsell Rock is 14 miles round trip with 2,600-foot gain

Riding the Palm Springs Aerial Tramway or driving the Palms to Pines Highway are two ways to view the astonishing change in vegetation that occurs with a change in elevation in the San Jacinto Mountains. A third way to observe the startling contrast between desert and alpine environments is to hike up the back side of the San Jacinto Mountains to aptly named Desert Divide. The imposing granite divide, which reminds some mountaineers of the High Sierra, offers far-reaching views of the canyons back of Palm Springs and of the Coachella Valley.

Most visitors to the San Jacinto Mountains begin their explorations in Idyllwild or from the top of the tramway. Few hike—or even think about—Desert Divide. Too bad, because this land of pine forest, wide meadows and soaring granite peaks has much to offer.

The trail begins in Garner Valley, a long meadowland bordered by tall pine. Meandering across the valley floor is the South Fork of the San Jacinto River, whose waters are impounded at the lower end of the valley by Lake Hemet. Splashing spring color across the meadow are purple penstemon, golden yarrow, owl's clover and tidy tips. Autumn brings a showy "river" of rust-colored buckwheat winding through the valley.

Spitler Peak Trail offers a moderate-to-strenuous route up to Desert Divide. You can enjoy the great views from the divide and call it a day right there, or join Pacific Crest Trail and continue to the top of Apache Peak or Antsell Rock.

Directions to trailhead: The hamlet of Mountain Center is some 20 miles up Highway 74 from Hemet and a few miles up Highway 243 from Idyllwild. From the intersection of Highway 243 (Banning-Idyllwild Highway) and Highway 74 in Mountain Center, proceed southeast on the latter highway. After 3 miles, turn left at the signed junction for Hurkey Creek County Park. Instead of turning into the park, you'll continue 1.75 mile on Apple Canyon Road to signed Spitler Peak Trail on the right. Park in the turnout just south of the trailhead.

The hike: Spitler Peak Trail begins among oak woodland and chaparral. The mellow, well-graded path contours quite some distance to the east before beginning a more earnest northerly ascent. Enjoy over-the-shoulder views of Lake Hemet and of Garner Valley. Actually, geologists say Garner Valley is not a valley at all but a graben, a long narrow area that dropped between two bordering faults.

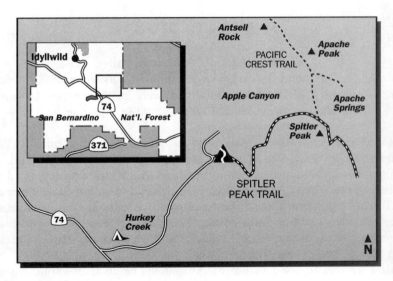

Garner Graben?

Nope, just doesn't have the right ring to it.

The trail climbs steadily into juniper-Jeffrey pine-Coulter pine forest. Most of the time your path is under conifers or the occasional oak. There always seem to be quite a number of deadfalls to climb over, climb under, or walk around along this stretch of trail.

About a mile from the divide the going gets steeper and you rapidly gain elevation. Finally you gain the windblown divide just northwest of Spitler Peak and intersect signed Pacific Crest Trail. Enjoy the vistas of forest and desert. Picnic atop one of the divide's many rock outcroppings.

PCT, sometimes known as Desert Divide Trail in these parts, offers the energetic a range of options. PCT heads north and soon passes through a section of ghost forest—the charred result of the 1980 Palm Canyon Fire that roared up these slopes from Palm Springs. After a half-mile you'll pass a side trail that descends steeply another 0.5-mile to Apache Springs. Another 0.5-mile along the PCT brings you to a side trail leading up to bare 7,567-foot Apache Peak.

Another mile brings you to a point just below 7,720-foot Antsell Rock. Unless you're a very good rock climber, stay off the unstable slopes and avoid the urge to ascend to the very top of the rock.

12. Palomar Mountains

THE PALOMAR MOUNTAINS, extending 25 miles along the northern boundary of San Diego County, are one of the few Southern California mountain ranges not bordering the desert. The range is an uplifted block with distinct fault lines on both the north and south sides. The north and south slopes are quite precipitous as a result of these faults.

Three major ridges make up the Palomars. A long ridge near the Observatory rises to the range's highest point, unimaginatively named "High Point" (6,126 feet). A western ridge, protected by a federal wilderness area, is called Agua Tibia and the rocky ridge east of high point is Aguanga Mountain.

Native peoples called the Palomars, "Pauuw," which means quite simply "mountains." The Spanish noticed a large number of band-tailed pigeons in the area and named the mountains Palomar, "pigeon roost."

During the 1890s the Palomars were a popular vacation spot. Hotels and a tent city welcomed mountain lovers. When automania took hold in the teens and twenties, vacationers were lured to farther and more exotic locales. The Palomars reverted to semi-wilderness, undeveloped land thick with private property signs.

The Palomars were dubbed the "Mystery Mountains" because few people lived there when plans for Palomar Observatory were formulated. Access to the range was difficult. Cars had to climb up a steep, nerve-wracking grade. Motorists descending the grade tied trees to their car bumpers to slow their descent. Trees discarded at the bottom of the hill supplied locals with firewood for a long time. A new south grade road, the "Highway to the Stars," was built to the observatory site and opened up the mountains to visitors.

The beauty of the Palomars is entrusted to Palomar Mountain State Park and the Cleveland National Forest. Considering the mountains' popularity with visitors, it's surprising that there isn't an extensive trail network. However, the few trails take hikers through diverse ecosystems. Moist high-altitude environments, characteristic of coastal ranges much farther north, are found on upper Palomar slopes. Lower, sun-drenched slopes host a chaparral community typical of Southern California mountains. Whether you hike through blue lupine on sunny slopes or tiger lilies in the shade, manzanita on dry slopes or azalea in damp canyons, a hike in San Diego County's "Mystery Mountains" is a memorable event.

AGUA TIBIA WILDERNESS

Dripping Springs Trail
From Dripping Springs to Giant Chaparral is 7 miles round trip is 1,200-foot elevation gain; to Palomar Divide Truck Trail is 13 miles round trip with 2,800-foot gain; Season: November-June

Agua Tibia Wilderness Area, located on the northwest crest of the Palomar Mountains is a rugged three-by-five-mile area that seems outwardly inhospitable. Stream erosion has carved deep and precipitous canyons in the slopes, which are blanketed in thorny chaparral. Temperatures exceed 100 degrees in summer and as much as two feet of snow may fall on an open ridge in winter.

Dripping Springs Trail takes you to an area of giant chaparral where manzanita have miraculously escaped the ravages of fire for more than 100 years. The trail continues to the abandoned Palomar Divide Fire Road and oak- and pine-dotted upper slopes that give panoramic views of the San Jacintos and San Bernardinos.

Directions to trailhead: From Interstate Highway 15, exit east on Highway 79. Proceed 10 miles to the Dripping Springs Campground on your right. Signed Dripping Springs Trail begins at the south end of the campground. Near the entrance to the campground is a Forest Service station, where you may obtain a wilderness permit.

The hike: The path immediately crosses the only water en route, Arroyo Seco Creek. It climbs south and southwest, switchbacking forever and ever up one false summit after another on the north side of Agua Tibia Mountain (4,779 feet). Enjoy views of Vail Lake and the mighty San Jacintos.

You arrive at the Giant Chaparral 3.5 miles from the trailhead.

A half-mile farther the trail descends and you get a view southeast over the Palomars. Crowning a far-off ridge, the silver dome of Palomar Observatory sparkles in the sun. Begin switchbacking again and rise above the chaparral to oak- and pine-dotted slopes. Three miles from the Giant Chaparral, the Dripping Springs Trail intersects the Palomar Divide Truck Trail. From the truck trail, you can look over distant peaks and valley and occasionally glimpse the Pacific Ocean, 40 miles away. If you turn left at the truck trail and walk yet another mile, you'll reach a primitive campsite, just as the truck trail begins to head west.

Palomar Mountain

Observatory National Recreation Trail
From Observatory Campground to Palomar Observatory is 4 miles round trip from 800-foot elevation gain

Astronomer George Hale will be remembered both for his scientific discoveries and his vision of constructing great observatories. His first vision materialized as the Yerkes Observatory with its 40-inch telescope, his second as Mt. Wilson Observatory with its 60- and 100-inch telescopes, and finally Palomar Observatory with its 200-inch telescope. The Great Glass at Palomar is the most powerful telescope in America and has done a great deal to increase our knowledge of the heavens.

Most visitors traveling to Palomar drive their cars all the way to the top, visit the Observatory and drive back down. Too bad! They miss a nice hike. Observatory Trail roughly parallels the road, but is hidden by a dense forest from the sights and sounds of traffic.

Palomar Mountain doesn't have the distinct cone shape of a stereotypical mountain top. It soars abruptly up from the San Luis River Valley to the south, but flattens out on top. Atop and just below the long crest, are oak valleys, pine forests, spring-watered grasslands and lush canyons.

All the great views from the top do not come from the Hale telescope. Palomar Mountain provides a bird's-eye view of much of Southern California. Miles and miles of mountains roll toward the north, dominated in the distance by peaks of the San Bernardino Mountains. Southward, Mt. Cuyamaca is visible, and even farther south, the mountains of Baja California. On the western horizon, orange sunset rays floodlight the Pacific.

Menhenhall Valley from Mt. Palomar Observatory Trail.

Observatory National Recreation Trail is a delightful introduction to the geography of the Palomar Mountains. It leads from Observatory Campground to the peak, where you can learn about the geography of the heavens.

Directions to trailhead: From Interstate Highway 15, exit on Highway 76 east. Proceed to Rincon Springs. For a couple of miles, S6 joins with Highway 76. Continue on S6, forking to the left at South Grade Road (Highway to the Stars). South Grade winds steeply to Observatory Campground and up to the Observatory. Turn right into Observatory Campground. The Forest Service charges a day use fee. The campground closes in mid-December for the winter. Follow the campground road until you spot the signed trailhead between campsites 19 and 20. The Forest Service booklet "Guide to the Observatory Trail," which highlights flora and fauna found along the trail, is available at the trailhead.

You could just as well hike the Observatory Trail from top to bottom and have a friend or family member pick you up at the bottom. To reach the upper trailhead, simply continue up the road to the Observatory parking area. The top of the trail is just outside the gates of the Observatory grounds.

The hike: The signed trail begins at the edge of the campground. You begin climbing over wooded slopes and soon get a grand view of Mendenhall Valley. You continue ascending over slopes watered by the headwaters of the San Luis Rey River. As the legend goes, young Indian girls visited one of the trickling mountain springs whose waters rushed over beautiful slender stones. The maidens would reach into the water to gather these stones, the number found indicating the number of children she would bear.

The last part of the trail climbs more abruptly up manzanita-covered slopes. Soon you see the silvery dome of the 200-inch Hale telescope. This obelisk of symmetry and precision dwarfs nearby trees. Ever-changing patterns of sunlight and shade play upon the top of the dome.

Visit the Observatory gallery to see the great telescope. And take a look at the nearby museum whose exhibits explain some of the mysteries unraveled by the 200-inch lens.

PALOMAR MOUNTAIN STATE PARK

Scott's Cabin Trail
From Silver Crest Picnic Area to Scott's Cabin; Cedar Grove Campground
and Boucher Lookout is a 3.5-mile loop with 800-foot elevation gain

Palomar Mountain is a state park for all seasons. Fall offers dramatic color changes, and blustery winter winds ensure far-reaching views from the peaks. In spring, the dogwood blooms, and during summer, when temperatures soar, the park offers a cool, green retreat.

A mixed forest of cedar, silver fir, spruce and black oak invites a leisurely exploration. Tall trees and mountain meadows make the park especially attractive to the Southern California day hiker in search of a Sierra Nevada-like atmosphere.

The discovery of bedrock mortars and artifacts in Doane Valley indicate that native peoples lived in this area of the Palomars for many hundreds of years. The mountains' pine and fir trees were cut for the construction of Mission San Luis Rey. Remote Palomar Mountain meadows were a favorite hiding place for cattle and horse thieves, who pastured their stolen animals in the high country until it was safe to sneak them across the border.

This day hike is a grande randonnée of the park, a four-trail sampler that leads to a lookout atop 5,438-foot Boucher Hill.

Directions to trailhead: From Interstate 5 in Oceanside, drive northeast on State Highway 76 about 30 miles. Take County Road S6 north; at S7, head northwest to the park entrance. There is a day use fee. Park in the lot at Silver Crest Picnic Area just inside the park. Scott's Cabin Trail takes off from the right side of the road about 20 yards beyond the lot entrance.

The hike: A trail sign points the way to Scott's Cabin, a 0.5-mile away. Noisome Stellar's jays make their presence known along this stretch of trail. Scott's Cabin, built by a homesteader in the 1880s, is found on your left. The crumpled remains aren't much to view.

Descend steeply through a white fir forest and reach the signed jucntion with the Cedar-Doane Trail, which heads right (east). This steep trail, formerly known as the Slide Trail because of its abruptness, takes the hiker down oak-covered slopes to Doane Pond. The pond is stocked with trout, and fishing is permitted. A pond-side picnic area welcomes the hiker.

Continue past the Cedar-Doane Trail junction a short distance to Cedar Grove Campground. Follow the trail signs and turn left on the campground road, and then right into the group campground. Look leftward for the signed Adams Trail, which cuts through a bracken fern-covered meadow. Once across the meadow, you'll encounter a small ravine where dogwood

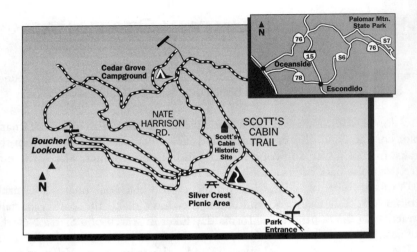

blooms during April and May. The trail winds uphill past some big cone spruce and reaches Nate Harrison Road.

The road is named in honor of Nathan Harrison, a Southern slave who followed his master to the California gold rush—and freedom—in 1849. Harrison laid claim to a homestead on the wild eastern edge of what is now state parkland, and had a successful hay-making and hog-raising operation, despite numerous run-ins with bears and mountain lions.

Across the road, your path becomes Boucher Trail, which ascends a north-facing slope through white fir, then through bracken ferns and black oaks, to the summit of Boucher Hill. Atop the hill is a fire lookout and microwave facility. From the summit, you get a view of the surrounding lowlands, including Pauma Valley to the west.

Return to the parking area via Oak Ridge Trail, which descends one mile between the two sides of the loop road that encircles Boucher Hill. The trailheads down an open ridgeline to a junction of five roads, where it's a mere hop, skip and a jump back to the Silver Crest Picnic Area.

13. Southern California Coast

FOR THE DAY HIKER, the Southern California Coast offers not only those white sand beaches depicted on postcards, but a wide variety of shoreline features—the palms of La Jolla and Santa Monica, the cliffs of Torrey Pines and Palos Verdes.

The air and water temperatures are Mediterranean, the place names Spanish. Southland beaches are an attraction for visitors (foreign and domestic) who come for the sun, the fun and depending on age and orientation, the historical romance or the cutting-edge trendiness of the coast.

Each of the Southland's five coastal counties—San Diego, Orange, Los Angeles, Ventura and Santa Barbara—has its own character. And each individual beach seems to have its own personality as well—best surfing, clearest water, panoramic view, most bird life, etc.

It is said that California began in San Diego, when Portuguese navigator Juan Rodríguez Cabrillo landed on Pt. Loma in 1542. The beaches near the Mexican border are wide sand strands. From Pt. Loma to La Jolla, rocks and reefs carve the oceanfront into a series of pocket beaches, dramatically altering waves and currents so that a few feet of movement can transport hikers from a safe swimming area to a paradise for surfers to a frothy, wave-swept cauldron.

Although it shares a single coastal plain with neighboring Los Angeles County, Orange County retains a distinct shoreline identity as a boating community (Newport Harbor), a surfing community (Huntington Beach), and as a place much sought-after for recreation and residence.

When the summer sun beats down on the metropolis and smog thickens, it seems half the Basin and San Fernando Valley flee to Los Angeles County's seventy-four miles of coastline. Perhaps a hundred million visits a year are made to county beaches although, as hikers soon discover, most cluster blanket to blanket on the same beaches, leaving less accessible areas to those willing to hike. Among the hike-able locales are Palos Verdes Peninsula and the rugged bluffs up-coast from Malibu.

Ventura County's 43 miles of shoreline offers several fine sandy beaches. The best ones are in the state parks: Point Mugu, McGrath, San Buenaventura and Emma Wood.

From Carpinteria west, the Santa Barbara County shoreline extends to Point Conception, one sandy and mellow beach after another. The coastline's southern exposure results in clearer water, smoother sand, warmer sun. In the northern part of the county some hidden beaches await those willing to venture off the beaten track.

Carpinteria Beach

Carpinteria Beach Trail
From Carpinteria State Beach to Harbor Seal Preserve
is 2.5 miles round trip; to Carpinteria Bluffs is 4.5 miles round trip;
to Rincon Beach County Park is 6 miles round trip

Carpinteria is one of the state park system's more popular beachfront campgrounds. A broad beach, gentle waves, fishing and clamming are among the reasons for this popularity. A tiny visitors center (open weekends only) offers displays of marine life and Chumash history, as well as a children-friendly tidepool tank.

Carpinteria residents boast they have "The World's Safest Beach" because, although the surf can be large, it breaks far out, and there's no undertow. As early as 1920, visitors reported "the Hawaiian diversion of surfboard riding." Surfers, hikers and bird-watchers have long enjoyed the bluffs, which rise about 100 feet above the beach and offer great views of Anacapa, Santa Cruz and Santa Rosa islands.

For more than two decades a battle raged between development interests with plans to build huge housing and hotel projects and local conservationists who wanted to preserve the bluffs, one of the last stretches of privately-held, undeveloped coastline between Los Angeles and Santa Barbara.

Activists led by Citizens for the Carpinteria Bluffs and the Land Trust for Santa Barbara, along with local merchants, school children, hundreds of Santa Barbara county citizens and the California Coastal Conservancy raised money for the purchase of the property in 1998.

The Carpinteria Tar Pits once bubbled up near Carpinteria Beach. Spanish explorers noted that the Chumash caulked their canoes with the asphaltum. Around 1915, crews mined the tar, which was used to pave the coast highway in Santa Barbara County. In order to dig the tar, workmen had to heat their shovels in a furnace; the smoking tar would slice like butter with the hot blade. Long ago, the tar pits trapped mastodons, saber-toothed tigers and other prehistoric animals. Unfortunately, the pits, which may have yielded amazing fossils like those of the La Brea Tar Pits in Los Angeles, became a municipal dump.

On August 17, 1769, the Captain Portola's Spanish explorers observed the native Chumash building a canoe and dubbed the location La Carpinteria, the Spanish name for carpenter shop. The Chumash used the asphaltum to caulk their canoes and seal their cookware.

The Carpinteria beach hike heads down-coast along the state beach to City Bluffs Park and the Chevron Oil Pier. A small pocket beach contains the Harbor Seal Preserve. From December through May this beach is seals-only. Humans may watch the boisterous colony, sometimes numbering as many as 150 seals from a blufftop observation area above the beach.

After seal-watching, you can then sojourn over the Carpinteria bluffs or continue down the beach to Rincon Point on the Santa Barbara-Ventura county line.

Directions to trailhead: From Highway 101 in Carpinteria, exit on Linden Avenue and head south (oceanward) 0.6 mile through town to the avenue's end at the beach. Park along Linden Avenue (free, but time restricted) or in the Carpinteria State Beach parking lot (fee).

The hike: Follow "The World's Safest Beach" down-coast. After a half-mile's travel over the wide sand strand you'll reach beach-bisecting Carpinteria Creek. During the summer, a sand bar creates a lagoon at the mouth of the creek. Continue over the sand bar or, if Carpinteria Creek is high, retreat inland through the campground and use the bridge over the creek.

Picnic at City Bluffs Park or keep walking a short distance farther along the bluffs past Chevron Oil Pier to an excellent vista point above the Harbor Seal Preserve.

From the seal preserve, you can walk another mile across the Carpinteria Bluffs. Time and tides permitting, you can continue still farther down-coast along the beach to Rincon Beach County Park, a popular surfing spot on the Santa Barbara-Ventura county line.

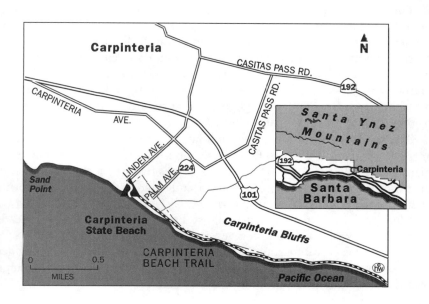

McGrath State Beach

McGrath Beach Trail
From State Beach to McGrath Lake is 4 miles round trip; to Oxnard Shores is 8 miles round trip; to Channel Islands Harbor is 12 miles round trip

McGrath State Beach and McGrath Lake were named for the McGrath family which had extensive land holdings in the Ventura coastal area dating from 1874. Located on the western city limits of Oxnard, the two-mile long state beach extends south from the Santa Clara River.

A small lake in the southern portion of the park helps to attract more than two hundred species of birds, including black-shouldered kites, northern harriers, owls and herons. Such rare birds as ospreys, white wagtails, black skimmers and peregrine falcons have been sighted here. The lake, which is partially on private property, was damaged by a 1993 oil spill caused by a ruptured pipeline.

The Santa Clara Estuary Natural Preserve on the northern boundary of the park offers a haven for birds and habitat for weasels, skunks, jackrabbits, opossum, squirrels and mice, plus tortoises and gopher snakes. Near the state beach entry kiosk, a small visitor center features exhibits about the area's plants and wildlife.

This walk takes you on a nature trail through the Santa Clara River Estuary, visits McGrath Lake and travels miles of sandy beach to Channel Islands Harbor.

Directions to trailhead: To reach McGrath State Beach, visitors southbound on Highway 101 take the Seaward Avenue offramp to Harbor Boulevard, turn south on Harbor and travel 4 miles to the park. Northbound visitors exit Highway 101 on Victoria Avenue, turn left at the light to Olivas Park Drive, then right to Harbor Boulevard. Turn left on Harbor and proceed 0.75 mile to the park. The signed nature trail leaves from the day use parking lot. Signposts along the nature trail are keyed to a pamphlet, available at the entry kiosk.

The hike: From the parking lot, follow the nature trail through the estuary. The riverbank is a mass of lush vegetation: willow, silverweed and yerba mansa. In 1980, the Santa Clara River area was declared a natural preserve, primarily to protect the habitat of two endangered birds—the California least tern and Belding's Savannah Sparrow.

When you reach nature trail signpost 11, join a nearby trail that leads atop an old levee, first along the river, then down-coast along the periphery of the state beach campground. This trail joins a dirt road and continues down coast, but the far more aesthetic route is along water's edge, so trudge over the low dunes and walk along the shoreline.

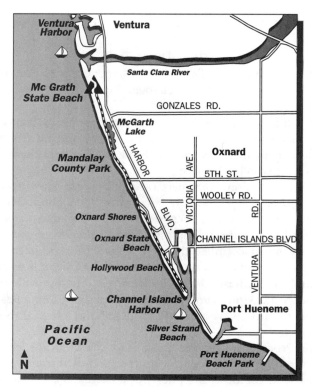

Along the beach, visitors enjoy sunbathing or surf fishing for bass, corbina, or perch. In two miles, if you head inland a short ways, you'll spot McGrath Lake, tucked away behind some dunes.

As you continue south, more sandy beach and dunes follow. You pass a huge old Edison power plant, and arrive at Oxnard Shores, a development famous for getting clobbered by heavy surf at high tide. The beach is flat and at one time was eroding at the phenomenal rate of 10 feet a year. Homes were built right on the shoreline, and many have been heavily damaged. New homes are built on pilings, so the waves crash under rather than through them.

Past Oxnard Shores, a mile of beach walking brings you to historic Hollywood Beach. The Sheik, starring that great silent movie idol Rudolph Valentino, was filmed on the desert-like sands here. Real estate promoters of the time attempted to capitalize on Oxnard Beach's instant fame and re-named it Hollywood Beach. They laid out subdivisions called Hollywood-by-the-Sea and Silver Strand, suggesting to their customers that the area was really a movie colony and might become a future Hollywood, but it never became a mecca for the stars or their fans.

This walk ends another mile down-coast at the entrance to Channel Islands Harbor.

POINT DUME

Zuma-Dume Trail
From Zuma Beach to Point Dume is 1 mile round trip; to Paradise Cove
is 3 miles round trip

Zuma Beach is one of the finest white sand strands in California. Zuma lies on the open coast beyond Santa Monica Bay and thus receives heavy breakers crashing in from the north. From sunrise to sunset, board and body surfers try to catch a big one.

This walk travels along that part of Zuma Beach known as Westward Beach, climbs over the geologically fascinating Point Dume Headlands for sweeping views of the coast, then descends to Paradise Cove, site of a romantic little beach and a fishing pier. During the whale-watching season (approximately mid-December through March), hikers ascending to the lookout atop Point Dume can spot migrating California gray whales.

Directions to trailhead: From Pacific Coast Highway, about 25 miles up-coast from Santa Monica and just down coast from Zuma Beach County Park, turn oceanward on Westward Beach Road and follow it to its end at a (fee) parking lot.

The hike: Proceed down-coast along sandy Westward Beach. Look for a distinct path leading up the point. The trail ascends through a community of sea fig and sage, coreopsis and prickly pear cactus to a lookout point.

From atop Point Dume, you can look down at Pirate's Cove, two hundred yards of beach tucked away between two rocky outcroppings. In past years, this beach was the scene of much dispute between nude beach advocates, residents and the county sheriff.

After enjoying the view and watching for whales, retrace your steps a short distance and continue on the main trail over the point, which has been set aside as a preserve under the protection of the California Department of Fish and Game. A staircase lets you descend to the beach.

A mile of beach-walking brings you to Paradise Cove, sometimes called Dume Cove. It's a secluded spot, and the scene of much television and motion picture filming. A restaurant and a private pier are located here.

Palos Verdes Peninsula

Palos Verdes Peninsula Trail
From Malaga Cove to Rocky Point is 5 miles round trip; to Point Vincente
Lighthouse is 10 miles round trip

Palos Verdes Peninsula is famous for its rocky cliffs, which rise from 50 to 300 feet above the ocean and for its thirteen wave-cut terraces. These terraces, or platforms, resulted from a combination of uplift and sea-level fluctuations caused by the formation and melting of glaciers. Today the waves, as they have for so many thousands of years, are actively eroding the shoreline, cutting yet another terrace onto the land.

This walk visits many beautiful coves, where whaling ships once anchored and delivered their cargo of whale oil. Large iron kettles, used to boil whale blubber, have been found in sea cliff caves. Native Americans, Spanish rancheros and Yankee smugglers have all added to the Peninsula's romantic history. Modern times have brought white-stuccoed, red-tiled mansions to the Peninsula bluffs, but the beach remains almost pristine. Offshore, divers explore the rocky bottoms for abalone and shellfish. Onshore, hikers enjoy the wave-scalloped bluffs and splendid tidepools.

Hiking this beach is like walking over a surface of broken bowling balls. The route is rocky and progress slow, but that gives you more time to look down at the tidepools and up at the magnificent bluffs. Check a tide table and walk only at low tide.

Directions to trailhead: Take Pacific Coast Highway to Palos Verdes Boulevard. Bear right on Palos Verdes Drive. As you near Malaga Cove Plaza, turn right at the first stop sign (Via Corta). Make a right on Via Arroyo, then another right into the parking lot behind the Malaga Cove School. The trailhead is on the ocean side of the parking area where a wide path descends the bluffs above the Flatrock Point tidepools. A footpath leaves from Paseo Del Mar, 0.1 mile past Via Horcada, where the street curves east to join Palos Verdes Drive West.

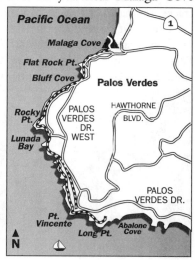

The hike: From the Malaga Cove School parking lot, descend the wide path to the beach. A sign indicates you're entering a seashore reserve and asks you to treat tidepool residents with respect.

To the north are sandy beaches for sedentary sun worshipers. Active rock-hoppers clamber to the south. At several places along this walk you'll notice that the great terraces are cut by steep-walled canyons. The first of these canyon incisions can be observed at Malaga Cove, where Malaga Canyon slices through the north slopes of Palos Verdes Hills, then cuts west to empty at the cove.

The coastline curves out to sea in a southwesterly direction and Flatrock Point comes into view. The jade-colored waters swirl around this anvil-shaped point, creating the best tidepool area along this section of coast. Above the point, the cliffs soar to 300 feet. Cloaked in morning fog, the rocky seascape here is reminiscent of Big Sur.

Rounding Flatrock Point, you pick your way among the rocks, seaweed and the flotsam and jetsam of civilization to Bluff Cove, where sparkling combers explode against the rocks and douse the unwary with their tangy spray. A glance over your right shoulder brings a view of Santa Moncia Bay, the Santa Monica Mountains in gray silhouette, and on the far horizon, the Channel Islands.

A mile beyond Bluff Cove, Rocky (also called Palos Verdes) Point juts out like a ship's prow. Caught fast on the rocks at the base of the point is the rusting exoskeleton of the Greek freighter *Dominator*, a victim of the treacherous reef surrounding the Peninsula.

Trek around Rocky Point to Lunada Bay, a good place to observe the terrace surfaces. From here you'll walk under almost perpendicular cliffs that follow horseshoe-shaped Lunada Bay. Shortly you'll round Resort Point, where fishermen try their luck. As the coastline turns south, Catalina can often be seen glowing on the horizon. Along this stretch of shoreline, numerous stacks, remnants of former cliffs not yet dissolved by the surf, can be seen.

The coast around the lighthouse has been vigorously scalloped by thousands of years of relentless surf. You'll have to boulder-hop the last mile to Point Vincente. The lighthouse has worked its beacon over the dark waters since 1926. Guided tours of the lighthouse are available by appointment.

Passage is usually impossible around the lighthouse at high tide; if passable, another 0.5 mile of walking brings you to an official beach access (or departure) route at Long Point.

Pt. Vicente Lighthouse warns mariners of the peninsula's rocky shores.

CORONA DEL MAR

Crown of the Sea Trail
From Corona del Mar Beach to Arch Rock is 2 miles round trip; to Crystal Cove is 4 miles round trip; to Abalone Point is 7 miles round trip

In 1904, George Hart purchased 700 acres of land on the cliffs east of the entrance to Newport Bay and laid out a subdivision he called Corona del Mar ("Crown of the Sea"). The only way to reach the townsite was by way of a long muddy road that circled around the head of Upper Newport Bay. Later a ferry carried tourists and residents from Balboa to Corona del Mar. Little civic improvement occurred until Highway 101 bridged the bay and the community was annexed to Newport Beach.

This hike explores the beaches and marine refuges of "Big" and Little Corona del Mar beaches and continues to the beaches and headlands of Crystal Cove State Park. Consult a tide table. Best beach-walking is at low tide.

Directions to trailhead: From Pacific Coast Highway in Corona del Mar, turn oceanward on Marguerite Avenue and travel a few blocks to the Corona del Mar State Beach parking lot.

The hike: Begin at the east jetty of Newport Beach, where you'll see sailboats tacking in and out of the harbor. Surfers tackle the waves near the jetty. Proceed down-coast along wide sandy Corona del Mar State Beach.

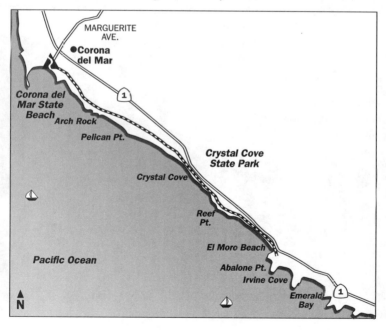

The beach narrows as you approach the cove that encloses Little Corona del Mar Beach. Snorkeling is good beneath the cliffs of "Big" and Little Corona beaches. Both areas are protected from boat traffic by kelp beds and marine refuge status.

A mile from the jetty, you'll pass well-named Arch Rock, which is just offshore, and can be reached at low tide. The beach from Arch Rock to Irvine Cove, 2.5 miles to the south, was purchased by the state from the Irvine Corporation and is now part of Crystal Cove State Park. Trails lead up the bluffs which, in winter, offer a good vantage point from which to observe the California gray whale migration.

Continuing your stroll down the undeveloped beach and past some tide-pools brings you to the tiny resort community of Crystal Cove, site of a few dozen beach cottages. The wood frame cottages, little altered since their construction in the 1920s are on the National Register of Historic Places. "Cove" is something of a misnomer; the beach here shows almost no coastal indentation.

Rounding Reef Point, you'll continue along El Moro Beach, a sand strand that's sometimes beautifully cusped. El Moro Point, a rocky promontory located just outside Laguna Beach city limits, is made of eroded lava and other volcanic material distributed in the San Joaquin Hills. It's capped by a grass-covered dome rising two hundred feet above the water.

Return the same way or ascend one of the coastal accessways to the blufftops of Crystal Cove State Park. Blufftop trails offer a scenic alternative for a portion of your return route.

Little Corona del Mar Beach is popular both onshore and off.

San Clemente State Beach

Trestles Trail
From State Beach to San Mateo Point is 3 miles round trip

"Our beach shall always be free from hurdy-gurdies and defilement. We believe beauty to be an asset as well as gold and silver, or cabbage and potatoes." This was the pledge of Norwegian immigrant Ole Hanson, who began the town of San Clemente in 1925. It was quite a promise from a real estate developer, quite a promise in those days of shameless boosterism a half-century before the California Coastal Commission was established.

Thanks in part to Hanson's vision, some of the peaceful ambiance of San Clemente, which he regarded as "a painting 5 miles long and a mile wide" has been preserved. And some of its isolation, too. Most everyone in the real estate community thought Hanson crazy for building in a locale 66 miles from San Diego, 66 miles from Los Angeles, but today this isolation attracts rather than repels. This isolation was one of the reasons President Richard Nixon (1969-74) established his Western White House on the bluffs above San Clemente Beach.

San Clemente State Beach is a great place for a walk. The beach is mercifully walled off from the din of the San Diego Freeway and the confusion of the modern world by a handsome line of tan-colored bluffs. Only the occasional train passing over Santa Fe Railroad tracks, located near the shore interrupt the cry of the gull, the roar of the breakers. The trestles located at the south end of the beach at San Mateo Point give Trestles Beach its name.

Trestles Beach is one of the finest surfing areas on the west coast. When the surf is up, the waves peel rapidly across San Mateo Point, creating a great ride. Before the area became part of the state beach, it was restricted government property belonging to Camp Pendleton Marine Base. During the 1960s and '70s, surfers carried on guerrilla warfare with U.S. Marines. Trespassing surfers were chased, arrested and fined, and on many occasions had their boards confiscated.

This walk's destination, San Mateo Point, is the northernmost boundary of San Diego County, the beginning of Orange County. When the original counties of Los Angeles and San Diego were set up in 1850, the line that separated them began on the coast at San Mateo Point. When Orange County was formed from southern Los Angeles County in 1889, San Mateo Point was established as the southern point of the new county.

The enthusiastic, with the time and inclination, can easily extend this beach-walk several miles south to San Onofre State Beach. Another option worth considering is to take the train to San Clemente and walk south from the Amtrak station.

Directions to trailhead: From the San Diego Freeway (5) in San Clemente, exit on Avenida Calafia and head west 0.5 mile to Calafia Beach Park, where there is metered parking. You can also park (for a fee) at San Clemente State Beach. A limited amount of free parking is available in the residential area near the state beach.

North-bound motorists on I-5 will exit at Cristianitos Road, turn left and go over the freeway onto Ave. Del Presidente and drive a mile north to Calafia Beach Park.

The hike: From Calafia Beach Park, cross the railroad tracks, make your way down an embankment and head south. As you'll soon see, San Clemente State Beach is frequented by plenty of shorebirds, as well as plenty of surfers, body surfers, and swimmers.

At distinct San Mateo Point, which marks the border of Orange and San Diego counties, you'll find San Mateo Creek. The headwaters of the creek rise way up in the Santa Ana Mountains above Camp Pendleton. A portion of the creek is protected by the Cleveland National Forest's San Mateo Canyon Wilderness. Rushes, salt grass and cattails line the creek mouth, where sand pipers, herons and egrets gather.

You can ford the creek mouth (rarely a problem except after winter storms) and continue south toward San Onofre State Beach and the giant domes of San Onofre Nuclear Power Plant. Or you can return the same way.

Or here's a third alternative, an inland return route: Walk under the train trestles and join the park service road, which is usually filled with surfers carrying their boards. The service road takes you up the bluffs, where you'll join the San Clemente Coastal Bike Trail, then wind through a residential area to an entrance to San Clemente State Beach Campground. Improvise a route through the campground to the park's entry station and join the self-guiding nature trail (brochures available at the station). The path descends through a prickly pear- and lemonade berry-filled draw to Calafia Beach Park and the trailhead. The wind- and water-sculpted marine terraces just south of the trailhead resemble Bryce Canyon in miniature and are fun to photograph.

DEL MAR BEACH

Del Mar Beach Trail
From Del Mar Train Station to Torrey Pines State Reserve is 6 miles round trip

Along Del Mar Beach, the power of the surf is awesome and cliff collapse unpredictable. At this beach, permeable layers of rock tilt toward the sea and lie atop other impermeable layers. Water percolates down through the permeable rock, settles on the impermeable rock and "greases the skids"—an ideal condition for collapsing cliffs.

On New Year's Day in 1941, a freight train suddenly found itself in midair. Erosion had undermined the tracks. A full passenger train had been delayed, so the freight train's crew of three were the only casualties.

This walk takes you along the beach, visits the superb Flat Rock tidepool, and detours up the bluffs to Torrey Pines State Reserve. At the Reserve, you'll see those relics from the Ice Age, Torrey pines, which grow only atop the Del Mar bluffs and on Santa Rosa Island; no other place in the world.

Consult a tide table and schedule your walk at low tide when there's more beach to walk and tidepool life is easier to observe.

Directions to trailhead: From Interstate 5 in Del Mar, exit on Via de la Valle. Continue west to Highway S21 and turn left (south) along the ocean past the race tracks and fairgrounds to reach the train station. If you can't find a place to park at the trail station, park in town.

By train: Board a south-bound train at Los Angeles' Union Station or another station along the line, and get off in Del Mar. Reservations are usually not necessary. Call Amtrak for fares and schedules.

The hike: From the train station, cross the tracks to the beach and begin hiking south. With the high cliffs on your left and the pounding breakers on your right, you'll feel you're entering another world. Follow the sometimes wide, sometimes narrow beach over sparkling sand and soft green limestone rock. Holes in the limestone are evidence of marine life that once made its home there.

You'll hike past a number of lifeguard towers. When you reach Tower 5, turn left and make a brief detour through the Highway S21 underpass to Los Penasquitos Lagoon, a saltwater marsh patrolled by native and migratory waterfowl. After observing the least terns and light-footed clapper rails, return to the beach trail.

After three miles of beachcoming, you'll see a distinct rock outcropping named, appropriately enough, Flat Rock. Legend has it that this gouged-out rock, also known as Bathtub Rock, was the site of a luckless Scottish miner's search for coal. Common tidepool residents housed in the rocks at the base of the bluff include barnacles, mussels, crabs and sea anemones.

Just north of Flat Rock, a stairwell ascends the bluffs to Torrey Pines State Reserve. Torrey pines occupy the bold headlands atop the yellow sandstone; these rare and graceful trees seem to thrive on the foggy atmosphere and precarious footing. The Reserve features superb nature trails, native plant gardens and interpretive exhibits.

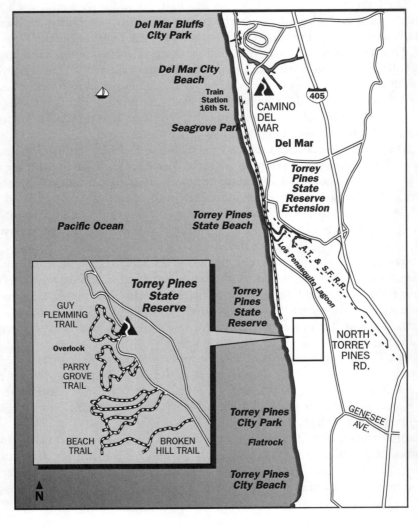

Cabrillo National Monument

Bayside Trail
From Old Point Loma Lighthouse to National Monument boundary
is 2 miles round trip

Cabrillo National Monument, located on the tip of Point Loma, marks the point where Portuguese navigator Juan Rodríguez Cabrillo became the first European to set foot on California soil. He landed near Ballast Point in 1542 and claimed San Diego Bay for Spain. Cabrillo liked this "closed and very good port" and said so in his report to the King of Spain.

One highlight of a visit to the national monument is the Old Point Loma Lighthouse. This lighthouse, built by the federal government, first shined its beacon in 1855. Because fog often obscured the light, the station was abandoned in 1891 and a new one was built on lower ground at the tip of Point Loma. The 1891 lighthouse is still in service today, operated by the U.S. Coast Guard. The 1891 lighthouse has been wonderfully restored to the way it looked when Captain Israel and his family lived there in the 1880s.

Bayside Trail begins at the old lighthouse and winds past yucca and prickly pear, sage and buckwheat. The monument protects one of the last patches of native flora in southernmost California, a hint at how San Diego Bay may have looked when Cabrillo's two small ships anchored here.

Directions to trailhead: Exit Interstate 5 on Rosecrans Street (Highway 209 south) and follow the signs to Cabrillo National Monument. Obtain a trail guide at the visitor center.

The hike: The first part of the Bayside Trail winding down from the old lighthouse is a paved road. At a barrier, you bear left on a gravel road, once a military patrol road. During World War II, the Navy hid bunkers and searchlights along these coastal bluffs.

Bayside Trail provides fine views of the San Diego Harbor shipping lanes. Sometimes when ships pass, park rangers broadcast descriptions of the vessels. Also along the trail is one of Southern California's most popular panoramic views: miles of seashore, 6,000-foot mountains to the east and Mexico to the south. The trail dead-ends at the park boundary.

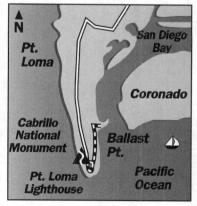

Anacapa Island's welcoming arches

Hikers get commanding views from San Miguel Island high points.

14. CHANNEL ISLANDS NATIONAL PARK

C HANNEL ISLANDS NATIONAL PARK is a preserve for what some have called the "American Galapagos." Top priority was given to protecting sea lions and seals, endemic plants like the Santa Cruz pine, rich archaeological digs, and what may be the final resting place of Portuguese navigator Juan Rodríguez Cabrillo, who explored the California coast for the Spanish crown in the 16th century.

Would-be adventurers enjoy the visitors center in Ventura Harbor as an exciting sneak preview of the splendid park out there in the Pacific, 12 to 60 miles away, a series of blue-tinged mountains floating on the horizon. The visitors center boasts excellent island history and ecology exhibits, and provides boat transportation information.

In 1980, five of the eight Channel Islands—Anacapa, San Miguel, Santa Barbara, Santa Cruz and Santa Rosa—became America's fortieth national park. (The U.S. Navy practices maneuvers on San Nicholas and San Clemente. Farther south, Santa Catalina, has pursued a destiny apart.) The waters surrounding the national park islands are protected as the Channel Islands National Marine Sanctuary.

From Anacapa, only 14 miles offshore from Ventura, you get the feeling that the Channel Islands may once have been connected to the mainland. Years ago, geologists had this same feeling, figuring that the Santa Monica Mountains, which bisect Los Angeles, marched out to sea and their peaks appeared offshore as the Channel Islands. This belief was based on the assumption that a land bridge was the only way terrestrial animals could have arrived. So it's now theorized that the islands rose out of the Pacific through volcanic action 14 million years ago, later sinking and rising many times as glaciation alternated with massive melting. The four northern islands were linked, until about twenty thousand years ago, into a super-island called Santaroasae, only to part company during the final glacial melt into the wave-sculpted islands we see today.

The islands' even sea-tempered climate has preserved plants that either were altered through evolution on the mainland, or have perished altogether. What you see on the islands is Southern California of a millennium ago.

Because of the fragile islands ecology, hiking on the islands is more regulated than it is in most places. You must always stay on the trail, and on some islands be accompanied by a national park ranger or Nature Conservancy employee.

Anacapa Island

Anacapa Island Loop Trail
2 miles round trip

Anacapa, 12 miles southwest of Port Hueneme, is the most accessible Channel Island. It offers the hiker a sampling of the charms of the larger islands to the west. Below the tall wind-and-wave-cut cliffs, sea lions bark at the crashing breakers. Gulls, owls, and pelicans call the cliffs home.

Anacapa is really three islets chained together with reefs that rise above the surface during low tide. West Anacapa is the largest segment, featuring great caves where the Chumash Indians are said to have collected water dripping from the ceiling. The middle isle hosts a wind-battered eucalyptus grove.

The east isle, where the National Park has a visitors center, is the light of the Channel Islands; a Coast Guard lighthouse and foghorn warn ships of the dangerous channel. It's a romantic approach to East Anacapa as you sail past Arch Rock.

What you find on top depends on the time of year. In February and March, you may enjoy the sight of 30-ton gray whales passing south on their way to calving and mating waters off Baja California. In early spring, the giant coreopsis, one of the island's featured attractions, is something to behold. It is called the tree sunflower, an awkward thick-trunked perennial that grows as tall as 10 feet.

Anacapa is small (a mile long and a quarter of a mile wide), but perfect-sized for the usual visit (2 to 3 hours). By the time you tour the lighthouse and visitor center, hike the self-guided trail and have lunch, it's time to board the boat for home.

Directions to trailhead: For the most up-to-date information about boat departures to Anacapa and to the other islands, contact Channel Islands National Park at (805) 658-5730 or the park concessionaire, Island Packers in Ventura Harbor at (805) 642-1393.

The hike: The nature trail leaves from the visitor center, where you can learn about island life, past and present.

Along the trail, a campground and several inspiring cliff-edge nooks invite you to picnic. The trail loops in a figure-eight through the coreopsis and returns to the visitor center.

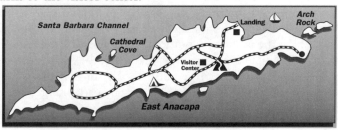

Santa Cruz Island

Cavern Point, Potato Harbor, Smugglers Cove Trails
From Scorpion Anchorage to Cavern Point is 1.2 miles round trip
with 300-foot elevation gain; to Potato Harbor is 4.5 miles round trip
with 300-foot elevation gain; to Smugglers Cove is 7 miles round trip
with 500-foot elevation gain

When viewed from Ventura or Santa Barbara shores, Santa Cruz Island doesn't look that big. However, hike a trail up to one of the commanding east isle promontories and the island appears massive: row upon row of mountains alternating with deep canyons, as well as a seemingly endless series of stark bluffs extending to the horizon. The first time I took in this view I figured I was looking at a neighboring island but no, it was all Santa Cruz, all 96 square miles and 62,000 acres of it. For you city-slickers, the isle measures about four times the size of Manhattan.

Santa Cruz definitely offers hikers plenty of room to roam, as well as a far-reaching trail system composed mainly of old ranch roads. The only limitation on the hiker seems to be time: day-trippers are allowed about five hours on the island before it's necessary to catch to boat back to Ventura Harbor.

For more time on the island, consider camping near the anchorage in Scorpion Canyon. Many campers contend that the eucalyptus-shaded campground is the national park's best because it's the only one with shade, and because it's a convenient base for so many excellent hikes.

A short walk from the Scorpion Anchorage leads to picnic tables, restrooms and a historic two-story ranch house In the 1880s, a colony of French and Italian immigrants led by Justinian Caire began a Mediterranean-style ranch here, raising sheep and cattle, growing olives and almonds, and even making wine. The Gherini family, descendants of Caire, owned the east end of the isle until 1997, when the property was added to the national park. Rangers intend to create a visitor center at the old ranch house.

Thanks to a new higher-speed boat, the national park's primary concessionaire, Island Packers, now transports hikers from Ventura Harbor to Scorpion Anchorage on the eastern end of Santa Cruz Island in about half the time required by the company's earlier, slower craft. The ride takes about an hour non-stop, 15 minutes or so longer if the captain pauses for a bit of whale-watching or to observe the many dolphins, seals and other marine life. In the strictly subjective opinion of this sea-sick prone passenger, the new boat seemed rather smooth, too.

Island day-trippers have a choice of three trails.

Cavern Point: The short, but steep, climb on Cavern Point Trail leads the hiker to a stunning viewpoint. Look for seals and sea lions bobbing in the waters around the point, as well as cormorants, pigeon guillemots and black oyster-catchers swooping along the rugged volcanic cliffs.

Potato Harbor: The jaunt to Potato Harbor begins on a right-forking road just beyond the upper end of the campground. After a heart-stirring half-mile climb, the road levels and heads west.

This hike parallels the mainland coast so it's fun to look back at the cities and civilization you left behind—a unique perspective indeed. Two miles out a spur trail leads oceanward to an overlook of the distinctly tater-shaped cove backed by rugged cliffs.

Smugglers Cove: The signed dirt road to Smugglers Cove climbs east then west as it passes a cypress grove. At the two-mile mark, a spur trail leads to San Pedro Point, a worthy destination for the time-short hiker.

The road descends to an airstrip, then down to the beach. Note the century-old eucalyptus and olive trees in the vicinity of Smugglers Cove.

An optional return route is by way of Scorpion Canyon Trail, which travels through the habitat of the Santa Cruz scrub jay, a bird that's about 30 percent bigger and a much brighter blue than its mainland cousin, and found nowhere else in the world.

There are two more accessible landings (and good hikes accompanied by The Nature Conservancy) on the island known as The Main Ranch Trip, which emphasizes human history and the Pelican Bay Trip, which stresses natural history.

Main Ranch Day Trip: From the landing at Prisoners Harbor, it's a

Ranch house

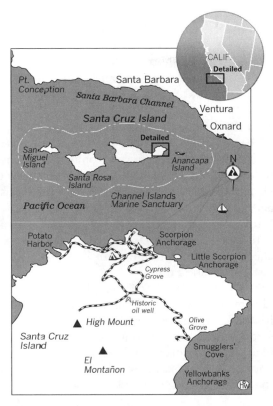

three-mile hike under old oaks and through eucalyptus groves along an old fennel-lined ranch road. Your party will be accompanied by a Nature Conservancy employee who will point out some of the botanical and historical highlights encountered en route.

Upon arrival at the ranch, visitors eat lunch around a pool. After lunch you can take a tour of the ranch buildings, including a tiny cabin converted into an anthropology museum, the main ranch house and some dilapidated winery buildings. A restored stone Catholic church celebrated its 100th anniversary in 1991 with a visit by Archbishop (now Cardinal) Roger Mahony. Next to the old church is a cemetery where both humans and ranch dogs rest in peace.

Pelican Bay Day Trip: After arrival at Pelican Bay, landing is by a small skiff onto a rocky ledge. You'll have to climb up a somewhat precipitous cliff trail to reach the picnic spot overlooking the bay.

A Nature Conservancy naturalist leads your group on an educational hike (about 3 miles round trip) along the north shore. Two special botanical delights are a bishop pine forest and a grove of Santa Cruz Island ironwood.

SANTA ROSA ISLAND

Lobo Canyon, East Point, Cherry Canyon Trails
5 miles round trip around Lobo Canyon; 1 mile around East Point;
3 miles around Cherry Canyon.

Grasslands cover much of Santa Rosa Island, which is cut by rugged oak- and ironwood-filled canyons. Torrey pines are found at Beecher's Bay.

Santa Rosa had a considerable Chumash population when explorer Juan Rodríguez Cabrillo sailed by in 1542. Scientists who have examined the island's extensive archeological record believe the island was inhabited at least 10,000 years ago.

After the Chumash era, during Spain's rule over California, the island was land granted to Don Carlos and Don José Carrillo. For many years their families raised sheep on the island and were known on the mainland for hosting grand fiestas at shearing time.

In 1902, Walter Vail and J.W. Vickers bought the island and raised what many considered some of the finest cattle in California. The island became part of Channel Islands National Park in 1986.

The national park service offers a couple of ranger-guided walking tours of the island. Hikers are transported to the more remote trailheads by four-wheel drive vehicles. (See Anacapa Island hike for visitor information)

Lobo Canyon (5 miles round trip): Hikers descend the sandstone-walled

Santa Rosa's beaches and bluffs are a delight for hikers.

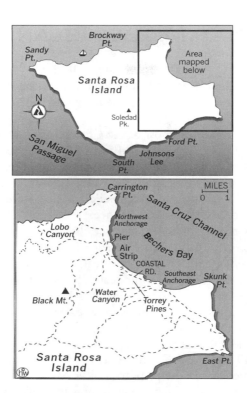

Canada Lobos, pausing to admire such native flora as island monkey-flower, dudleya and coreopsis. At the mouth of the canyon, near the ocean, is a Chumash village site. The hike continues, as the trail ascends the east wall of the canyon, then drops into Cow Canyon. At the mouth of Cow Canyon is an excellent tidepool area.

East Point Trail (1 mile round trip): Here's an opportunity for hikers to visit a rare stand of Torrey pines, and a large freshwater marsh where bird-watchers will enjoy viewing shorebirds and waterfowl. Trail's end is one of Santa Rosa's beautiful beaches.

The Torrey pines are an easy 3-mile round trip walk from the camp-ground; the stand is located on a hillside. From the top of this hill are spectacular views of Beecher's Bay.

Cherry Canyon Trail (3 miles round trip): Walking Cherry Canyon offers the opportunity to see some plants and animals that are found nowhere else. The trailheads two miles up the canyon to an oak grove. On the return trip, the trail offers far-reaching views of the interior, roaming deer and Roosevelt elk, and the dramatic sweep of Beecher's Bay. Trail's end is the island's historic ranch complex.

SAN MIGUEL ISLAND

San Miguel Island Trail
From Cuyler Harbor to Lester Ranch is 3 miles round trip
with 700-foot elevation gain

San Miguel is the westernmost of the Channel Islands. Eight miles long, four miles wide, it rises as a plateau, 400 to 800 feet above the sea. Wind-driven sands cover many of the hills which were severely overgrazed by sheep during the island's ranching days. Owned by the U.S. Navy, which once used it as a bombing site and missile tracking station, San Miguel is now managed by the National Park Service.

Three species of cormorants, storm petrels, Cassin's auklets, and pigeon guillemot nest on the island. San Miguel is home to six pinniped species: California sea lion, northern elephant seal, steller sea lion, harbor seal, northern fur seal and Guadalupe fur seal. The island may host the largest elephant seal population on earth. As many as 15,000 seals and sea lions can be seen basking on the rocks during mating season.

A trail runs most of the way from Cuyler Harbor to the west end of the island at Point Bennett, where the pinniped population is centered. The trail passes two round peaks, San Miguel and Green Mountain, and drops in and out of steep canyons to view the lunar landscape of the caliche forest. You must hike with the resident ranger and stay on established trails because the island's vegetation is fragile.

Directions to trailhead: Plan a very long day—or better yet, an overnight trip to San Miguel. It's at least a five-hour boat trip from Ventura.(See Anacapa hike on page 266 for more visitor information).

The hike: Follow the beach at Cuyler Harbor to the east. The harbor was named after the original government surveyor in the 1850s. The beach around the anchorage was formed by a bight of volcanic cliffs that extend to bold and precipitous Harris Point, the most prominent coastal landmark.

Snoozing elephant seal, one of thousands that bask on San Miguel's beaches.

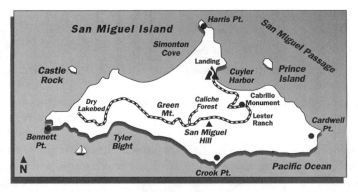

At the east end of the beach, about 0.75 mile from anchoring waters, a small footpath winds its way up the bluffs. It's a relatively steep trail following along the edge of a stream-cut canyon. At the top of the canyon, the trail veers east and forks. The left fork leads a short distance to Cabrillo Monument.

You can anchor and come ashore at "The Palm Trees" during rough weather or under heavy swell conditions. In calm weather, however, come ashore at Gull Rock right in front of Nidever Canyon. You will be able to see the trail above the east side of the canyon. When you get to the top of the canyon the ranger station and pit toilet are straight ahead. Instead of going straight you can turn east, The trail ascends a short distance to the Cabrillo Monument. The Lester Ranch is a short distance beyond that.

Juan Rodríguez Cabrillo, Portuguese explorer, visited and wrote about San Miguel in October 1542. While on the island he fell and broke either an arm or a leg (historians are unsure about this). As a result of this injury he contracted gangrene and died on the island in January 1543 and it's believed (historians disagree about this, too) he was buried here. In honor of Cabrillo, a monument was erected in 1937.

The right fork continues to the remains of a ranch house. Of the various ranchers and ranch managers to live on the island, the most well-known were the Lesters. They spent 12 years on the island and their adventures were occasionally chronicled by the local press. When the Navy evicted the Lesters from the island in 1942, Mr. Lester went to a hill overlooking Harris Point, in his view the prettiest part of the island, and shot himself. Within a month his family moved back to the mainland. Not much is left of the ranch now. The buildings burned down in the 1960s and only a rubble of brick and scattered household items remain.

For a longer 14-mile round trip the hiker can continue on the trail past the ranch to the top of San Miguel Hill (861 feet), down, and then up again to the top of Green Mountain (850 feet). Ask rangers to tell you about the caliche forest, composed of fossil sand casts of ancient plants. Calcium carbonate reacted with the plants' organic acid, creating a ghostly forest.

Santa Barbara Island

Signal Peak Loop Trail
Loop around isle is 2-5 miles round trip with 500-foot elevation gain.

Only one square mile in area, Santa Barbara is the smallest Channel Island. It's located some 38 miles west of San Pedro—or quite a bit south of the other islands in the national park.

Geologically speaking, Santa Barbara arose a bit differently from the other isles. The island is a volcano, leftover from Miocene times, some 25 million years ago, and shares characteristics with Mexico's Guadalupe Islands.

To bird-watchers, Santa Barbara means seabirds, lots of them—gulls, cormorants, pelicans and black-oyster catchers. And the island boasts some rare birds, too: the black storm-petrel and the Xantus murrelet.

Besides the birds, another reason to bring binoculars to the island is to view sea lions and elephant seals. Webster Point on the western end of the isle is a favorite haul-out area for the pinnipeds.

Early in this century, the isle's native flora was all-but destroyed by burning, clearing, and planting nonnative grasses, followed by sheep grazing. Besides the grasses, iceplant, a South African import, began to spread over the island. Even when the hardy iceplant dies, it hurts the native plant community because it releases its salt-laden tissues into the soil, thus worsening the odds for the natives. Park service policy is to re-introduce native plants and eliminate nonnatives.

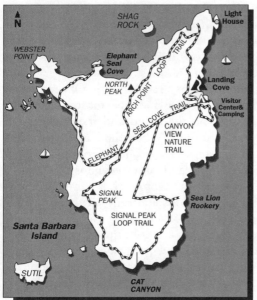

Six miles of trail criss-cross the island. A good place to start your exploration is Canyon View Nature Trail. Request an interpretive brochure from the resident ranger and enjoy learning about island ecology.

Directions to trailhead: Santa Barbara Island is infrequently serviced by boat, but it is possible to join a trip. Contact park headquarters.

15. Catalina Island

ONE OF MY FAVORITE VIEWS OF Los Angeles is from the top of Catalina Island's Hermit Gulch Trail. All the beautiful topographical features of Southern California—the Santa Monica and San Gabriel mountains, the coastal bluffs—are visible, but not a single building or freeway. Catalina offers the sunny, unspoiled Southland of a century ago, an island far removed from the bustle of modern life.

Catalina first floated into America's consciousness during the Big Band era when live music was broadcast from Avalon's Casino Ballroom. A generation later the Four Preps immortalized the island's appeal when they sang:

Twenty-six miles across the sea,
Santa Catalina is awaiting for me,
Santa Catalina, the island of
Romance, romance, romance, romance . . .

Actually, Catalina is only 19 miles off the Southern California coast (less than a two-hour ferry ride), but it's so quiet that it seems like a million miles from the L.A. megalopolis. It's as popular and as romantic as ever—especially among we hikers who've discovered the isle's secluded beaches, splendid backcountry and breathtaking Pacific vistas.

When viewed from the island's extensive network of dirt roads and footpaths, Catalina's terrain reminds me of a Greek island; one of the Cyclades perhaps. One of the major differences, however, is the local wildlife; roaming the hills and savannas with visiting hikers are the island's resident buffalo (brought here by Hollywood moviemakers in the 1920s), deer, rabbits and wild boar.

While I hike wearing an L.A. Dodger cap, my hat goes off to chewing gum magnate and Chicago Cubs owner William Wrigley who purchased most of the island in 1919. Wrigley intended to place Avalon on the map as a world-class destination while at the same time conserving the island's special natural resources. These days the nonprofit Santa Catalina Conservancy, dedicated to preserving the island environment, now administers 86 percent of Catalina. The Conservancy has an active interpretive program and coordinates wildlife efforts, including the reintroduction of bald eagles to the island.

Avalon has everything a resort town should have—from B & Bs to bikini shops—-and is the information and transportation hub for ventures into the isle's interior. The Catalina Island Conservancy Office in Avalon dispenses (free) hiking permits along with trail suggestions, campsite reservations and safety tips. A shuttle bus (very few cars are allowed) services destinations near and far and allows the hiker to choose among a variety of trails.

AVALON CANYON

Avalon Canyon, Memorial Road, Divide Road, Hermit Gulch Trails
From Avalon to Botanical Garden is 3 miles round trip with 200-foot
elevation gain; return via Hermit Gulch Trail is 6.5 miles round trip
with 1,000-foot gain

Botanical Garden is a showcase for plants native to Catalina, and to the
Channel Islands. At the head of the canyon is the imposing Wrigley
Memorial, a huge monument honoring chewing gum magnate William
Wrigley, who purchased most of the island in 1919.

Families with children, and those visitors looking more for a walk than a
hike, will enjoy the trip as far as Botanical Garden. More adventurous hikers
will undertake the second, more strenuous part of this loop trip; it utilizes
fire roads and Hermit Gulch Trail and offers a sampling of Catalina's rugged
and bold terrain.

Directions to trailhead: Several boat companies offer ferry service to
Catalina, with departures from San Diego, Newport Beach, Long Beach and
San Pedro. The 22-mile crossing to Catalina takes about two hours. For
more information about ferryboat schedules, island services and accommodations, call the Catalina Island Chamber of Commerce.

If you intend to hike into the Catalina backcountry (anywhere past the
Botanical Garden) you must secure a free hiking permit from the Catalina
Island Conservancy Office in Avalon.

The hike: Head uphill along Catalina Street, which soon joins Avalon
Canyon Road, passes a few residences, and begins a 1.5 mile ascent toward the
Botanical Garden. On your right, watch for one of William Wrigley's many
contributions to the island, Bird Park, which once held thousands of unusual
birds in the "largest bird cage in the world." Bird Park is now a campground.
On the left side of the road, bleacher bums sill stop and pay homage to the
one-time spring training camp of Wrigley's beloved Chicago Cubs.

At the end of the road is Botanical Garden (fee for entry). The garden
began in the 1920s, when Wrigley's wife Ada began planting native and
exotic plants in Avalon Canyon. More recently, the garden has greatly
expanded, emphasizing native Southern California flora. Particularly interesting are plants endemic to Catalina, including Catalina mahogany,
Catalina manzanita, Catalina live-forever, and Catalina ironwood.

Proceed up the dirt path to the Wrigley Memorial. At one time, Wrigley's
body was entombed here. Climb up the many stairs to the 232-foot-wide,
130-foot-high monument, and enjoy the great view of Avalon Harbor.

At this point, intrepid hikers will pass through the unlocked gate below
and to the right of the memorial and stride up Memorial Road. Scrub oak,

manzanita and lemonade berry—and many more of the native plants featured in the botanical garden—grow wild along the fire road.

The vigorous ascent on Memorial Road offers better and better views of Avalon Harbor. It's likely your approach will flush a covey or two of quail from the brush. Practiced birders might recognize the Catalina quail, a slightly larger and slightly darker subspecies than its mainland relatives.

Memorial Road reaches a divide and, appropriately enough, intersects Divide Road. Bear right. From the 1,000-foot high divide, partake of commanding views of both sides of the island and of the mainland.

Continue along the divide, which bristles with prickly pear cactus. The slopes below are crisscrossed with trails made by the island's many wild goats. After about 0.75 mile of walking atop the divide, bear right on unsigned Hermit Gulch Trail. This trail is difficult to spot and the early going is steep. The trail descends 2.4 miles along a waterless canyon back to Avalon Canyon Road, at a point a few hundred yards below the Botanical Garden. Turn left and saunter downhill back to Avalon.

Avalon then (above) and now.

Black Jack

Black Jack Trail
From Black Jack Junction to Little Harbor is 8 miles one way
with 1,500-foot elevation loss.

Catalina's terrain is rugged and bold, characterized by abrupt ridges and V-shaped canyons. Many of the mountaintops are rounded, however, and the western end of the island is grassland and brush, dotted with cactus and seasonal wildflowers. Bison, deer, boar and rabbits roam the savannas.

This walk is a good introduction to the island; it samples a variety of terrain on the island, inland and coastal. Transportation logistics are a bit complex, but the trail is easy to follow.

Directions to trailhead: From Avalon, travel to the trailhead via the Catalina Island Interior Shuttle Bus (fee), which departs from the information center in Island Plaza. Secure the necessary hiking permit (free) from the center.

The hike: At signed Black Jack Junction, there's a fire phone and good views of the island's precipitous west ridges.

The trail, a rough fire road, ascends for one mile over brush- and cactus-covered slopes. You'll pass the fenced, but open shaft of the old Black Jack Mine (lead, zinc and silver). On your left a road appears that leads up to Black Jack Mountain, at 2,006 feet in elevation the island's second highest peak. Continue past this junction.

Ahead is a picnic ramada with a large sunshade and a nearby signed junction. You may descend to Black Jack Camp, which is operated by Los Angeles County. Here you'll find tables, shade, and water. Set in a stand of pine, the camp offers fine channel views.

Buffalo have a home and place to roam on Catalina.

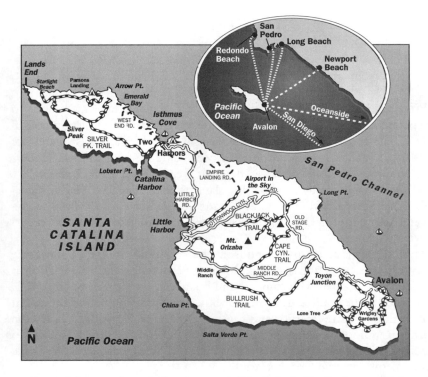

Bear right on signed Cottonwood/Black Jack Trail. A second junction soon appears. Continue straight downhill. (The other trail ascends 2,097-foot Mt. Orizaba, Catalina's highest peak.

The trail drops through a steep walled canyon, whose vegetation—chaparral and grassland—is favored by a large herd of wild goats. At the bottom of the canyon, pass through three gates of a private ranch. (Close all gates behind you.)

The trail reaches the main road connecting Little Harbor with Airport-in-the-Sky. You may bear left at this junction and follow the winding road 3.5 miles to Little Harbor. For a more scenic route of about the same distance, turn right on the road. Hike about 200 yards to the end of the ranch fence line, then bear left, struggling cross-country briefly through spiny brush and intersect a ranch road. This dirt road follows the periphery of the fence line on the east side of the ranch to the top of a canyon. You bear left again, still along the fence line. Ascend and then descend, staying atop this sharp shadeless ridge above pretty Big Springs Canyon. When you begin descending toward the ocean, you'll spot Little Harbor.

Little Harbor is the primary campground and anchorage on the Pacific side of the island. It's a good place to relax while you're waiting for the shuttle bus, or to refresh yourself for the hike through buffalo country to Two Harbors.

LITTLE HARBOR

Little Harbor Trail
From Little Harbor to Two Harbors is 7 miles one way

From a distance, the mountainous land on Catalina's east end appears to be separated from a smaller portion on the west end; in fact, it's an optical illusion. The eye is tricked by a low-lying isthmus, the narrowest section of the island. Catalina Harbor lies on the ocean side of this isthmus, Isthmus Cove on the channel side, and together this area is called Two Harbors.

As the Wrigley family opened the island to tourism, Two Harbors pursued a destiny apart from Avalon. During the 1920s and 1930s, it was a peaceful sanctuary for Hollywood celebrities and the elite Southland yachting set.

This hike leads across the island from the Pacific side to the Channel side and offers fine views and a chance to observe buffalo. Your destination is Two Harbors, popular with campers and boaters.

Directions to trailhead: A shuttle bus transports you across the island from Avalon to Little Harbor and can pick you up in Two Harbors for the return to Avalon. If you purchased a ferry ticket from the mainland to Avalon, it's possible to leave the island from Two Harbors if you make arrangements with the ferry company.

The hike: From Little Harbor, a onetime stagestop turned popular campground and anchorage, join Little Harbor Road and begin ascending higher and higher into Little Springs Canyon.

Buffalo graze both sides of the canyon and two reservoirs have been developed for the animals. In 1924, when Hollywood moviemakers were filming Zane Grey's classic Western, The Vanishing American, 14 buffalo were brought to the island. Recapturing them after filming proved impossible so the beasts were left to road. The animals adapted well to life on Catalina and quickly multiplied. Today's population is held at 400 to 500, the ideal number for available pasturage.

At an unsigned junction a mile past Lower Buffalo Reservoir, bear left on Banning House Road, which leads 3.25 miles to Two Harbors. (Little Harbor Road continues north, then west, to Two Harbors if you prefer to stick to this road.) Rough Banning House Road ascends very steeply up a canyon roamed by wild boar. At the windswept head of the canyon, hikers are rewarded with superb views of the twin harbors of Catalina Harbor and Isthmus Cove, and can see both the eastern and western fringes of the island.

A steep northeasterly descent brings you to the outskirts of Two Harbors. Improvise a route past ranchettes and private clubs to the ferry building.

16. West Mojave Desert

Topographically, the East and West Mojave are quite different. The West presents great sandscapes, with many flat areas and some isolated ridges and buttes. The East Mojave is more mountainous.

Situated south of the Tehachapi Mountains and northwest of the San Gabriel Mountains, the Antelope Valley makes up the western frontier of the Mojave Desert. The rapidly expanding cities of Palmdale, Lancaster and Victorville are located here.

The Antelope Valley's natural attractions include a reserve for the state's official flower—the California poppy—and another reserve for the endangered desert tortoise. Other parks preserve a Joshua tree woodland (Saddleback Butte State Park) and display the remarkable earthquake-fractured geology of this desert (Devil's Punchbowl County Park).

Joshua trees thrive in the valley. Palmdale, established in 1886 was named for the Joshuas; settlers mistakenly figured the spiky trees were palms. Saddleback Butte was originally named Joshua Tree State Park when it was created in 1960. The name was changed to avoid confusion with Joshua Tree National Park.

The Spartan-looking valley once supported thousands of pronghorn antelope—hence the name Antelope Valley—and the numerous native people who hunted them. The railroad tracks interrupted the antelope's migration, thus dooming the animals. The antelope could easily cross the tracks, but instinct prevented them from doing this; they soon perished from exposure to harsh winters and the shrinkage of their habitat.

The California poppy blooms on many a grassy slope in the Southland, but only in the Antelope Valley does the showy flower blanket whole hillsides in such brilliant orange sheets. Surely the finest concentration of California's state flower (during a good wildflower year) is preserved at the California State Poppy Reserve in the Mojave Desert west of Lancaster.

Vasquez Rocks

Geology, Pacific Crest Trails
From 1 to 3 miles round trip.

Chances are, you've seen the rocks on TV and the big screen many times—from old Westerns to modern sci-fi films. And you've probably seen Vasquez Rocks while motoring along the Antelope Valley Freeway; the famed formations are a short distance from California 14.

But the best place to see the Southland's most famous geological silhouette is Vasquez Rocks County Park Natural Area in Agua Dulce. Hiking trails circle the rocks, which are not only enjoyable to view, but fun to climb.

Through a camera lens, and from a distance, the rocks look insurmountable; actually, they're rather easy to climb. The rocks are only about 100 to 150 feet high, and you can find safe and mellow routes to the top of the sandstone outcrops.

The rocks themselves are tilted and worn sandstone, the result of years of earthquake action and erosion by elements. The big beds of sedimentary rock known as the Mint Canyon Formation were laid down some eight to 15 million years ago. The Vasquez Rocks Formation is composed of coarser, redder layers underneath.

Tataviam Indians occupied the area until the late 1700s, when their culture was overwhelmed and eventually extinguished by the soldiers, settlers and missionaries of the San Fernando Mission.

During the 1850s and 1860s, notorious highwayman Tiburcio Vasquéz used the rocks and canyons as a hide-out from the Los Angeles lawmen who were pursuing him. Even before he was hung for his crimes in 1875, the area was known as Vasquez Rocks.

The trail system at Vasquez Rock is a bit informal. Because of the open nature of the terrain, hikers can—and do—tend to wander where their rock fancy takes them. If you remember that the park entrance/office is more or less to the north and the Antelope Valley Freeway to the south, you'll stay fairly well oriented.

A favorite route of mine, a clockwise tour of three miles or so, is described below; however, part of the fun of Vasquez Rocks is going your own way.

Directions to trailhead: From the Antelope Valley Freeway (14), a few miles northeast of the outskirts of Canyon Country, exit on Agua Dulce Road. Head north 1.5 miles. Agua Dulce Canyon Road swings west and you join Escondido Canyon Road, proceeding 0.25 mile to the signed Vasquez Rocks County Park entrance on your right. You can park just inside the entrance at the small parking area near the park office, or continue to the main lot near the largest of the rock formations.

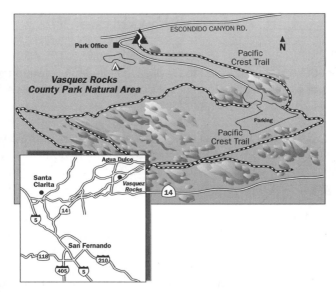

The hike: Begin at the signed trailhead for Geology Trail just across the park road from the parking lot. (Pick up an interpretive brochure, as well as a trail map, from the office.) Soon after you begin your trail-side study of strata, Geology Trail intersects Pacific Crest Trail and you'll head right.

The mile-long stretch of PCT through the park is part of a segment that connects the San Gabriel Mountains to the south with the Sierra Pelona area of Angeles National Forest to the north. The path parallels the park road. To your left are some scattered residences and the open desert beyond; to your right are some of the most famous of the Vasquez Rocks.

Pacific Crest Trail joins a dirt road at the edge of the picnic area and continues west atop the north wall of Escondido Canyon. Very few park visitors, it seems, hike here, though the rock formations are stunning and a seasonal creek flows through the canyon. Only the annoying hum of the nearby Antelope Valley Freeway disturbs the natural beauty.

You can cross the creek with the PCT, double back along the other side of Escondido Canyon, and continue your exploration of the little-known southern part of the park. But to continue to the main rock formations, stay west with the dirt road and you'll soon reach a junction with the park's horse trail. You can take this trail if you wish, or continue a short distance farther and join the foot trail.

The Vasquez Rocks area is a transition zone between mountain and desert environments. Yucca, buckwheat, sage and California juniper are among the plants you'll pass en route.

The footpath drops northwestward then heads east to visit the most dramatic of the Vasquez Rocks.

DEVIL'S PUNCHBOWL

Punchbowl Trail

From South Fork Campground to Devil's Chair is 6 miles round trip with
1,000-foot elevation gain; to park headquarters is 12 miles round trip;
Season: October-May

Southern California has many faults, and the mightiest of these is the San Andreas. Nowhere is the presence of this fault more obvious than in Devil's Punchbowl County Park. The dun-colored rocks have been tilted every which way and weathered by wind and rain. They are a bizarre sight to behold.

Punchbowl Trail takes you into the Devil's domain, a satanically landscaped rock garden on the desert side of the San Gabriel Mountains. The trip offers views of the Punchbowl Fault and the San Jacinto Fault—part of what seismologists call the San Andreas Rift Zone. If you're superstitious, you'll want to carry a good-luck charm in your day pack when you hike to the monstrous mass of white rock known as the Devil's Chair.

Winter is a fine time to visit the Punchbowl. Winds scour the desert clean and from the Devil's Chair, you can get superb views of this land, as well as the seemingly infinite sandscape of the Mojave.

Note that the six-mile-long Punchbowl Trail may be hiked from two directions. For aesthetic and logistical reasons, I prefer the route from the Forest Service's South Fork Campground to Devil's Chair.

The leg-weary or families with small children may wish to proceed directly to Devil's Punchbowl County Park. A 0.3-mile-long nature trail, Pinyon Pathway, introduces visitors to park geology and plant life, and a one-mile loop trail offers grand views of the Punchbowl.

Directions to trailhead: From Pearblossom Highway (Highway 138) in Pearblossom, turn south onto Longview Road, then briefly left on Fort Tejon Road and right on Valyermo Road. Continue three miles to Big Rock Creek Road. Two-and-a-half miles past this junction, turn right on a signed

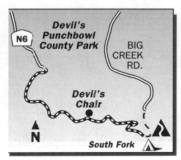

dirt road to South Fork Campground and proceed one mile to the special day use/hiker's parking lot below the campground. The road is suitable for passenger cars, but on occasion, Big Rock Creek may be too high for a low-slung car to ford; you may have to walk an extra mile to the trailhead. The signed trail departs from the parking area.

If you want to go directly to Devil's

Punchbowl County Park, turn south on County Road N6 from Highway 138 in Pearblossom and follow it to the county park. Punchbowl Trail begins near the picnic area.

The hike: From the parking area below South Fork Campground, join the signed trail. Almost immediately, you'll reach a trail junction. (Steep South Fork Trail ascends the canyon cut by the South Fork of Big Rock Creek up to the Angeles Crest Highway at Islip Saddle.)

Stay on Punchbowl Trail and boulder-hop across the creek. If your imagination has already run away with you, perhaps the mythological Charon the Ferryman (who conveyed the dead to Hades over the River Styx) will carry you across this watercourse.

Take a seat on the Devil's Chair and marvel at the Punchbowl's bizarre geology.

The trail climbs through manzanita and heat-stunted pinyon pine to a saddle where there's a view of the park and its faults. Descend from the saddle, down chaparral-covered slopes and over to Holcomb Canyon. Along the way, notice the strange dovetailing of three plant communities: yucca-covered hills, oak woodland, and juniper and piney woods.

You may wish to take a break near Holcomb Creek crossing. Oaks and big cone spruce shade the creek.

From Holcomb Creek, the trail ascends steeply up another ridge through a pinyon pine forest to the Devil's Chair. From a distance, those with fanciful imaginations can picture the devil himself ruling over this kingdom of fractured rock. Below the chair, there's an awesome panorama of the Punchbowl and its jumbled sedimentary strata. The somersaulted sandstone formation resembles pulled taffy. If you look west to the canyon wall, you can see the vertical crush zone of the fault, marked by white rocks.

While visiting the Devil's Chair, stay behind the protective fence; people have taken a plunge into the Punchbowl. Return to the trailhead the way you came or continue on the Punchbowl Trail to county park headquarters.

Above Devil's Chair, the trail contours west and offers close-up views of the Punchbowl. A mile-and-a-half from the Chair, your route crosses Punchbowl Creek, briefly joins a dirt road, then bears right on the trail leading to the Punchbowl parking area.

RED ROCK CANYON

Hagen, Red Cliffs Trails
1 to 2 miles round trip; Season: October-May

The view of Red Rock Canyon may very well seem like déjà vu. Cliffs and canyons in these parts have appeared in the background of many a Western movie.

A black-and-white movie of Red Rock Canyon would be dramatic: shadow and light playing over the canyon walls. Technicolor, however, might more vividly capture the aptly named red rock, along with the chocolate brown, black, white and pink hues of the pleated cliffs.

Gold fever in the 1890s prompted exploration of almost all the canyons in the El Paso Mountains. During this era, Rudolph Hagen acquired much land in the Red Rock area. He named the little mining community/stage stop Ricardo after his son Richard. The Ricardo Ranger Station is located at the site of the once-thriving hamlet.

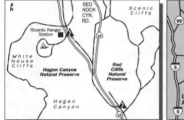  Red Rock Canyon became a state recreation area in 1969; when it became obvious off-road vehicles were damaging the hills and canyons, Red Rock was upgraded to park status in 1982.

Best places to hike are in the park's two preserves. You'll find some trails to hike, but this park lends itself to improvisation.

Hagen Canyon Natural Preserve is a striking badlands, with dramatic cliffs capped by a layer of dark basalt. A primitive one-mile loop trail explores the canyon.

Red Cliffs Natural Preserve protects the 300-foot sandstone cliffs east of Highway 14. No developed trail exists; however hikers can enjoy a mile or so of cross-country travel through the preserve.

The park nature trail, a 0.75-mile path tells the geologic story of the area, and points out typical desert flora. It's keyed to an interpretive pamphlet available at the trailhead. Join the nature trail at the south end of the park campground.

Directions to trailhead: Red Rock Canyon State Park is located 25 miles north of the town of Mojave off Highway 14. Turn northwest off 14 onto the signed road for the park campground. Follow this road a short mile to Ricardo Ranger Station. The station has a small visitor center with nature exhibits.

SADDLEBACK BUTTE

Saddleback Butte Trail
From Campground to Saddleback Peak is 4 miles round trip
with 1,000-foot elevation gain; Season: October-May

Rarely visited Saddleback Butte State Park, located on the eastern fringe of Antelope Valley, is high-desert country, a land of creosote bush and Joshua trees. The park takes the name of its most prominent feature—3,651-foot Saddleback Butte, a granite mountaintop that stands head and shoulders above Antelope Valley.

The park's short nature trail is a good introduction to the Joshua tree and other plant life found in this corner of the desert. The trail to the boulder-strewn summit of Saddleback Peak takes a straight-line course, with most of the elevation gain occurring in the last half-mile. From atop the peak, enjoy far-reaching desert views.

Directions to trailhead: From Highway 14 (Antelope Valley Freeway) in Lancaster, take the 20th Street exit. Head north on 20th and turn east (right) on Avenue J. Drive 18 miles to Saddleback Butte State Park. Follow the dirt park road to the campground, where the trail begins. Park (day use fee) near the trail sign.

The hike: The signed trail heads straight for the saddle. The soft, sandy track, marked with yellow posts leads through an impressive Joshua tree woodland. After 1.5 miles, the trail switchbacks steeply up the rocky slope of the butte. An invigorating climb brings you to the saddle of Saddleback Butte. To reach the peak, follow the steep leftward trail to the summit.

From the top, you can look south to the San Gabriel Mountains. At the base of the mountains, keen eyes will discern the California Aqueduct, which carries water to the Southland from the Sacramento Delta. To the east is the vast Mojave Desert, to the north is Edwards Air Force Base. To the west are the cities of Lancaster and Palmdale and farther west, the rugged Tehachapi Mountains.

ANTELOPE VALLEY
CALIFORNIA POPPY RESERVE

Antelope Loop Trail
From Visitors Center to Antelope Butte Vista Point is 2.5 miles round trip
with 300-foot elevation gain; Season: March-May

The California poppy blooms on many a grassy slope in the Southland, but only in the Antelope Valley does the showy flower blanket whole hillsides in such brilliant orange sheets. Surely the finest concentration of California's state flower (during a good wildflower year) is preserved at the Antelope Valley California Poppy Reserve in the Mojave Desert west of Lancaster.

The poppy is the star of the flower show, which includes a supporting cast of fiddlenecks, cream cups, tidy tips and gold fields. March through Memorial Day is the time to saunter through this wondrous display of desert wildflowers.

The poppy has always been recognized as something special. Early Spanish Californians called it Dormidera, "the drowsy one," because the petals curl up at night. They fashioned a hair tonic/restorer by frying the blossoms in olive oil and adding perfume.

At the reserve, you can pick up a map at the Jane S. Pineiro Interpretive Center, named for the painter who was instrumental in setting aside an area where California's state flower could be preserved for future generations to admire. Some of Pineiro's watercolors are on display in the center, which also has wildflower interpretive displays and a slide show.

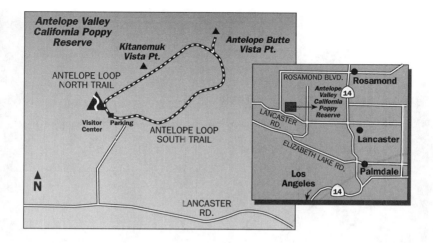

Built into the side of a hill, the center boast an award-winning solar design, windmill power and "natural" air conditioning."

Antelope Loop Trail—and all trails in the reserve—are easy walking and suitable for the whole family. Seven miles of gentle trails crisscross the 1,760-acre reserve; many hikers take every trail in the park without getting too tired.

Directions to trailhead: From the Antelope Valley Freeway (California 14) in Lancaster, exit on Avenue I and drive west 15 miles. Avenue I becomes Lancaster Road a few miles before the Poppy Reserve. The reserve (day use fee) is open 9 A.M. to 4 P.M. daily.

Spring wildflower displays are always unpredictable. To check on what's blooming where, call the park at (805) 724-1180 before making the trip.

The hike: Begin on the signed Antelope Loop Trail to the left of the Visitors Center. The trail passes through an orange sea of poppies and fiddlenecks, then climbs briefly to Kitanemuk Vista Point, 0.75 mile from the Visitors Center. Atop Vista Point are those flowery symbols of faithfulness and friendship, forget-me-nots, and an unforgettable view of the Mojave Desert and the snow-covered Tehachapis.

After enjoying the view, continue on to Antelope Butte Vista Point, where another lookout offers fine desert panoramas. From here, join the south loop of the Antelope Loop Trail and return to the visitors center.

After you've circled the "upper west side" of the Poppy Reserve, you may wish to extend your hike by joining the Poppy Loop Trail and exploring the "lower east side."

Thousand Palms Oasis

17. PALM SPRINGS

IN THE EARLY YEARS OF THIS CENTURY, it was called a "Desert Eden," "Our Araby," and "A Garden in the Sun." Now it's called a "Desert Hollywood," "Fairway Living," and "Rodeo Drive East."

Palm Springs today means different things to different people, but one thing is for certain—the golf courses, condos and country clubs of the resort are a far cry from what the first residents of Agua Caliente intended.

What most Palm Springs pioneers intended was to leave this desert land more or less alone. Turn-of-the-century health-seekers and nature lovers recognized their discovery for what it was—a true oasis. Here was a palm-dotted retreat where an ancient hot springs gushed forth. Here was nature, simple and unadorned.

Some residents championed the creation of Palm Canyon National Monument, in order to preserve the canyons on the outskirts of Palm Springs known collectively as the Indian Canyons—Palm, Murray and Andreas. The national monument was approved by Congress in 1922 but no funds were ever allocated and the palm canyons never did win National Park Service protection. Finally, however, in 1990, a sizable portion of the palm canyons, as well as the surrounding mountains came under federal protection with the establishment of the Santa Rosa Mountains National Scenic Area, administered by the U.S. Bureau of Land Management.

Fortunately, for the modern visitor, there yet remains a wild side of Palm Springs—parks, preserves and special places that offer opportunities to see the desert of old. Palm Springs wildlife, not to be confused with the Palm Springs wild life enjoyed by thousands of college students who come here during spring break, can be viewed in a number of quiet and picturesque locales, both near town and in the surrounding Coachella Valley.

"Essentially, the desert is Nature in her simplest expression," wrote nature writer and Palm Springs resident Joseph Smeaton Chase. The Living Desert Preserve, Palm Canyon, Big Morongo Canyon and the Coachella Valley Preserve are places for the hiker to commune with this simple nature.

BIG MORONGO CANYON

Big Morongo Canyon Trail
To waterfall is 2.5 miles round trip; to canyon mouth is 12 miles round trip
with 1,900-foot elevation loss; Season: October-May

For many centuries native peoples used Big Morongo Canyon as a passage-way between the high and low deserts. The last of these nomads to inhabit the canyon were a group of Serrano Indians known as the Morongo, for whom the canyon is named. When white settlers entered the area in the mid-19th century, the Morongos were forced onto a reservation and the canyon became the property of ranchers. Today, Big Morongo Canyon is managed and pro-tected by the Nature Conservancy and the U.S. Bureau of Land Management.

The relative abundance of water is the key to both Big Morongo's long human history and its botanical uniqueness. Several springs bubble up in the reserve and one of the California desert's very few year-around creeks flows through the canyon. Dense thickets of cottonwood and willow, as well as numerous water-loving shrubs line Big Morongo Creek. This lush, crowded riparian vegetation sharply contrasts with the well-spaced creosote community typical of the high and dry slopes of the reserve and of the open desert beyond.

The oasis at Big Morongo is a crucial water supply for the fox, bobcat, raccoon, coyote and bighorn sheep. Gopher snakes, rosy boas, chuckawallas and California tree frogs are among the amphibians and reptiles in resi-dence. The permanent water supply also makes it possible for the showy western tiger swallowtail and other butterflies to thrive, along with several species of dragon flies and water bugs.

Big Morongo Canyon is best known for its wide variety of birds, which are numerous because the canyon is not only at the intersection of two deserts, but also at the merging of two climate zones—arid and coastal. These climates, coupled with the wet world of the oasis, means the preserve is an attractive stopover for birds on their spring and fall migrations.

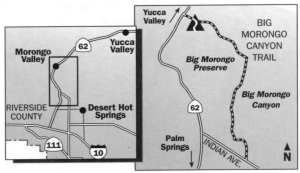

More than two hundred bird species have been sighted, including the rare vermilion flycatcher and the least Bell's vireo. Commonly seen all-year residents include starlings, house finches and varieties of quail and hummingbirds.

For the hiker, the preserve offers several short loop-trails ranging from a quarter to one mile long. Some of the wetter canyon bottom sections of trail are crossed by wooden boardwalks, which keep hikers dry and fragile creekside flora from being trampled. Desert Wash, Cottonwood, Willow, Yucca Ridge and Mesquite Trails explore the environments suggested by their names.

A longer path, Canyon Trail, travels the 6-mile length of Big Morongo Canyon. You could make this a one-way, all downhill journey by arranging a car shuttle or by having someone pick you up on Indian Avenue. Families with small children or the leg weary will enjoy a 2.5-mile round trip canyon walk to a small waterfall.

Directions to trailhead: From Interstate 10, 15 miles east of Banning and a bit past the Highway 111 turnoff to Palm Springs, exit on Highway 62. Drive 10 miles north to the signed turnoff on your right for Big Morongo Wildlife Preserve. Turn east and after 0.10 mile you'll see the preserve's service road leading to a parking area.

To reach the end of the trail at the mouth of Big Morongo Canyon, you'll exit on Highway 62 on Indian Avenue and drive exactly a mile to a dirt road on your left. A dip sign precedes the turnoff and a pump enclosed by a chain link fence suggests your parking space.

The hike: From the parking lot, you may pick up the trail by the Preserve's interpretive displays or join the dirt road that leads past the caretaker's residence.

Off to the right of the old ranch road, you'll see a pasture lined with cottonwood and a barn built in the 1880s. Often the road is muddy, so detour with the signed and aptly named Mesquite Trail which utilizes a wooden boardwalk to get over the wet spots. As you stand on the boardwalk in the midst of Big Morongo Creek, take a moment to listen to the sound of running water, the many chirping birds and croaking frogs.

Canyon Trail meanders with the creek for a gentle mile or so and arrives at a corrugated metal check dam that has created a small waterfall. For the less energetic, this is a good turnaround point. The trail continues descending through the canyon with Big Morongo Creek until a bit over three miles from the trailhead, the creek suddenly disappears. Actually, the water continues flowing underground through layers of sand.

The canyon widens and so does the trail. About 5 miles from the trailhead is the south gate of the preserve. Compensating for Big Morongo's somewhat inglorious end is a stirring view of snow-capped Mt. San Jacinto, which lies straight ahead. Stick to your right at every opportunity as you exit the canyon and a dirt road will soon deliver you to Indian Avenue.

Thousand Palms Oasis

McCallum, Smoke Tree Ranch, Indian Palms Trails
1 to 5-mile loop; Season: October-May

If it looks like a movie set, don't be surprised. Thousand Palms Oasis was the setting for Cecil B. DeMille's 1924 silent film epic, *King of Kings* and the 1969 movie *Tell Them Willie Boy is Here* starring Robert Redford and Katherine Ross. The oasis is something special, and deserving of protection, but that's not why Coachella Valley Preserve was established. The reserve's raison d'être is habitat for the threatened Coachella Valley fringe-toed lizard.

For the most part, Uma inornata goes about the business of being a lizard beneath the surface of sand dunes, but scientists have been able to discover some of the peculiar habits of this creature, which manages to survive in places where a summer's day surface temperature may reach 160 degrees.

The eight-inch reptile is also known as the "sand swimmer" for its ability to dive through sand dunes. Its entrenching tool-shaped skull rams through the sand, while round scales on its skin reduce friction as it "swims." Fringes (large scales) on its toes give the lizard traction —as well as its name.

Alas, all is not fun in the sun for the fringe-toed lizard. The creature must avoid becoming dinner for such predators as roadrunners, snakes and loggerhead shrikes. But the biggest threat to the lizards continues to be real estate development and consequent loss of habitat.

Fortunately for the fringe-toed lizard, real estate developers, the U.S. Bureau of Land Management, Congress, the California Department of Fish and Game, the U.S. Wildlife Service and the Nature Conservancy were able to find a common ground and establish a 13,000-acre preserve in 1986. Some conservationists believe the $25 million price tag may be the most expensive single species preservation effort of all time.

Still, the reserve would be something special even without its namesake lizard. It protects flora and fauna once common in the Coachella Valley before it grew grapefruit, golf courses and subdivisions.

Thousand Palms Oasis is California's second-largest collection of native California fan palms. Thousand Palms, along with Indian Palms, Horsehoe Palms and a couple of other oases in the reserve came into existence as the result of earthquake faults which brought water to the surface.

Before the reserve was set aside, the Thousand Palms area was purchased by turn of the century rancher Louis Wilhelm and his family. The Wilhelms built "Palm House" (now the reserve's visitors center) and by the 1930s were using it as a commissary for campers, scientists, scout troops and anyone else who wanted to enjoy a weekend in one of their palm-shaded cottages.

Hikers can explore Coachella Valley Reserve on a half dozen trails. Three of these trails depart from Thousand Palms Oasis. Shortest (a fifteen minute walk) is Smoke Tree Ranch Trail, which encircles the palms oasis. Good bird-watching is possible in the mesquite thickets and among the smoke trees. Watch for the smoke tree's bright blue/purple flowers in May or June.

Don't miss McCallum Trail, a 1.5-mile round trip nature trail. It meanders by a jungle of willows, palms, cottonwoods and mesquite. At the trailhead, pick up an interpretive pamphlet that's keyed to numbered posts along the path.

Indian Palms Trail leads 0.5 mile to small Indian Palm Oasis.

More ambitious hikers will head for Wash Trail which, true to its name, winds through washes in the northern portion of the reserve. You can also visit Bee Rock Mesa, where Malpais Indians camped 5,000 years ago, hike into adjoining Indio Hills County Park, and visit more oases—Horseshoe Palms and Pushawalla Palms.

Directions to trailhead: From Interstate 10, about ten miles east of where Highway 111 leads off to Palm Springs, exit on Washington Street/Ramon Road. Head north on Washington Street, which bends west and continues as Ramon Road. Soon after the bend, turn right (north again) onto Thousand Palms Canyon Road. Continue to the entrance to Coachella Valley Preserve and park in the dirt lot.

PALM SPRINGS DESERT MUSEUM

Lykken Trail

From Palm Springs Desert Museum to Desert Riders Overlook is 2 miles
round trip with 800-foot elevation gain; to Ramon Drive is 4 miles round trip
with 800-foot gain; Season : October-May

Museum and Lykken Trails offer a good overview of the resort. This
hike begins at Palm Springs Desert Museum, where natural science exhibits
recreate the unique ecology of Palm Springs and the surrounding Colorado
Desert.

Steep Museum Trail ascends the western base of Mt. San Jacinto and
junctions with Lykken Trail, which winds through the Palm Springs hills
north to Tramway Road and south to Ramon Road. Lykken Trail honors
Carl Lykken, Palms Springs pioneer and the town's first postmaster. Lykken,
who arrived in 1913, owned a general merchandise store, and later a department/hardware store.

Directions to trailhead: From Highway
111 (Palm Canyon Drive) in the middle of
downtown Palm Springs, turn west on
Tahquitz Drive, then a right on Museum
Drive. Park in Palm Springs Desert Museum's
north lot.

The trail begins back of the museum,
between the museum and an administration
building, by a plaque honoring Carl Lykken.
The trail is closed during the summer months
for health reasons (yours).

The hike: The trail ascends the rocky slope above the museum. Soon
you'll intersect a private road, jog left, then resume trail walking up the
mountainside. As you rapidly gain elevation, the view widens from the
Desert Fashion Plaza to the outskirts of Palm Springs to the wide-open
spaces of the Coachella Valley.

A mile's ascent brings you to a picnic area, built by the Desert Riders,
local equestrians whose membership included Carl Lykken. One Desert
Rider, former Palm Springs Mayor Frank Bogart is a real trail enthusiast
whose efforts have contributed much to the state's trail system. Bear left
(south) on Lykken Trail, which travels the hills above town before descending to Ramon Road near the mouth of Tahquitz Canyon.

THE LIVING DESERT

Jaeger Nature Trail
2-mile loop through Living Desert Reserve; return via Eisenhower Trail
and Eisenhower Mountain is 5 miles round trip with 500-foot elevation gain;
Season: October-May

A superb introduction to desert plant life and wildlife, The Living Desert is a combination zoo, botanic garden and hiking area. The 1,200-acre, nonprofit facility is dedicated to conservation, education and research. Gardens represent major desert regions including California's Mojave, Arizona's Sonoran and Mexico's Chihuahuan. Wildlife-watchers will enjoy observing coyotes in their burrows and bighorn sheep atop their mountain peak. The reserve also has a walk-through aviary and a pond inhabited by the rare desert pupfish.

Nature and hiking trails provide an opportunity to form an even closer acquaintance with an uncrowded, undeveloped sandscape. Easy trails lead past the Arabian Oryx and bighorn sheep, past desert flora with name tags and ecosystems with interpretive displays, and over to areas that resemble the open desert of yesteryear.

Presidents Eisenhower, Nixon, Ford and Reagan relaxed in Palm Springs. Eisenhower spent many winters at the El Dorado Country Club at the base of the mountain that now bears his name. Palm Desert boosters petitioned the Federal Board of Geographic Names to name the 1,952 (coincidentally, 1952 was the year of his election)-foot peak for part-time Palm Springs resident Dwight D. Eisenhower.

Bighorn sheep roam the Living Desert.

The first part of the walk through The Living Desert uses a nature trail named after the great naturalist Edmund Jaeger. It's keyed to a booklet available from the entrance station. An inner loop of two-thirds of a mile and an outer loop of 1.5 miles lead past a wide array of desert flora and 60 interpretive stops. A longer loop can be made using Canyon Trail and Eisenhower Trail. The hike to Ike's peak ascends about halfway up the bald mountain and offers great views of the Coachella Valley.

Directions to trailhead: From Highway 111 in Palm Desert, turn south on Portola Avenue and drive 1.5 miles south to the park. Hours: 9 A.M. to 5 P.M.; closed mid-June to the end of August.

The hike: The trail begins at the exhibit buildings. Follow either the numbered nature trail, beginning at number one, or make a short rightward detour to the bighorn sheep enclosure. The trail junctions once more and you begin heading up the alluvial plain of Deep Canyon. Walking up the wash, you'll observe the many moisture-loving plants that thrive in such environments, including smoke trees, desert willows and palo verde.

Stay right at the next junction and begin the outer loop of the Jaeger Nature Trail. You'll pass plenty of that common desert dweller, the creosote bush, and wind along the base of some sand dunes.

The trail climbs out of the wash and into a kind of plain that true desert rats call a "bajada." Here you'll find a quail guzzler which stores rainwater to aid California's state bird in the hot summer months. And here you'll find a junction with Canyon Trail (the south loop of the Eisenhower Trail).

Canyon Trail heads up the bajada. After climbing through a little canyon, the trail winds up the south slope of Eisenhower Mountain to a picnic area and a plaque describing the region's date industry.

From the picnic area, you'll descend Eisenhower Mountain, getting good views of the mountains and the Coachella Valley. After passing the signed Eisenhower trailhead, you'll reach the north loop of the Nature Trail and begin heading west down the brittlebush-dotted floodplain back to the exhibit buildings and the central part of the preserve.

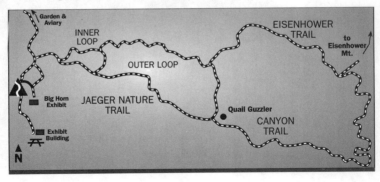

MURRAY AND ANDREAS CANYONS

Murray Canyon Trail
From Andreas Canyon to Murray Canyon is 2 miles round trip
with 200-foot elevation gain; Season: October-May

In the foothills above Palm Springs are two lovely palm-lined canyons—Andreas and Murray. Both have hundreds of palms, crystalline streams and dramatic rock walls. Andreas, with about 700 native California fan palms and Murray with about 1,000 palms, are among the most populous palm groves in the state. The two canyons are tributaries of nearby Palm Canyon, undisputed king of California's palm oases.

Both canyons honor Palm Springs pioneers. Andreas is named after a Cahuilla Indian chieftain of the late 1800s, while Murray honors irascible Scotsman and dedicated botanist Dr. Welwood Murray, who built a hotel/health resort in the very early days of Palm Springs. Many of those making their way to the Murray Hotel came for the curative climate and the rejuvenation of their health, but a number of literary figures also visited and these scribes soon spread the word that Palm Springs was a very special place indeed.

Andreas Canyon was once a summer retreat for the Agua Caliente band of the Cahuilla. The Indians spent the winter months in the warm Coachella Valley then sought the relative coolness of Andreas and other palm canyons during the warmer months.

Unlike most palm oases, which are fed by underground springs or sluggish seeps, Andreas is watered by a running stream. Fortunately for the palms and other canyon life, settlers were legally prevented from diverting this stream to the emerging village of Palm Springs. Ranchers and townspeople had to turn to the larger, but notoriously undependable Whitewater River.

Meandering through the tall Palms, hikers can travel a ways upstream through Andreas Canyon. Adding to the lush scene are alders and willows, cottonwoods and sycamores.

Murray Canyon

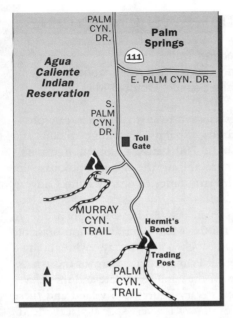

The trail between Andreas Canyon and Murray Canyon is only a mile long, but you can travel a few more miles up the canyons themselves.

Directions to trailhead: From the junction of State Highway 111 and South Palm Canyon Drive in Palm Springs, proceed south on the latter road for 1.5 miles, bearing right at a signed fork. After another mile you'll reach the Agua Caliente Indians Reservation tollgate.

Just after the tollgate, bear right at a signed fork and travel 0.75 mile to Andreas Canyon picnic ground. The trail begins at the east end of the splendid picnic area. A sign suggests that Murray Canyon is "20 min" away.

The hike: Notice the soaring, reddish-brown rocks near the trailhead. At the base of these rocks are grinding holes once used by the Cahuilla.

The trail extends south along the base of the mountains. A dramatic backdrop to the path is the desert-facing side of the San Jacinto Mountains.

It's an easy walk, occasionally following a dry streambed. Here, away from water, you encounter more typical desert flora: cholla, hedgehog cacti, burrobush.

When you reach Murray Canyon, you can follow the palms and stream quite a ways up-canyon. Joining the palms are willows, cottonwoods, mesquite, arrowweed and desert lavender. Mistletoe is sometimes draped atop the mesquite and attracts lots of birds.

As you take the trail back to Andreas Canyon you can't help noticing the luxury housing and resort life reaching toward the palm canyons. And you can't help being thankful that these tranquil palm oases are still ours to enjoy.

PALM CANYON

Palm Canyon Trail
From Hermit's Bench to turnaround is 4 miles round trip with 200-foot elevation gain; Season: October-May

The hills and canyons bordering Palm Springs have the greatest concentration of palm trees in the U.S., and in number of trees, Palm Canyon is the uncrowned king of America's desert oases. A meandering stream and lush undergrowth complement over three thousand palms, creating a jungle-like atmosphere in some places.

Palm fans will enjoy viewing the largest concentration of California fan palms while visiting the Agua Caliente Indian Reservation.

Directions to trailhead: From Interstate 10, exit on Highway 111 (Palm Canyon Drive) and proceed to downtown Palm Springs. Continue through town on Palm Canyon Drive. At a fork, Highway 111 veers east and becomes known as East Palm Canyon Drive. You head straight ahead, on South Palm Canyon Drive, following the signs to "Indian Canyons." You reach the Aqua Caliente Indians tollgate, where you must pay a fee to enter tribal lands. The reservation is open daily from 8:30 A.M. to 5 P.M. Parking is a short distance beyond the tollgate at the head of Palm Canyon at Hermit's Bench, where there is a trading post and a good view north into Palm Springs. Many signs remind visitors that they must be off the reservation before 5 p.m.

The hike: From the trading post, the trail descends into the canyon. Some of the palms stand 60 feet tall, with three-foot trunk diameters. The trail follows the canyon for two miles to a tiny grotto that seems an ideal place to turn around.

Hearty adventurers will relish the challenge of proceeding up Palm Canyon seven more miles, gaining 3,000 feet in elevation, before reaching a junction with Highway 74, the Palms-to-Pines Highway. Note: This extremely strenuous hike is best done by beginning at the Highway 74 trailhead, hiking down Palm Canyon, and convincing a friend to pick you up at Hermit's Bench. Contact the BLM in Palm Springs for the latest trail advice.

Tahquitz Canyon

Tahquitz Canyon Trail
A ranger-guided hike of 2 miles round trip with 350-foot elevation gain

After a 30-year closure, the lovely canyon named after the banished Cahuilla shaman Tahquitz has been reopened on a limited basis to hikers. Tribal rangers lead four interpretive hikes per day through the storied canyon, located just two miles as the phainocepla flies from downtown Palm Springs.

Guided hike highlights include ancient rock art, diverse desert flora, an early irrigation system and a 60-foot waterfall featured in Frank Capra's classic 1937 film, *Lost Horizon* starring Ronald Coleman and Jane Wyatt. Hikers are ushered into the Tahquitz Canyon Visitor Center screening room for a viewing of "The Legend of Tahquitz Canyon" video, then step past bottled water and snack vending machines onto the trail.

As legend has it, Tahquitz, the Cahuilla's first shaman, at first practiced his art to good effect, but soon became increasingly mischievous, then downright dangerous. He is known, even today, as one who steals people and eats their souls. Some local tribe members refuse to enter the shaman's home canyon. Such is his power that he can appear to people in downtown Palm Springs or manifest himself as an earthquake or as a fireball in the sky.

The Cahuilla closed the canyon to the public in 1969 when a rowdy crowd left a Canned Heat rock concert and descended into Tahquitz Canyon for several days of partying. In later years, "No Trespassing" signs, locked gates and fences slowed, but did not stop visitors. Most of the hikers and skinny-dippers enjoyed the picturesque falls and were respectful to the serene scene, but a number of vandals dumped garbage on the canyon floor and spray-painted graffiti on the rocks and boulders. Hippies, hermits, hobos and homeless folks took up residence in the canyon's caves.

The Agua Caliente band of the Cahuilla built a visitor center with educational and cultural exhibits and, after a three-year cleanup effort, reopened the canyon about a year ago. As tribal ranger Robert Hepburn succinctly explains the rationale behind the guided hike program: "We can keep the bad people out and let the good people in."

The canyon is chock-full of native plants including brittle bush, creosote, cholla, hedgehog cactus, Mormon tea and desert lavender. Tour leaders detail the many ways the Cahuilla used the canyon's plants for food and medicine.

The hiker's view down-canyon over the sometimes smog-obscured Coachella Valley sprawl can be a bit discouraging; up-canyon vistas, however, are glorious. From Tahquitz Peak, a subsidiary summit of Mt. San

Jacinto, a lively creek tumbles through an impressive gash in the towering rock walls.

I recommend getting an early start (Tahquitz Canyon Visitor Center opens at 7:30 A.M.) and arriving in time to watch the rising sun probe the dark recesses of the high walls of Tahquitz Canyon. If you take the first (8 A.M.) tour of the day, you'll beat the crowds, beat the heat, and have the best chance of spotting wildlife.

At just two-miles long, the hike is family-friendly one; however, because it's an interpreted hike that proceeds at a very slow pace, it's not suitable for all ages, particularly for children under 6, who will not appreciate the tribal ranger's narrative, and may become a distraction to their parents and other hikers. Some restless older kids (and many adults, too) may prefer a self-guided hike through nearby Palm Canyon for a look at the largest collection of our native California fan palm.

Canyon hiking tours depart from the Tahquitz Canyon Visitor Center at 8 A.M., 10 A.M., 12 noon and 2 P.M. There is a cost for both adults and children, and reservations are strongly recommended.

Directions to trailhead: From Highway 111 in Palm Springs, head south on Palm Spring Drive through downtown to Mesquite Avenue. Turn right (west) and proceed 0.5 mile to the parking area below the Tahquitz Canyon Visitor Center.

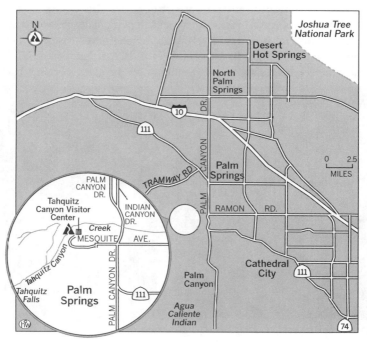

SANTA ROSA WILDERNESS

Cactus Springs Trail

From Pinyon Flat to Horsethief Creek is 5 miles round trip with a 900-foot loss; to Cactus Spring is 9 miles round trip with a 300-foot gain; Season: October-May

The Santa Rosas are primarily a desert range and a unique blend of high and low desert environments. Desert-facing slopes of these mountains are treeless—scorched and sparse as the desert itself. Throughout the foothills and canyons, lower Sonoran vegetation—chamise, barrel cactus, ocotillo and waxy creosote—predominate. In some of the canyons with water on or near the surface, oases of native California fan palms form verdant islands on the sand. With an increase in elevation, the wrinkled canyons and dry arroyos give way to mountain crests bristling with pine and juniper.

The Santa Rosa Wilderness, set aside in 1984, lies within the boundaries of the San Bernardino National Forest. Trails are few in the Santa Rosas; most are faint traces of Cahuilla Indian pathways. The ancients climbed the mountains to hunt deer, gather pinyon pine nuts, and escape the desert heat. When the snows began, they descended from the high country to the gentle, wintering areas below.

Cactus Spring Trail, an old Indian path overhauled by the Forest Service, gives the hiker a wonderful introduction to the delights of the Santa Rosas.

The trail first takes you to Horsethief Creek, a perennial waterway that traverses high desert country. A hundred years ago, horse thieves pastured their stolen animals in this region before driving them to San Bernardino to sell. The cottonwood-shaded creek invites a picnic. Continuing on the Cactus Spring Trail, you'll

Horsethief Creek crossing Cactus Spring Trail.

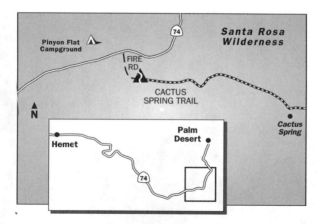

arrive at Cactus Spring. Along the trail is some wild country, as undisturbed as it was in 1774 when early Spanish trailblazer Juan Bautista de Anza first saw it.

Directions to trailhead: From Highway 111 in Palm Desert, drive 16 miles up Highway 74 to the Pinyon Flat Campground. (From Hemet, it's a 40-mile drive along Highway 74 to Pinyon Flat Campground.) Opposite the campground is Pinyon Flat Transfer Station Road, also signed "Elks Mountain Retreat." You'll follow this road about 0.75 mile. Just before reaching the (trash) Transfer Station. a rough dirt road veers to the left. Follow this road 200 yards to road's end.

The hike: Follow the dirt road east a short distance to Fire Road 7S01, then head south for 0.25 mile. You'll then take the first road on your left. A sign reassures you that you are indeed on the way to Cactus Spring, and you'll soon pass the abandoned Dolomite Mine, where limestone was once quarried. Approximately 0.25 mile past the mine site, the dirt road peters out and the trail begins. Here you'll find a sign and a trail register.

The trail bears east to the east and dips in and out of several (usually) dry gullies. A half-mile past the sign-in register, a sign welcomes you to the Santa Rosa Wilderness. Cactus Spring Trail does not contour over the hills, but zigs and zags, apparently without rhyme or reason. The bewitching, but easy-to-follow trail finally drops down to Horsethief Creek. At the creek crossing, Horsethief Camp welcomes the weary with flowing water and shade.

Return the same way, explore up and down the handsome canyon cut by Horsethief Creek, or continue to Cactus Spring.

To reach Cactus Spring, cross the creek, then climb east out of the canyon on a rough and steep trail past sentinel yuccas guarding the dry slopes. The trail stays with a wash for a spell (the route through the wash is unmarked except for occasional rock ducts), then gently ascends over pinyon pine-covered slopes. It's rolling wild country, a good place to hide out. Alas, Cactus Spring, located a few hundred yards north of the trail, is almost always dry.

18. JOSHUA TREE NATIONAL PARK

OR MANY VISITORS, THE JOSHUA TREES are not only the essence but the whole of their park experience. Joshua Tree National Park, however, is much more than a tableau of twisted yucca and beckons the explorer with a diversity of desert environments, including sand dunes, native palm oases, cactus gardens and jumbles of jumbo granite.

The Joshua tree's distribution defines the very boundaries of the Mojave Desert. Here in its namesake national park, it reaches the southernmost limit of its range.

The park area is sometimes known as the "connecting" desert because of its location between the Mojave and the Colorado Desert, and because it shares characteristics of each. The Mojave, a desert of mountains, is (relatively) cooler-wetter-higher and forms the northern and western parts of the park. Southern and eastern sections of the park are part of the hotter-drier-lower Colorado Desert, characterized by a wide variety of desert flora, including, ironwood, smoketree and native California fan palms. Cacti, especially cholla and ocotillo, thrive in the more southerly Colorado Desert (a part of the larger Sonoran Desert).

In 1994, under provisions of the federal California Desert Protection Act, Joshua Tree was "upgraded" to national park status and expanded by about a quarter-million acres. The park attracts campers, hikers, and especially rock-climbers. From Hidden Valley to the Wonderland of Rocks, the park has emerged as one of the world's premiere rock-climbing destinations. The park offers about 3,000 climbing routes, ranging from the easiest of bouldering to some of the sport's most difficult technical climbs.

The visitor center is located alongside one of JTNP's four palm oases—the Oasis of Mara, also know as Twenty-nine Palms. For many hundreds of years native Americans lived at "the place of little springs and much grass."

Two paved roads explore the heart of the park. The first loops through the high northwest section, visiting Queen and Lost Horse Valleys, as well as the awesome boulder piles at Jumbo Rocks and Wonderland of Rocks. The second angles northwest-southeast across the park, and crosses both the Mojave Desert Joshua tree woodland and cactus gardens of the Colorado Desert.

RYAN MOUNTAIN

Ryan Mountain Trail
From Sheep Pass to Ryan Mountain is 4 miles round trip
with 700-foot elevation gain

This walk tours some Joshua trees, visits Indian Cave and ascends Ryan Mountain for a nice view of the rocky wonderland in this part of Joshua Tree National Park. Ryan Mountain is named for the Ryan brothers, Thomas and Jep, who had a homestead at the base of the mountain.

The view from atop Ryan Mountain is to be savored, and is one of the finest in the National Park.

Directions to trailhead: From the Joshua Tree National Park Visitor Center at Twentynine Palms, drive 3 miles south on Utah Trail Road (the main park road), keeping right at Pinto Y junction and continuing another 8 miles to Sheep Pass Campground on your left. Park in the Ryan Mountain parking area. You may also begin this hike from the Indian Cave Turnout just up the road. Be sure to visit Indian Cave; a number of bedrock mortars found in the cave suggests its use as a work site by its aboriginal inhabitants.

The hike: From Sheep Pass Campground, the trail skirts the base of Ryan Mountain and passes through a lunar landscape of rocks and Joshua trees.

Soon you intersect a well-worn side trail coming up from your right. If you like, follow this brief trail down to Indian Cave, typical of the kind of shelter sought by the nomadic Cahuilla and Serrano clans that traveled this desert land.

Ryan Mountain Trail

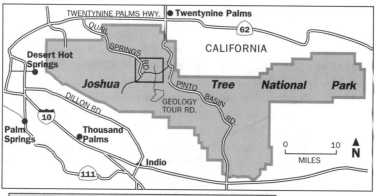

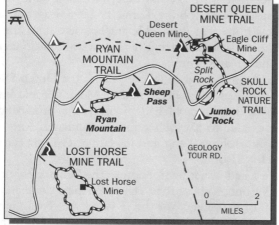

Continuing past the junction, Ryan Mountain Trail ascends moderately-to-steeply toward the peak. En route, you'll pass some very old rocks which make up the core off this mountain and the nearby Little San Bernardino range. For eons, these rocks have, since their creation, been metamorphosed by heat and pressure into completely new types, primarily gneiss and schist. No one knows their exact age, but geologists believe they're several hundred million years old.

Atop Ryan Mountain (5,470 feet) you can sign the summit register, located in a tin can stuck in a pile of rocks that marks the top of the mountain. From the peak, you're treated to a panoramic view of Lost Horse, Queen, Hidden and Pleasant valleys. There's a lot of geologic history in the rocks shimmering on the ocean of sand below. Not all the rocks you see are as ancient as the ones on Ryan Mountain. Middle-aged rocks, predominately quartz monzonite, are found at Hidden Valley, Jumbo Rocks and White Tank. Younger rocks made of basaltic lava are mere infants at less than a million years old; they are found in Pleasant Valley.

LOST HORSE MINE

Lost Horse Mine Trail
To Lost Horse Mine is 3.5 miles round trip with 400-foot elevation gain

Lost Horse Mine was the most successful gold mining operation in this part of the Mojave. More than 9,000 ounces of gold were processed from ore dug here in the late 1890s. The mine's 10-stamp mill still stands, along with a couple of large cyanide settling tanks and a huge winch used on the main shaft. The trail to the mine offers a close-up look back into a colorful era and some fine views into the heart of the national park.

Many are the legends that swirl like the desert winds around the Lost Horse Mine. As the story goes, Johnny Lang in 1893 was camping in Pleasant Valley when his horse got loose. He tracked it out to the ranch belonging to Jim McHaney, who told Lang his horse was "no longer lost" and threatened Lang's health and future.

Lang wandered over to the camp of fellow prospector Dutch Diebold, who told him that he, too, had been threatened by McHaney and his cowboys. A pity too, because he, Diebold had discovered a promising gold prospect, but had been unable to mark his claim's boundaries. After sneaking in to inspect the claim, Johnny Lang and his father, George, purchased all rights from Diebold for $1,000.

At first it looked like a bad investment, because the Langs were prevented by McHaney's thugs from reaching their claim. Partners came and went, and by 1895, Johnny Lang owned the mine with the Ryan brothers, Thomas and Jep. Peak production years for the mine were 1896 through 1899. Gold ingots were hidden in a freight wagon and transported to Indio. The ruse fooled any would-be highwaymen.

But thievery of another sort plagued the Lost Horse Mine. The theft was of amalgam, lumps of quicksilver from which gold could later be separated. Seems in this matter of amalgam, the mill's day shift, supervised by Jep Ryan, far out-produced the night shift, supervised by Lang. One of Ryan's men espied Lang stealing the amalgam. When Ryan gave Lang a choice—sell his share of the mine for $12,000 or go to the penitentiary—Lang sold out.

Alas, Johnny Lang came to a sad end. Apparently, his stolen and buried amalgams supported him for quite some time, but by the end of 1924, he was old, weak and living in an isolated cabin. And hungry. He had shot and eaten his four burros and was forced to walk into town for food. He never made it. His partially mummified body wrapped in a canvas sleeping bag was found by prospector/rancher Bill Keys alongside present-day Keys View Road. He was buried where he fell.

Directions to trailhead: From the central part of Joshua Tree National

Lost Horse Mine

Park, turn south from Caprock Junction on Keys Road and drive 2.5 miles. Turn left on a short dirt road. Here you'll find a Park Service interpretive display about Johnny Lang's checkered career. (You can also visit Lang's grave, located a hundred feet north of the Lost Horse Mine turnoff on Keys Road.) The trail, a continuation of Lost Horse Mine Road, begins at a road barrier.

The hike: The trail, the old mine road, climbs above the left side of a wash.

An alternative route, for the first (or last) mile of this day hike, is to hike from the parking area directly up the wash. Pinyon pine and the nolina (often mistaken for a yucca) dot the wash. Nolina leaves are more flexible than those of yucca, and its flowers smaller. The wash widens in about 0.75 mile and forks; bear left and a short ascent will take you to the mine road. Turn right on the road and follow it to the mine.

A few open shafts remain near the Lost Horse, so be careful when you explore the mine ruins. Note the stone foundations opposite the mill site. A little village for the mine workers was built here in the late 1890s. Scramble up to the top of the hill above the mine for a panoramic view of Queen Valley, Pleasant Valley and the desert ranges beyond.

WONDERLAND OF ROCKS

Barker Dam Loop Trail
From Parking Area to Barker Dam is 1.25 mile round trip

One of the many wonders of Joshua Tree National Park is the Wonderland of Rocks, 12 square miles of massive jumbled granite. This curious maze of stone hides groves of Joshua trees, trackless washes and several small pools of water.

Perhaps the easiest, and certainly the safest way to explore the Wonderland is to follow the Barker Dam Loop Trail. The first part of the journey is on a nature trail that interprets the botanical highlights of the area. The last part of the loop trail visits some Indian petroglyphs.

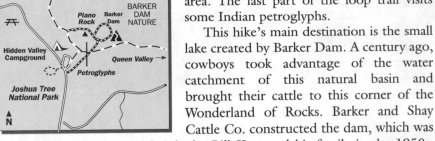

This hike's main destination is the small lake created by Barker Dam. A century ago, cowboys took advantage of the water catchment of this natural basin and brought their cattle to this corner of the Wonderland of Rocks. Barker and Shay Cattle Co. constructed the dam, which was later raised to its present height by Bill Keys and his family in the 1950s. Family members inscribed their names atop the dam's south wall and renamed it Bighorn Dam; however, Barker was the name that stuck.

The trail to Barker Dam, while interesting, is not likely to occupy much of a day for the intrepid day hiker. One way to explore a little more of the Wonderland of Rocks is to pick up the Wonderland Wash Ranch Trail to the Astrodomes. Departing from the next spur road and parking area past the Barker Dam trailhead, this path leads to the ruins of a pink house known as the Worth Bagley House. From the back corner of the house, you'll pick up a wash and follow an intermittent trail through boulder clusters. The trail is popular with rock climbers, who use this trail to reach the Astrodomes—steep, 300-foot tall rocks that tower above the wash.

A myriad narrow canyons and washes lead into the Wonderland, but route-finding is extremely complex and recommended only for the very experienced with map and compass skills.

By park service regulation, the area is open only from 8 A.M. to 6 P.M.; this restriction is designed to allow the shy bighorn sheep a chance to reach water without human interference.

Directions to trailhead: From I-10, a little east past the Highway 111 turnoff to Palm Springs, take Highway 62 northeast to the town of Joshua Tree. Continue 4 miles south to the park entrance, then another 10 miles to

Hidden Valley Campground. A dirt road leads 2 miles from Hidden Valley Campground to Barker Dam parking area.

The hike: From the north end of the parking area, join the signed trail that immediately penetrates the Wonderland of Rocks. You'll pass a special kind of oak, the turbinella, which has adjusted to the harsh conditions of desert life. The oaks are habitat for a multitude of birds and ground squirrels.

For the first 0.5 mile, interpretive signs point out the unique botany of this desert land.The path then squeezes through a narrow rock passageway and leads directly to the edge of the lake. Bird-watching is excellent here because many migratory species not normally associated with the desert are attracted to the lake. The morning and late afternoon hours are particularly tranquil times to visit the lake, and to contemplate the ever-changing reflections of the Wonderland of Rocks on the water.

The trail is a bit indistinct near Barker Dam, but resumes again in fine form near a strange-looking circular water trough, a holdover from the area's cattle ranching days. A toilet-like float mechanism controlled the flow of water to the thirsty livestock.

The path turns southerly and soon passes a huge boulder known as Piano Rock. When this land was in private ownership, a piano was hauled atop this rock and played for the amusement of visitors and locals.

Beyond Piano Rock the trail enters a rock-rimmed valley. A brief leftward detour at a junction brings you to the Movie Petroglyphs, so named because in less-enlightened times, the native rock art was painted over by a film crew in order to make it more visible to the camera's eye.

Back on the main trail, you'll parallel some cliffs, perhaps get a glimpse of some Indian bedrock mortars, and loop back to the parking area.

Barker Dam

Black Rock Canyon

Black Rock Canyon Trail
From Black Rock Campground to Warren Peak is 6 miles round trip with 1,000-foot elevation gain

A hike through Black Rock Canyon has just about everything a desert hike should have: plenty of cactus, pinyon pine-dotted peaks, a sandy wash, dramatic rock formations, a hidden spring, grand vistas. And much more.

Tucked away in the northwest corner of the park, the Black Rock Canyon area also hosts forests of the shaggy Joshuas. Yucca brevifolia thrive at the higher elevations of this end of the national park.

More than two hundred species of birds, including speedy road-runners, have been observed in and around Black Rock Canyon. Hikers frequently spot mule deer and rabbits—desert cottontails and black-tailed jack rabbits. Bighorn sheep are also sighted occasionally. A bit off the tourist track, Black Rock Canyon rarely makes the "must see" list of natural attractions at the national park. Ironically though, while Black Rock is often overlooked, it is one of the easiest places to reach. The canyon is close to Yucca Valley's commercial strip, very close to a residential neighborhood.

Maybe we nature-lovers practice a curious logic: If a beautiful place is near civilization it can't be that beautiful, right? In Black Rock Canyon's case, our logic would be faulty. The canyon matches the allure of much more remote regions of the national park.

Black Rock Canyon Trail follows a classic desert wash, then ascends to the crest of the Little San Bernardino Mountains at Warren Peak. Desert and mountain views from the peak are stunning.

Directions to trailhead: From Highway 62 (Twentynine Palms Highway) in Yucca Valley, turn south on Joshua Lane and drive five miles through a residential area to Black Rock Ranger Station. Park at the station. The station has some interpretive displays and sells books and maps. Ask rangers for the latest trail information.

Walk uphill through the campground to campsite #30 and the trailhead.

The hike: From the upper end of the campground, the trail leads to a water tank, goes left a very short distance on a park service road, then angles right. After a few hundred yards, the trail splits. The main trail descends directly into Black Rock Canyon wash. (An upper trail crests a hill before it, too, descends into the wash.)

A quarter-mile from the trailhead, the path drops into the dry, sandy creekbed of Black Rock Canyon. You'll bear right and head up the wide canyon mouth, passing Joshua trees, desert willow and cholla.

A mile of wash-walking leads you to the remains of some so-called "tanks," or rock basins that were built by early ranchers to hold water for their cattle.

Another quarter-mile up the wash is Black Rock Spring, sometimes dry, sometimes a trickle. Beyond the spring, the canyon narrows. You wend your way around beaver tail cactus, pinyon pine and juniper.

(Near the head of the canyon, the trail splits. Turning left [east] cross-country will lead along a rough ridge to Peak 5195.)

If you follow the right fork of the rough trail, you'll climb to a dramatic ridge crest of the Little San Bernardino Mountains, then angle right (west) along the crest. A steep, 0.25-mile ascent past contorted wind-blown juniper and pinyon pine brings you to the top of Warren Peak.

Oh what a grand clear-day view! North is the Mojave Desert. To the west is snowy Mt. San Gorgonio, Southern California's highest peak, as well as the San Bernardino Mountains and the deep trough of San Gorgonio Pass. Southwest lies mighty Mt. San Jacinto and to the south (this is often the murky part of the view) Palm Springs and the Coachella Valley. The peaks of the Little San Bernardino Mountains extend southeast, marching toward the Salton Sea.

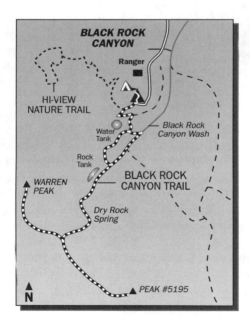

FORTYNINE PALMS

Fortynine Palms Trail
To Fortynine Palms Oasis is 3 miles round trip with 400-foot elevation gain

Fortynine Palms Oasis has retained a wonderful air of remoteness. From the parking area, an old Indian trail climbs a steep ridge and offers the hiker expansive views of the Sheephole and Bullion mountain ranges.

On the exposed ridge, barrel cacti, creosote, yucca, and brittlebush brave the heat. As the trail winds up and over a rocky crest, the restful green of the oasis comes into view. At the oasis, nature's personality abruptly changes and the dry, sunbaked ridges give way to dripping springs, pools, and the blessed shade of palms and cottonwoods.

Unlike some oases, which are strung out for miles along a stream, Fortynine Palms is a close-knit palm family centered around a generous supply of surface water. Seeps and springs fill numerous basins set among the rocks at different levels. Other basins are supplied by "rain" drip-drip-dripping from the upper levels. Mesquite and willow thrive alongside the palms. Singing house finches and croaking frogs provide a musical interlude.

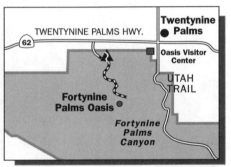

Perched on a steep canyon wall, Fortynine Palms Oasis overlooks the town of Twentynine Palms, but its untouched beauty makes it seem a lot farther removed from civilization.

Directions to trailhead: From Interstate 10, a few miles east of the Highway 111 turnoff going to Palm Springs, bear north on Highway 62. After passing the town of Yucca Valley, but before reaching the outskirts of Twentynine Palms, turn right on Canyon Road. (Hint: Look for an animal hospital at the corner of Highway 62 and Canyon Road) Follow Canyon Road 1.75 miles to its end at a National Park Service parking area and the trailhead.

The hike: The trail rises through a Spartan rockscape dotted with cacti and jojoba. After a brisk climb, catch your breath atop a ridgetop and enjoy the view of Twentynine Palms and the surrounding desert.

The trail leads down slopes dotted with barrel cactus and mesquite. Soon the oasis comes into view. Lucky hikers may get a fleeting glimpse of bighorn sheep drinking from oasis pools or gamboling over nearby steep slopes.

Mastodon Peak

Mastodon Peak Trail
3-mile loop trail with 400-foot elevation gain

Mastodon Peak Trail packs a lot of sight-seeing into a three-mile walk: a cottonwood-shaded oasis, a gold mine and a grand desert view.

Mastodon Peak, named by early prospectors for its behemoth-like profile, was the site of the Mastodon Mine, a gold mine worked intermittently from 1919 to 1932. The ore was of high quality; however, the main ore body was cut off by a fault.

A mile down the trail from the mine is Winona, where some concrete foundations remain to mark the former mill and little town. Winona was home to workers at the Mastodon Mine, as well as workers at the mill, which processed ore from a number of nearby mines.

Views from elephantine-shaped Mastodon Peak include the Cottonwood Springs area and the Eagle Mountains. Clear-day panoramas extend from Mt. San Jacinto above Palm Springs to the Salton Sea.

Directions to trailhead: Entering the national park from the south (via Interstate 10), travel eight miles north of the park boundary to Cottonwood Spring Campground. Park at the Cottonwood Spring day use area.

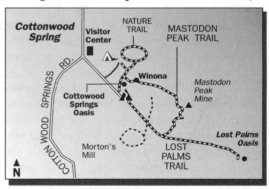

The hike: From the parking area, the path proceeds immediately to Cottonwood Spring, a collection of cottonwoods, California fan palms and cattails crowded around a trickling spring.

The path continues 0.5 mile, following a wash to a junction. Lost Palms Trail heads right, but you take the left fork to ascend Mastodon Peak. A short spur trail leads to the summit. Enjoy the views from Cottonwood Campground just below to the Coachella Valley beyond.

The main trail descends to the shafts and ruins of Mastodon Mine. Another mile of travel brings you to Winona. Some shady trees—including eucalyptus planted by miners—offer a pleasant rest stop. A last 0.25-mile brings you to a fork in the road. The right fork leads to the campground; the left fork returns to Cottonwood Spring parking lot.

Lost Palms Oasis

Lost Palms Oasis Trail
From Cottonwood Springs Campground to Lost Palms Oasis is 8 miles
round trip with 300-foot elevation gain.

Lost Palms Oasis Trail passes through a cactus garden, crosses a number
of desert washes, and takes you to the two southern oases in the National
Park: Cottonwood and Lost Palms.

Largely manmade, Cottonwood Spring Oasis was once a popular
overnight stop for freight-haulers and prospectors during the mining years
of 1870 to 1910. Travelers and teamsters journeying from Banning to the
Dale Goldfield east of Twentynine Palms, rested at the oasis.

Lost Palms Oasis is a hidden gem. Nearly 100 palms are found in the
deep canyon whose steep igneous walls sparkle in the desert sun.

Directions to trailhead: From the south end of Joshua Tree National
Park, follow the park road 8 miles to Cottonwood Spring Campground.
Park your car at the campground. The trailhead is at the end of the camp-
ground.

The hike: Leaving Cottonwood Spring Campground, the trail ambles
through a low desert environment of green-trunked palo verde, ironwood
and cottonwood trees, spindly ocotillo plants and cholla cactus. Park Service
identification plaques describe the area's flora and fauna.

The trail, a bit difficult to follow through the sandy wash, brings you to
Cottonwood Spring Oasis in 0.5 mile. Cottonwood Spring is home to a
wide variety of birds and a large number of bees.

From Cottonwood Spring, the trail marches over sandy hills, past heaps
of huge rocks and along sandy draws and washes. A number of Park Service
signs point the way at possibly confusing junctions. Finally, you rise above
the washes and climb to a rocky outcropping overlooking the canyon har-
boring Lost Palms Oasis. From the overlook, descend the steep path around
the boulders to the palms.

Little surface water is present at Lost Palms Oasis, but enough is underground for the palms to remain healthy. Lost Palms remained relatively
untouched throughout the mining years, though some of its water was
pumped to settlements eight miles to the south at Chiriaco Summit.
Adjacent to Lost Palms Canyon is a handsome upper canyon called Dike
Springs.

Shy and reclusive desert bighorn sheep are often seen around this oasis—
particularly in hot weather when they need water more often.

19. ANZA-BORREGO
DESERT STATE PARK

W HEN BUTTERFIELD OVERLAND STAGECOACHES sped from St. Louis through the Colorado Desert toward Pueblo de Los Angeles in the 1850s, the serpentine canyons and jagged mountains that are now part of Anza-Borrego Desert State Park stood as the last obstacle to the trip across the continent. Stagecoach passengers were only too happy to leave behind this vast desolate wilderness. Since the 1930s however, when a half million acres of palm oases, cactus flats and fantastic badlands were preserved in a state park, this very vastness and desolation have attracted visitors.

East-west highway 78 crosses the state park and reveals a land as intriguing as its names: Earthquake Valley, Grapevine Hills, Nude Wash, and Angelina Spring, Narrows Earth Trail and Burro Bend. At Yaqui Well grow the spiny ironwood trees and at Split Canyon grow those botanical oddities, the puffy-looking elephant trees. At Split Mountain the road penetrates the middle of the mountain and offers an inside-out look at hundreds of sedimentary layers of ancient sea bottoms and fossil shell reefs.

Another long desert highway, S-22, the Salton Sea Parkway, also crosses the park from east to west. S-22 offers access to lonely Seventeen Palms Canyon, where a desert seep enables a group of fan palms to survive, and to the twisted sandstone formations of Calcite Canyon, where calcite, useful for making gun sights, was mined during World War II.

Anza-Borrego Desert State Park includes virtually every feature visitors associate with a desert: washes, badlands, mesas, palm oases and much more. This diverse desert park boasts more than 20 palm groves and year-around creeks, great stands of cholla and elephant trees, slot canyons and badland formations.

Anza-Borrego is diverse, and it is huge; more than three times the size of Zion National Park. The 600,000-acre park stretches almost the whole length of San Diego County's eastern border between Riverside County and Mexico. Its elevation ranges from 100 feet below sea level near the Salton Sea to 6,000 feet above sea level atop San Ysidro Mountain. California's largest state park preserves a 60-mile long, 30-mile wide stretch of Colorado Desert from the Santa Rosa Mountains to the Mexican border.

Travelers are welcomed to Anza-Borrego by what is probably the best visitors center in the state park system. Numerous self-guided nature trails and automobile tours allow visitors to set their own pace. An active natural history association and foundation sponsors many regularly scheduled ranger- and naturalist-led activities.

BORREGO PALM CANYON

Borrego Palm Canyon Trail
To Falls is 3 miles round trip with 600-foot elevation gain; to South Fork is 6.5 miles round trip with 1,400-foot gain; Season: October-May

Borrego Palm Canyon is the third-largest palm oasis in California, and was the first site sought for a desert state park back in the 1920s. It's a beautiful, well-watered oasis, tucked away in a rocky V-shaped gorge.

The trail visits the first palm grove and a waterfall. A longer option takes you exploring farther up-canyon. In winter, the trail to the falls is one of the most popular in the park. In summer, you'll have the oasis all to yourself. Watch for bighorn sheep, which frequently visit the canyon.

Directions to trailhead: The trail begins at Borrego Palm Canyon Campground, located one mile north of park headquarters. Trailhead parking is available at the west end of the campground near the campfire circle.

The hike: Beginning at the pupfish pond, you walk up-canyon past many plants used by the Indians for food and shelter. Willow was used for home-building and bow-making; brittle bush and creosote were used for their healing qualities; honey, along with mesquite and beavertail cactus, was a food staple. Notice the shallow Indian grinding holes in the granite.

The broad alluvial fan at the mouth of the canyon narrows and the sheer rock walls of the canyon soon enclose you as the trail continues along the healthy, but seasonal stream. Already surprised to learn how an apparently lifeless canyon could provide all the Indians' necessary survival ingredients, you're surprised once more when Borrego Palm Oasis comes into view. Just beyond the first group of palms is a damp grotto, where a waterfall cascades over huge boulders. The grotto is a popular picnic area and rest stop.

From the falls, you may take an alternate trail back to the campground. This trail takes you along the south side of the creek, past some magnificent ocotillos, and give you a different perspective on this unique desert environment. By following the optional route, you can continue hiking up the canyon. Hiking is more difficult up-canyon after the falls, with lots of dense undergrowth and boulders to navigate around.

To South Fork: From the "tourist turnaround" continue up the canyon. The creek is a fairly dependable water supply and is usually running late in the fall. The canyon is wet, so watch your footing on the slippery, fallen palm fronds. The canyon narrows even further and the trail dwindles to nothing. Parallel the streambed and boulder-hop back and forth across the water. The canyon zigs and zags quite a bit. The hike is well-worth the effort though, because most of the 800 or so palms in the canyon are found in its upper reaches. Sometimes you'll spot rock-climbers practicing their holds on the steep red-rock cliffs above you.

The canyon splits 1.75 miles from the falls. Straight ahead, to the southwest, is South Fork. The rocky gorge of South Fork, smothered with bamboo, is in possession of all the canyon's water. It's quite difficult to negotiate. South Fork ascends to the upper slopes of San Ysidro Mountain (6,417 feet). The Middle Fork (the way you came) of Borrego Palm Canyon is dry and more passable. It's possible to hike quite a distance first up Middle Fork, then North Fork of Borrego Palm Canyon, but check with park rangers first. It's extremely rugged terrain.

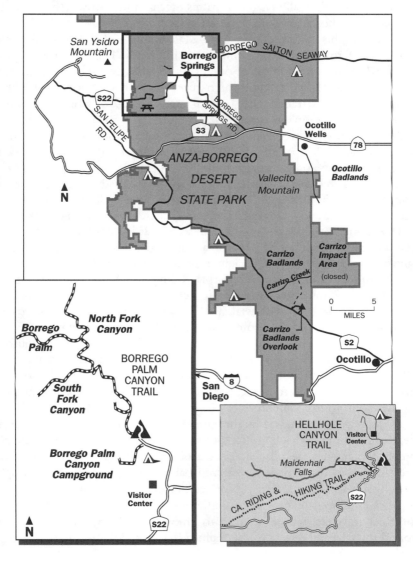

HELLHOLE CANYON

Hellhole Canyon Trail
From S-22 to Maidenhair Falls is 5 miles round trip
with 900-foot elevation gain; Season: October-May

Add Hellhole Canyon to the list of great geographical misnomers. Just as Greenland is anything but green, Hellhole Canyon is far from, well . . . hellish. Cottonwood, California fan palms, ferns and mosses thrive in the canyon, which hosts a blissful waterfall.

Certainly this hike's destination—Maidenhair Falls—is no misnomer. Maidenhair ferns enshroud the thirty-foot high falls. The presence of a lush, fern-filled grotto in the midst of one of the West's most parched landscapes is a small miracle, an example of nature's mysterious ways. Not only is Hellhole Canyon attractive, it's convenient—just a few miles as the cactus wren flies from the Anza-Borrego Desert State Park visitors center.

An intermittent trail travels through the long and deep canyon. Caution: While the canyon's riparian growth is easy on the eye, it's difficult to penetrate; expect slow-going through the thick vegetation.

Begin your trek to Hellhole Canyon from the park visitors center or from a trailhead located just off S-22. I recommend the latter trailhead, which shaves a mile from the hike and avoids the sometimes congested visitors center parking lot.

Directions to trailhead: From its intersection with Palm Canyon Drive, proceed 0.7 mile southwest on Montezuma Valley Road to the parking area on the right (west) side of the road. A bulletin board features trail and nature information.

The hike: Follow signed California Riding and Hiking Trail some 200 yards to a junction; the CRHT splits left, while you bear right, heading southwest over the broad alluvial fan. The well defined, sandy trail crosses a desert garden of cholla, creosote bush, desert lavender and ocotillo.

A bit more than a mile out, the path angles toward the mouth of Hellhole Canyon, distinguished by riparian trees and palms (and altogether different-looking than that smaller, drier tributary canyon to its right (north). The trail stays to the left of the fan, as should the hiker until entering the mouth of the canyon.

Once in the canyon, you might find yourself walking next to a wet or dry (depending on the season) watercourse. Try to steer clear of the very bottom of the canyon, an obstacle course of brush, boulders and fallen trees. The thickest of the canyon's scattered palm groves, and the narrowing of the canyon's walls signal that you're nearing Maidenhair Falls.

Ultra-ambitious hikers can continue bushwhacking up Hellhole Canyon, but most travelers will be content to enjoy the soft light and tranquillity around the falls and return to the trailhead.

CALCITE CANYON

Calcite Canyon Trail
From County Road S-22 to Calcite Mine is 4 miles round trip with 500-foot elevation gain; Season: October-May

Nature's cutting tools, wind and water, have shaped the ageless sandstone in Calcite Canyon into steep, bizarre formations. The cutting and polishing of the uplifted rock mass has exposed calcite crystals. Calcite is a common enough carbonate and found in many rocks, but only in a few places are the crystals so pure.

It was the existence of these crystals, with their unique refractive properties that brought prospectors to this part of the desert. The jeep trail was built in the mid-1930s for miners to gain access to Calcite Canyon, as it came to be called. Because of their excellent double refraction properties, calcite crystals were useful in the making of gun sights. Mining activity increased during World War II.

The calcite was taken from the canyon in long trenches, which look as if they were made yesterday. The desert takes a long time to heal.

This walk takes the jeep road to its dead end at the mine. You'll see the Calcite Mine Area up-close and get a good overlook of the many washes snaking toward the Salton Sea. A return trip through Palm Wash and its tributaries lets you squeeze between perpendicular walls and gives a unique perspective on the forces that shape the desert sands. The awesome effects of flash flooding are easily discerned by the hiker and suggest a narrow wash is the last place in the world you want to be in a rainstorm.

Directions to trailhead: Follow County Road S-22 west from Highway 86, or 20 miles from the Christmas Circle to Calcite

Nature and industry have sculpted Calcite Canyon.

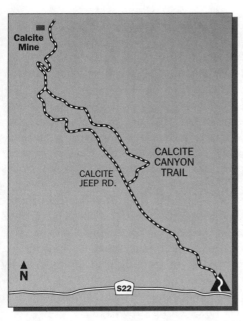

Jeep Road. The jeep road is just west of a microwave tower.

The hike: Follow the jeep road, which first drops into the south fork of Palm Wash, then begins to climb northwest. Along the road you'll see long, man-made slots cut into the hillsides for the removal of calcite. Calcite Jeep Road dips a final time, then climbs a last 0.5 mile toward the mine. Two miles from the trailhead, the road ends at the mining area.

Calcite crystal fragments embedded in the canyon walls and scattered on the desert floor glitter in the sun. Behind the mining area, to the northeast, is a gargantuan hunk of white sandstone dubbed "Locomotive Rock." The imaginative can picture a great locomotive chugging up a steep grade. If you look carefully, you'll be able to see Seventeen Palms and some of the palms tucked away in Palm Wash in a bird's-eye view of the east side of the state park.

You can return the same way or descend through tributaries of the middle fork of Palm Wash. Take a last look at the steep ravines and washes to get your bearings. Middle Fork is but a hop, skip and a jump from the mine, but the jump's a killer—a 50-foot plunge to a deep intersecting wash. To get into the wash, you need to descend 0.5-mile down Calcite Road to a small tributary wash. Descend this wash, which is fairly steep at first. The sandstone walls close in on you. One place, "Fat Man's Misery," allows only one fat man (or two skinny day hikers) to squeeze through at a time. When you reach the middle fork, a prominent canyon, follow it 0.25 mile to the brief jeep trail connecting the wash to Calcite Road. Hike back up Calcite Road 0.1 mile to the parking area.

ELEPHANT TREES

Elephant Trees Discovery Trail
1.5 miles round trip with 100-foot elevation gain; Season: October-May

A rarity in California deserts, the odd elephant tree is much admired by visitors to Anza-Borrego Desert State Park. Its surreal color scheme (was this tree designed by committee?) of green foliage, red-tan twigs, yellow-green peeling parchment-like bark, white flowers and blue berries, is something to behold. The stout trunk and the way the branches taper, vaguely suggests an elephant, but lots of imagination is required.

Enjoy this hike by following the 1.5 mile nature trail and/or by trekking along an alluvial fan to some elephant trees. A herd estimated at five hundred elephant trees grow at this end of the state park. Birsera microphylla is more common in Baja California and in the Gila Range of Arizona. The park has three populations of elephant trees, but the one off Split Mountain Road is the most significant one.

Elephant Trees Discovery Trail (brochure available), interprets various desert flora and geological features of this part of the Colorado Desert.

Directions to trailhead: From Ocotillo Wells (located about 40 miles west of Brawley and 78 miles east of Escondido on Highway 78), turn south on Split Mountain Road and proceed 6 miles to the signed turnoff for the Elephant Trees Area. Follow a dirt road 1 mile to the trailhead.

The hike: Follow the nature trail until signpost #10, where you'll see the first elephant tree on the hike.

(Those experienced hikers who wish to see more elephant trees will leave the trail here and hike west up the broad alluvial fan. You'll encounter bits of trail, but really the route is cross-country. Keep the mountains on the western horizon in your sight. A mile's walk brings you to some elephant trees.)

Return the way you came back to the nature trail, which follows the numbered posts through a dry streambed and loops back to the trailhead.

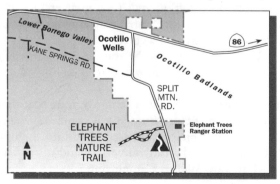

BOW WILLOW CANYON

Rockhouse Canyon Trail
Bow Willow Campground to Rockhouse is 7 miles round trip with a 700-foot gain; Season: October-May

This enjoyable day hike, for more experienced hikers, explores two intriguing canyons—Bow Willow and Rockhouse.

A turn-of-the-century miner, Nicolas Swartz, boasted he took $18,000 worth of gold from his remote desert mine. In the great tradition of Lost Mine Legends, he died without leaving a map. In 1906, Swartz built a rock house in an anonymous canyon that soon picked up the name of his structure.

This looping day hike takes you climbing through a single palm canyon, visits the rock house and its canyon and returns via the wash on the bottom of Bow Willow Canyon. Spring scatters color in the wash. Monkeyflowers, desert stars and a host of wildflowers brighten the sands and gravel bars. Even ocotillo changes its fit-only-for-firewood appearance and displays its new green leaves and flaming red flowers.

Directions to trailhead: From Interstate 8 in Ocotillo, take County Road S-2 sixteen miles to the turnoff for Bow Willow Canyon and Campground.

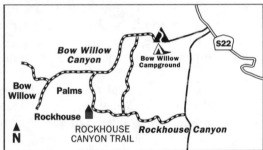

Follow the good hardpack sand road 1.5 miles to the campground. Park in the campground, but don't take a campsite someone could use.

The hike: Hike up Bow Willow Canyon on the signed jeep trail. Before you get much past the campground, make a 90-degree left turn (south) across a few hundred yards of wash to pick up the foot trail. One-quarter mile up the trail is a beleaguered palm tree. You begin climbing steadily through a desert garden of granite boulders, agave and cholla cactus.

As you near Rockhouse Canyon, the trail descends briefly and intersects Rockhouse Canyon Jeep Trail. Follow the Jeep Trail west for one mile to Swartz's abandoned rock house.

From the rock house, you follow a tentative foot trail that drops down into Bow Willow Canyon. Before long you'll come to a barrier across the wash preventing off-road vehicles from ascending into the upper reaches of the canyon. Past the barrier, the canyon widens and it's an easy 2-mile hike over soft sand back to Bow Willow Campground.

AGUA CALIENTE SPRINGS

Squaw Pond, Moonlight Canyon Trails
1.5 to 2.5 miles round trip; Season: October-May

Nothing like a good soak after a good hike. At Agua Caliente Springs in the middle of Anza-Borrego Desert State Park, you can have both—an inspiring walk and a soothing mineral bath. A hot spring, along with a good-sized campground, a store and the natural beauty of the Tierra Blanca Mountains, combine to make Agua Caliente County Park a popular weekend retreat.

Seismic activity (an offshoot of the Elsinore Fault) that long ago shaped the surrounding mountains also boosted water to the surface to form the mineral springs. The natural springs in the area give life to mesquite, willows and palms and also attract many animals and birds.

Today's visitors can soak away their cares in a large shallow outdoor pool, geothermally heated to 96 degrees and in an indoor pool, boosted to more than one hundred degrees and equipped with Jacuzzi jets.

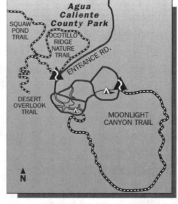

Two trails explore the county park and visit undeveloped tiny springs (seeps) in the surrounding hills. Squaw Pond Trail visits mesquite-filled Squaw Canyon; Moonlight Canyon Trail fulfills the promise of its name.

Squaw Pond Trail ascends a mesquite-dotted slope above the park's campfire circle and soon comes to a junction. Desert Overlook Trail branches left and climbs a steep 0.25 mile to a panorama of the surrounding mountains. Ocotillo Ridge Trail, an abandoned nature trail, weaves through abundant desert flora and returns to the park entry road.

Continue on signed Squaw Pond Trail which descends a teddy-bear cholla-lined draw and soon arrives at Squaw Pond, a boggy, willow-lined area nurturing a single palm tree.

From the campground, Moonlight Canyon Trail ascends briefly, but steeply to a rocky saddle, curves east, then descends into a narrow wash. After passing a willow-lined seep in the midst of the canyon, the trail circles back to the park campground.

Directions to trailhead: Agua Caliente County Park is located on Highway S-2, some 22 miles southeast of Highway 78. Parking for Squaw Pond Trail is right next to the park entry station (day use fee) in a picnic area. Moonlight Canyon Trail begins at Campsite 140 next to the shuffle-board courts.

THE HIKER'S INDEX

Celebrating the Scenic, the Sublime, and the Ridiculous in Southern California

- **Only spot on U.S. mainland attacked by the Japanese Navy during World War II:**
  Goleta Beach, February 23, 1942
- **Spiritual Journeys:**
  Mt. Zion (San Gabriel Mountains), Solstice Canyon (Santa Monica Mountains), Holy Jim Trail (Santa Ana Mountains)
- **First federally funded Wilderness Area set aside by the Wilderness Act of 1964:**
  San Rafael Wilderness (Los Padres National Forest)
- **Southwesternmost point in the contiguous forty-eight states:**
  International Boundary Marker, Border Field State Park
- **Largest national forest in California:**
  Los Padres National Forest
- **Best swimmin' hole:**
  Santa Ynez River (Los Padres National Forest)
- **Best historical hike:**
  Mt. Lowe Railway Trail (San Gabriel Mountains)
- **California's most expensive state park:**
  Chino Hills State Park ($47 million spent by the time it opened in 1986)
- **Least-inspirational name:**
  (Three-way tie) Inspiration Point (San Gabriel Mountains), Inspiration Point (Santa Ynez Mountains), and Inspiration Point (Santa Monica Mountains).
- **Southland's smallest island:**
  Santa Barbara Island
- **Southland's largest island:**
  Santa Cruz Island
- **Best Autumn Color:**
  Sycamore Canyon (Pt. Mugu State Park) and Aspen Grove (San Bernardino Mountains).
- **Most inappropriate place name:**
  Sandstone Peak—it's granite (Santa Monica Mountains)
- **Second most inappropriate place name:**
  Crystal Cove—nothing is crystalline, and there's neither a cove nor coastal indentation of any kind (Orange County)
- **Best close-up view of the San Andreas Fault:**
  Devil's Punchbowl County Park

- **We'll Be Dead Before It's Done Award:**
  To the Santa Monica Mountains' Backbone Trail; after three decades of struggle, the 65-mile long trail is still incomplete.
- **Best wildflower-watching:**
  Antelope Valley Poppy Reserve, Nicholas Flat (Santa Monica Mountains), and Torrey Pines State Reserve
- **Tallest Lodgepole Pine:**
  World champion lodgepole in San Bernardino Mountains
- **Remembering Republican Presidents:**
  Eisenhower Peak (outside Palm Springs), Reagan Ranch (Santa Monica Mountains), (Grover) Cleveland National Forest, Richard M. Nixon's San Clemente Beach Trail
- **Most palms in a Palm Oasis**
  Palm Canyon (Palm Springs)
- **Second-most palms in a Palm Oasis**
  Thousand Palms (Coachella Valley)
- **Third-most palms in a Palm Oasis**
  Borrego Palm Canyon (Anza-Borrego Desert State Park)
- **Pardon the obvious:**
  Ocean Beach (Santa Barbara Co.), High Point (Palomar Mountains)
- **Devil of a time:**
  Devil's Punchbowl County Park, Devil's Backbone Trail (to Mt. Baldy), Devil's Slide Trail (San Jacinto Mountains), Devil's Canyon (San Gabriel Mountains), Devil's Gateway and Devil's Elbow (Los Padres National Forest), Devil's Pit (San Bernardino Mountains)
- **Honoring Southland naturalists:**
  Edmund Jaeger Trail (The Living Desert), Dick Smith Wilderness (Los Padres National Forest)
- **But seriously, they're fun places:**
  Rattlesnake Canyon (Santa Ynez Mountains), Suicide Rock (San Jacinto Mountains), Hellhole Canyon (Anza-Borrego Desert State Park) and Prisoners Bay (Santa Cruz Island)
- **Least lyrical place name:**
  Peak 9775 (San Bernardino Mountains); runners-up: Peak 7114 (Los Padres National Forest) Peak 5195 (Joshua Tree National Park)
- **They Must Know We're Coming Award:**
  Group award to the many national forest and state park ranger stations and visitor information centers that are closed on the weekends—the time when 95 percent of us go for a hike.

Information Sources

Angeles National Forest (Supervisor's Office)
701 N. Santa Anita Ave.
Arcadia, CA 91006
(626) 574-5200
Los Angeles River District
4600 Oak Grove Drive
Flintridge, CA 91011
(818) 790-1151
Santa Clara/Mojave Rivers District
30800 Bouquet Canyon Road
Saugus, CA 91350
(661) 296-9710
Chilao Visitor Center
(626) 796-5541
Mt. Baldy Visitor Center
(909) 982-2829

Anza-Borrego Desert State Park
200 Palm Canyon Drive
Borrego Springs, CA 92004
(760) 767-5311

Big Morongo Preserve
P.O. Box 780
Morongo Valley, CA 92256
(760) 363-7190

Border Field State Park
c/o San Diego Coast District
3990 Old Town Ave. #300-C
San Diego, CA 92110
(619) 428-3034

Catalina Island Chamber of
Commerce and Visitors Bureau
(310) 510-1520
Cabrillo National Monument
1800 Cabrillo Memorial Drive
P.O. Box 6670
San Diego, CA 92106
(619) 557-5450

Carbon Canyon Regional Park
442 Carbon Canyon Road
Brea, CA 92621
(714) 996-5252

Caspers Wilderness Park
33401 Ortega Highway
San Juan Capistrano, CA 92675
(949) 728-0235 / 728-3420

Channel Islands National Park
1901 Spinnaker Drive
Ventura, CA 93001
(805) 658-5730

Chino Hills State Park
1879 Jackson St.
Riverside, CA 92504
(909) 780-6222

Cleveland National Forest
Trabuco Ranger District
1147 East 6th Street
Corona, CA 91719
(909) 736-1811

Crystal Cove State Park
8471 Pacific Coast Highway
Laguna Beach, CA 92651
(949) 494-3539

Devil's Punchbowl Co. Reg. Park
28000 Devil's Punchbowl Road
Pearblossom, CA 93553
(661) 944-2743

Joshua Tree National Park
74485 National Park Drive
Twentynine Palms, CA 92777
(760) 367-5500

Leo Carrillo State Park
(818) 880-0350

The Living Desert
47900 Portola Avenue
Palm Desert, CA 92260
(760) 346-5694

Los Padres National Forest
6755 Hollister Avenue
Goleta, CA 93117
(805) 961-5793

Ojai Ranger District
1190 E. Ojai Avenue
Ojai, CA 93023
(805) 646-4348

Malibu Creek State Park
(818) 880-0350

McGrath State Beach
901 S. San Pedro
Ventura, CA 93001
(805) 654-4611

Mojave Desert State Parks
43779 15th Street West
Lancaster, CA 93545-4754
(661) 942-0662
Mt. San Jacinto State Park
P.O. Box 308
Idyllwild, CA 92549
(909) 659-2607

O'Neill Regional Park
30892 Trabuco Canyon Road
Trabuco Canyon, CA 92678
(714) 858-9366

Palomar Mountain State Park
c/o Cuyamaca Ranch State Park
(760) 765-0755

Saddleback Butte State Park
17102 E. Avenue J
Lancaster, CA 93535
(760) 942-0662

San Bernardino National Forest
(Forest Supervisor's Office)
1824 S.Commercenter Circle
San Bernardino, CA 92408
(909) 383-5588
Arrowhead Ranger District
P.O. Box 7
Rimforest, CA 92378
(909) 337-2444
Big Bear Ranger District
P.O. Box 290
Fawnskin, CA 92333
(909) 866-3437
San Gorgonio Ranger District

Mill Creek Ranger Station
34701 Mill Creek Rd.
Mentone, CA 92359
(909)794-1123
San Jacinto Ranger District
P.O. Box 518
Idyllwild, CA 92349
(760) 659-2117

Santa Monica Mountains National
Recreation Area
401 Hillcrest Drive
Thousand Oaks, CA 91360
(805) 370-2301

Santiago Oaks Regional Park
2145 North Windes Drive
Orange, CA 92669
(714) 538-4400

Silverwood Lake State Recreation Area
14651 Cedar Circle
Hesperia, CA 92345
(760) 389-2303

Topanga State Park
20829 Entrada Rd.
Topanga, CA 90290
(310) 455-2465

Torrey Pines State Reserve
12000 N. Torrey Pines Park Rd.
San Diego, CA 92008
(619) 755-2063

Tucker Wildlife Sanctuary
29322 Modjeska Canyon Rd.
Orange, CA 92667
(714) 649-2760

Will Rogers State Historic Park
1501 Will Rogers State Park Rd.
Pacific Palisades, CA 90272
(310) 454-8212

Vasquez Rocks County Park
10700 West Escondido Canyon Rd.
Saugus, CA 91350
(661) 268-0840

INDEX

JOHN MCKINNEY is the author of a dozen books about walking, hiking, and nature, including *Happy Trails: Hiking the Trailmaster Way*. The Trailmaster writes articles and commentaries about walking for national publications, promotes hiking and conservation on radio and TV, and serves as a consultant to a hiking vacation company.

Contact him at www.thetrailmaster.com